British Social Attitudes
the 1985 report

British Social
Attitudes

the
1985
report

Edited by
Roger Jowell &
Sharon Witherspoon

Gower

SCPr

SOCIAL AND COMMUNITY PLANNING RESEARCH

Published by
Gower Publishing Company Limited,
Gower House,
Croft Road,
Aldershot,
Hants GU11 3HR
England

Gower Publishing Company,
Old Post Road,
Brookfield,
Vermont 05036,
U.S.A.

Typeset by
Graphic Studios (Southern) Ltd, Godalming, Surrey.

Printed by Billing & Sons Limited, Worcester

Cover photograph supplied by *Community Care*

.

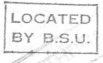
British Library Cataloguing in Publication Data

British social attitudes: the 1985 report.
   1. Public opinion — Great Britain   2. Great Britain — Social conditions — 1945-
   I. Jowell, Roger   II. Witherspoon, Sharon
   941.085'8   HN400.P8

Contents

Editors' introduction

This book is the second annual report of a series of surveys started by SCPR in 1983 and now core-funded until at least 1987–88. Its purpose, like that of its predecessor, is to provide readers with a guided tour around some of the survey's principal findings within about nine months of the appearance of initial tabulations. Within the same timetable we are also committed to lodging a fully documented dataset of each year's survey in the ESRC's Data Archive at the University of Essex, so that others in the social science community may do further analytic and interpretative work of their own.

Each chapter in this report is therefore only the first phase in what we envisage as a continuing analytic process. Our aim here is to document, to summarise and briefly to comment on a selection of findings from the 1984 survey and, where appropriate, to compare them with those obtained in 1983.

In his foreword to last year's report, Sir Claus Moser argued that

> What makes the series so important is precisely that it is a series. It is from the monitoring and understanding of *trends* in attitudes that one can learn most about what is happening in a society, and this new series promises to be much more enlightening than findings from isolated and unrelated surveys. Now we can look forward to a sustained look at trends . . .

It was for these reasons that we sought support for a series of surveys which would have the potential to increase understanding incrementally, rather than for a single 'definitive' study. We decided upon *annual* intervals not because we believed naïvely that most social attitudes would change much from one year to the next, but because one of our principal aims is to examine the relative rates at which different sorts of attitudes change – from the anticipated gradual movements in people's underlying values, to comparatively rapid fluctuations in those opinions that depend more on circumstances than on ideology.

Although the survey takes place each spring, not all questions or groups of questions (modules) are included in each fieldwork round. The modules we carry annually tend either to be on subjects where we anticipate fairly rapid movements in attitudes – and for which a year-on-year trend line is therefore likely to be helpful – or on variables such as demographic characteristics or party identification which are needed for interpreting other answers. In any event, constraints of space (we confine ourselves to an average of an hour-long interview each year, with a shorter self-completion supplement), the need for economy, and our wish to insert at least one fresh module into the question-naire every year for the time being, combine to limit the frequency with which each group of questions can be carried; but all questions are scheduled for regular repetition.

For many of the same reasons, each annual book does not include chapters on all the topics covered in the survey to which it refers. Instead we highlight here only a selection of the findings. We do, however, show the aggregate answers to every question (see Appendix III); as we have noted, we lodge the complete datatape at Essex; from the summer of 1985 we have arranged for 'on-line' access through the Data Library at the University of Edinburgh; and we offer extra tabulations (at cost) through SCPR. We thus try to ensure that anyone who wants access to the dataset (or parts of it) should be able to achieve it with the minimum of inconvenience. And we are very encouraged by the number of social scientists who are already quarrying the dataset in the way we hoped they would. We anticipate, therefore, that many of the most interesting findings are yet to emerge and will not be revealed in our annual reports. Instead they will appear in specialist papers (or further books) that are able to deal in a more focused and reflective way with subsets of the data. For the moment, however, readers will have to rely on this general overview.

As was the case last year, a few of our questions did not seem to work very well despite contrary indications at the pilot stage. We mention our misgivings when we refer to the responses to such questions. But other questions which do appear to have worked may also have flaws which only become apparent after several readings. Many survey series face these sorts of difficulties and their resolution is by no means straightforward. To change or remove unsatisfactory questions would sacrifice continuity and comparability between one reading and the next; to retain them would run the risk of producing (and reproducing) misleading information. Neither practice is desirable but one or other is unavoidable. Whenever we do tinker with question wording between one insertion and the next, we point this out both in the text and in the archived documentation to alert readers and users to the possibility of artefactual change.

Social surveys ought routinely to reveal their provenance and sources of funding, since such information sometimes helps to explain their content or emphasis. We wish in any case to do so, so that we can publicly express our appreciation of the support the series is receiving from a number of sources.

'Seed funding' for the study came in 1983 from the Nuffield Foundation. Envisaged initially as a development project, the sample size at that stage was to be relatively small. In the event, the ESRC then agreed to supplement the grant to enable the first year's survey to be a full-scale benchmark study (with a probability sample of around 1,700 respondents). By the end of 1983, the Monument Trust (a Sainsbury foundation) had guaranteed core-funding for a further three years. This large and long-term commitment transformed what was then an *ad hoc* survey into a series, enabling us to introduce and rotate questions and topics systematically. We also received supplementary contributions towards the series from Marks and Spencer plc and Shell UK Ltd. At around the same time, the Department of Employment, who had already expressed interest in our employment-related questions, agreed to provide funds to enhance the coverage of these topics over a three-year period. The continuation of the project was thus assured.

Subsequent support for the series enabled the 1984 survey (reported in this volume) to expand its scope. In particular, The Nuffield Foundation and the University of Pittsburgh agreed jointly to fund the introduction of a new module on public and private morality, the initial results of which are reported in Chapter 5. In addition, the ESRC agreed to fund the introduction of a panel element into the series, enabling us to return to half of the 1983 respondents as a means of measuring individual as distinct from aggregate changes in attitudes. This added an intriguing new dimension to the project, and the initial findings are reported in Chapter 7.

As we go to press, the series is entering its third year and contains several new features. First, ESRC funding of the panel element has been renewed for a further round, so we are about to interview a random subset of around 500 of our 1983 respondents for the third year running. By placing these findings alongside the cross-sectional findings we expect to learn a great deal not only about the nature of attitudinal movements but also about the respective results of cross-sectional and panel designs, and about the stability or otherwise of various kinds of attitudinal measures.

Second, we have now introduced an international dimension into the series, following the Nuffield Foundation's agreement to fund SCPR to convene a series of meetings at which we could confer with our counterparts (doing similar studies) in the USA, the Federal Republic of Germany, and Australia. Our aim was to devise identical (or closely comparable) questions which each of the four countries would agree to carry. The result is that we now have a self-completion module – this year on attitudes towards government intervention of various kinds – which each country is putting into the field in 1985. The preliminary cross-national findings will appear in next year's book. Funding permitting, our intention is that each country will include a similar module – on a fresh topic – in 1986 and 1987, and then in future years will return to our initial topics to look for changes.

Third, arising out of their interest in attitudes towards housing and towards the countryside respectively, the Department of the Environment and the Countryside Commission have now provided funds to enhance the coverage of those subjects in 1985 and beyond. Chapters on these topics will appear in next year's book.

Further developments are also in store for 1986 and beyond, thanks once again to the interest and generosity of the Monument Trust. Principally, the sample size from 1986 onwards is to be increased to around 3,000 respondents each year. We plan to divide the questionnaire in some (as yet undefined) way so that some questions will be asked of the total sample and others of only half, thus creating more questionnaire room for new modules. The larger sample size will greatly increase the analytic potential of the data, especially in relation to the attitudes and characteristics of smaller subgroups and minorities.

The Monument Trust has also decided to award three or four small bursaries in the academic year 1985/86 to social scientists who wish to re-analyse parts of the British Social Attitudes datasets with particular theoretical or policy questions in mind. These bursaries are intended to facilitate such work (for instance, through the funding of part-time research assistance), not to support it fully. Details of the scheme will be announced shortly.

In addition, core-funding for the British Social Attitudes series is from now on to be placed on a three-year 'rolling' basis. Thus at the end of *each* year the Trust will decide whether or not to add a further year to the two remaining. By this means, reasonable warning will be given if funding is to be reduced or withdrawn, a vital consideration in planning a series but one which is too often absent.

We owe an enormous debt of gratitude to the trustees of the Monument Trust and to the other sponsors for their support of and confidence in the series. They deserve the credit for helping to establish – only two years after a relatively shaky start – a new British data resource which appears to be in considerable demand already. That they have given such support during a period of ever-reducing funds for the social sciences is both impressive and encouraging.

The funders should not, however, get the blame for the survey's content (still less for its deficiencies). We must take full responsibility for that, especially as – in this series – a condition of funding is that it carries with it no control over either question design or reporting. We are grateful to our government and quasi-government sponsors in particular for accepting that condition.

Our other debts are much too numerous to catalogue here. For instance, we cannot single out colleagues in SCPR, almost all of whom have, in one way or another, contributed to the project. To our fellow researchers, field controllers and programmers, to those responsible for sampling, booking-in, editing, checking, typing and so on, we can pay only a blanket tribute in the knowledge that it is their work and advice that have made the project run smoothly. The same is true of the armies of interviewers and coders on whose professionalism and conscientiousness we continue to depend so heavily. And we are deeply indebted, as always, to the 2,200 or so anonymous respondents who gave their time so generously to complete our demanding questionnaires.

We continue also to rely heavily on advice from outside SCPR. Some of those whose help we have drawn upon are acknowledged at the ends of chapters. Others are not. In particular, the very existence of the series owes a great deal to the support and encouragement we have received from Sir Claus Moser. His enthusiasm for the project when it was first mooted and his role in helping us to turn it into a reality have been invaluable. His continuing advice is greatly appreciated and very influential. Hugh de Quetteville has equally been a persuasive and powerful supporter of the project. His advocacy has been a key factor in consolidating the series and we have depended a great deal on his guidance. We acknowledged last year the role that James Cornford and Pat Thomas played in getting the series started. We are equally grateful to them for their continuing help and advice which enabled us to expand its scope to allow cross-national comparisons.

Finally, we wish to express our gratitude to June Hoad for her sterling work as a research assistant on this project during the past year and, in particular, for her conscientiousness and skill in helping to produce this book in the time available.

RMJ
SW

1 Shades of opinion

*Ken Young**

In his introduction to the 1984 Report, Roger Jowell set down one of the basic premises on which this series is founded: that "the term 'public opinion' is itself misleading . . . there are actually several publics and many opinions" (Jowell and Airey, 1984, p.8). This chapter sets out to explore this diversity and to identify some (and only some; there are indeed many) of these significant publics. Its aim is to show, by selections from the new dataset, how certain groups in the population differ from one another on a range of major themes.

This is not to suppose that groups differ consistently across all issues. There are good grounds for supposing *a priori* that (for example) those employed in private sector manufacturing would differ from those employed in public sector services on the question of state aid to industry, but there is no particular reason to suppose that they would differ on issues of policing or personal morality. However, for the larger social groups such *a priori* assumptions may be a poor guide. Indeed, a close examination of larger groups can bring to light surprising findings and pose further questions. Thus, we may find the views of men and women to be substantially similar on a particular issue. But when we examine the views of young, middle-aged and older men, and those of young, middle-aged and older women we may find striking differences of view which, because they cut across age and gender, are obscured at more general levels of analysis.

Subject only to constraints of sample size and composition we can divide the population into endless numbers of categories only some of which will be fruitful for more than a few issues. Some social groups with coherent and distinctive views will necessarily be represented by too few cases for the purposes of this type of analysis, constituting as they do small minorities of the

---

* Senior Fellow, Policy Studies Institute.

population at large. No-one will doubt that the exploration of 'public opinion' usually neglects such minorities. Equally the assumption of a single 'majority' public also glosses over a complex plurality of opinion and deep divisions of attitude.

We shall not here pursue these divisions for more than a few basic social groups and in respect of a few major issues. It is for others in the social research community to explore the constellations of issues more rigorously and comprehensively.

Some key social groups

In selecting key social groups whose views are to be explored it is wise to pay some regard to those characteristics which encapsulate distinct life experiences and might thus be expected to find expression in different interpretations and therefore in different attitudes. Four such major lines of division come to mind immediately as representing distinct social experiences.

The first of these divisions is income, a major determinant of life-chances and of advantage. We established the annual gross income of the respondent's household within various bands. For the purpose of analysis, these were then grouped into four categories which are shown below together with the frequency distributions.

Annual gross household income

	Number	%
Under £5,000	493	30
£5,000–7,999	377	23
£8,000–11,999	292	18
£12,000 and over	281	17
No information	201	12

The second major line of division is that of Social Class. The class groups are based upon the occupational status rankings introduced by the Registrar General in 1921. Respondents were assigned to categories according to their present job, or their last job if they were not currently in work. We depart from this convention only to make comparisons with the 1983 survey, where a slightly different rule for allocating those currently looking after a home was used. In the interests of more satisfactory analysis, we have generally collapsed the very small extreme categories – Social Classes I and V – into their adjacent groups, while for certain purposes we also confine our discussion to the broad distinction between those in manual and non-manual occupations. We refer too, as and when it seems useful to do so, to self-rated social class.*

From time to time we refer to self-rated social mobility, by which we mean a difference between the self-rated class of the respondent's parents when the

* The debate about social classifications of various kinds is not addressed here. We have chosen for simplicity to refer only to Social Class. But we have collected and processed the data so that others can use different classifications such as socio-economic group or variants of it.

Social Class

	Number	%
I (professional) and II (intermediate)	341	21
III (non-manual)	378	23
III (manual)	369	22
IV (partly skilled) and V (unskilled)	380	23
Never worked/not classifiable	177	11

Self-rated social class

	Number	%
Upper middle/middle	438	27
Upper working	319	19
Working	789	48
Poor	47	3
Don't know/not answered	53	3

respondent was a young child, and his or her current self-rated status; however, only 11% of respondents assessed themselves as having achieved upward social mobility, and five per cent downward. The great majority considered themselves to have remained within their parents' class.

The third and fourth of these primary discriminators are age and sex. As the 1984 Report showed, clear divisions emerge between men and women on some issues. On others, age is a more important source of difference. But there are also differences between men and women within particular age groups. For some purposes, then, we shall refer to age; for others to sex; and for yet others to age/sex differences. The table below shows the basic age groupings, but for many purposes we shall wish to refer simply to younger, middle-aged or older men and women.

Age within sex

	Total		Men		Women	
	number	%	number	%	number	%
18–24	213	13	108	7	105	6
25–34	311	19	146	9	165	10
35–44	293	18	142	9	151	9
45–54	223	14	105	6	118	7
55–59	130	8	62	4	68	4
60–64	146	9	65	4	81	5
65 and over	315	19	144	9	171	10

We turn now to those divisions that might be expected to exert a less generalised influence upon social attitudes. The first of these is *sectoral location* which derives from the Standard Industrial Classification of the respondent's present job. In order to avoid having small numbers of respondents in particular cells, and in order to bring out those aspects of sectoral location that may be expected to bear upon the broader life experience and thereby to shape attitudes, we have collapsed these categories into a basic distinction between public and private, manufacturing and services, on the basis of respondents' current job (for those who have one).

Sectoral location

	number	%
Public sector:		
Services	237	14
Manufacturing and transport	55	3
Private sector:		
Non-manufacturing	307	19
Manufacturing	239	15
Working, but no information	14	1
Not working/not classified	793	48

The next division which we shall refer to occasionally is housing tenure. The influence of tenure upon social and political attitudes is subject to much speculation, not least because of the substantial expansion of home ownership in recent years, particularly among former council tenants. The variable we use is, strictly speaking, the accommodation of the household and to speak of respondents as 'owner occupiers' is an inescapable compression. These categories conflate those who are buying their own homes with those who own them outright, a distinction which could well prove to be important on, for example, economic issues.

Housing tenure of household

	number	%
Owner occupiers	1,081	66
Public rented (local authority or new town)	420	26
Rented from housing association	15	1
Other rented	122	7
No information	7	*

We are also concerned, so far as the nature of the data permits, to explore regional variations. It is, however, necessary to exercise considerable caution in doing so, owing to the very small numbers in some of the regional cells and the

Region and type of area

	number	%
Scotland	177	11
North	440	27
Midlands	283	17
Wales	94	6
South	495	30
Greater London	157	10
Metropolitan areas	576	35
Non-metropolitan areas	1,069	65

clustering of the sample. Although we have classified respondents into 10 standard regions, it is in many cases preferable to compress the variable, as shown above. In other instances, we distinguish only between those living in metropolitan and in non-metropolitan areas.

Finally, we turn to the sole measure which we use both as an attitude dimension itself and as a basic discriminator in exploring other attitudes: party identification. While people's strength of attachment to a particular party (or to none) is an interesting topic for exploration, particularly nowadays when the class basis of party support is said to be diminishing, the attitudes of different party identifiers to social, economic and political issues is also of considerable interest. For that reason we treat party identification as an analysis variable as well.

Party identification

	number	%
Conservative	635	39
SDP/Liberal/Alliance	219	13
Labour	575	35
Other party	28	2
Non-aligned	102	6
Other/don't know/not answered	86	5

These then are the basic social divisions with which we shall be concerned: income, class, age and sex, sector, tenure, region and party identification. All but the last (and the rarely used self-rated class) are measures of people's characteristics or attributes which locate the respondent within the social order and which may be expected to shape his or her attitudes to the world. Whether and how far distinct social attitudes are associated with these social divisions is the concern of the remaining parts of this chapter.

The selection of issues and themes for investigation is necessarily an arbitrary matter. This chapter is based on a number of themes that cut across the more specific issues to which a survey of this type is normally addressed. Each theme draws upon a group of questions which are loosely related to one another and which can be explored through each of the basic social divisions in turn. The themes explored here are: party identification and partisanship; political efficacy; intervention and the role of the state; and class and income equality.

Party identification and partisanship

Party identification, or the individual's sense of allegiance to a political party, is an important axis along which to analyse the responses to other attitudinal questions, for it bears directly upon the relationship between a party's policies and the views of those who, in varying measure, support it. Clearly, a party which is at odds with its supporters either on specific issues or in terms of broad dispositions or images stands to lose support either by abstention or by the transfer of allegiance to the 'next nearest' party. The formation of the Liberal/SDP Alliance heightens the possibilities of such transfer of allegiance at the margin of either main party's supporters (see Chapter 7 for evidence of such transfer). Thus the prospects of a major political realignment in Britain may turn upon the extent to which the least committed adherents of a major party are tempted to detach themselves from it. Strength of attachment to party is then of interest both to those who wish to speculate about long-term political change and to those whose interest centres on polarisation – the deepening of attitudinal differences between the more intense supporters of the two major parties.

Our approach to measuring the distribution and strength of party identification followed the practice adopted in the first of these surveys. We asked up to three questions in order to elicit a party preference. We asked first: *Do you think of yourself as a supporter of any one political party?* Where the reply was in the negative we asked: *Do you think of yourself as a little closer to one political party than to the others?* Where the respondents did not, we asked finally: *If there were a general election tomorrow which political party do you think you would be most likely to support?*

Some explanation of the particular terminology we adopted is in order at this point, for it is repeated through succeeding chapters. Those who chose a party in response to any one of these three questions we term *identifiers,* although stylistic considerations will sometimes lead us to speak of 'adherents', 'followers of' or 'those professing an attachment to' a party. Those who immediately identified themselves as supporters in response to the first question we term *partisans* and, as we shall see, these respondents often do feel more intensely about issues that divide the parties than do the rest of the sample. Those who thought themselves 'a little closer' to a party we term *sympathisers.* Those who profess no more than a voting preference we term *residual identifiers.* Too much should not be made of the distinction between the second and third categories of party identifiers, and for many purposes we shall confine our intra-party analyses to 'partisans' and 'others'. This rather inquisitorial approach to identifying political allegiances produced a quite widespread declaration of preference, more in fact than would be expected to translate itself into turnout at election time. Even so, six per cent of the sample resisted our invitations and declared no allegiance, and we term these the *non-aligned.* In the tables that follow their numbers are generally added to those – a further two per cent – who supported smaller parties.

We turn now to the social basis of party identification and partisanship. The following table shows the relationship between party identification and Social Class, calculated (unlike the procedure followed for class categorisations elsewhere in this report) on an identical basis to that used last year. This slight departure from standard usage allows direct comparison with the findings of our initial survey.

Comparison with the table on page 13 of last year's report shows that the familiar relationship between Social Class and party support continues, although the results suggest an increase in support for the Labour party among skilled manual workers since the 1983 survey (38% to 47%), largely at the expense of the Alliance and the non-aligned.

We also looked for changes in the proportion of *partisans,* that is the proportion of a party's adherents who immediately identify themselves as supporters. There has been little change in the proportions of Conservative and Alliance identifiers falling into the partisan category; but there was a remarkable 13 point increase in the proportion of Labour identifiers who were willing to describe themselves as supporters without further prompting. Moreover, this increase is not the by-product of a falling off of the more marginal adherents; it represents a switch. The changes since the 1983 general election seem therefore to have produced an intensification of Labour support within a stable electoral base; future years will show whether or not this is a short-term effect, possibly of the intervening changes in Labour's leadership.

Party identification by Social Class

		Social Class		
	I/II	III non-manual	III manual	IV/V
	%	%	%	%
Conservative identifiers	51	48	31	25
Alliance identifiers	16	17	10	11
Labour identifiers	22	23	46	52
Non-aligned/others	5	6	9	7

The patterns of party identification can also be related to the other major social divisions. There were, for example, clear relationships between household income and party identification, with the wealthier groups more likely to support the Conservative party than Labour, and *vice versa*. But it is perhaps more remarkable that, while the direction of the relationship is clear, there remain very sizeable minorities who did not support their 'expected' party; in the highest income group, about half the respondents supported the Conservative party, a quarter Labour, and the remainder either identified with the Alliance or were non-aligned. It is, however, worth stressing that no party's support was very closely associated with a particular income group at the expense of others.

Party identification by household income

	Less than £5,000	£5,000– £7,999	£8,000– £11,999	£12,000 and over
	%	%	%	%
Conservative	30	33	45	49
Alliance	11	16	14	17
Labour	47	37	32	24
Non-aligned	8	9	4	7

Nor was it surprising to find that there was a strong relationship between the occupancy of public housing and a Labour vote. Housing policy has rarely enjoyed bi-partisan consensus and the decline of the private rental sector has contributed to the partisan polarisation of housing tenure, a pattern which has possibly been reinforced by income polarisation as the better-off tenants move into owner occupation. As the table shows, there was strong support for the Labour party among those renting from a local authority or new town corporation; indeed, this is the sole social group of any size in which Labour actually had majority support.

Party identification by housing tenure

	Owner occupiers %	Public renters %	Other tenures %
Conservative	47	19	34
Alliance	15	10	12
Labour	27	54	42
Non-aligned	6	12	7

The Labour party is also popularly identified with the public sector, both the nationalised industries and public sector services. Overall, the relationship revealed by our results suggests that such a popular association does not, however, translate directly into employee support: public sector employees as a group did prefer Labour to the Conservatives, but only by a ratio of about four to three, a ratio that was reversed among private sector employees. Alliance support was unusually high among those in the public sector. Moreover, there were sharp distinctions to be found within these 'ownership' sectors according to whether or not the individual was employed in manufacturing or service industries.

Party identification by industrial sector

	Public sector		Private sector	
	manufacturing (and transport) %	services %	manufacturing %	services %
Conservative	21	34	36	48
Alliance	15	21	12	11
Labour	52	35	39	26
Non-aligned	9	6	6	9

The numbers in some of these categories are small, and too much weight should not be placed upon the distribution of party support in public sector manufacturing and transport in particular. Overall it would appear that location in service industries and in the private sector are both somewhat associated with support for the Conservative party, while location in manufacturing and in the public sector are somewhat associated with support for Labour. But these are not strong relationships, and they are likely to be compounded by the fact that the manufacturing sector and the service sector contain very different distributions of occupational class categories whose allegiances – as we have seen – are different. How far sectoral location actually exercises an independent influence upon party identification must be determined from larger sample bases or from more sophisticated multivariate analysis techniques. There are indications in our findings that occupational sector and housing tenure may combine to have a powerful effect, with public sector tenants who work in the public sector having some fairly distinctive views; but again the numbers are far too small to yield confident conclusions.

Although age and sex will be seen to be important axes in the patterning of opinion on specific issues, there are no very strong indications of this in the distribution of support for the various parties, except for somewhat greater support for Conservatives among older women.

Party identification by age group within sex

	Men		Women	
	under 35	35 and over	under 35	35 and over
	%	%	%	%
Conservative	38	38	35	41
Alliance	10	14	13	14
Labour	39	36	35	33
Non-aligned	8	7	14	6

We turn now from the distribution of party support among the various social groups to consider strength of attachment and engagement in 'mainstream' party politics, and to draw comparisons between the first and second year's findings. Monitoring attitudinal change over time is a primary function of this series of surveys, but we did not anticipate that year-on-year changes would be very large.

It is of course easy to mistake short-term fluctuations in political alignment for long-term shifts, although our own data, derived as they are from systematic probing, may be rather more robust than forced choice responses to routine opinion polls. They also have the advantage of being gathered annually, unlike the data from the (equally searching) British Election Studies. Some standard measures of political change may therefore be noted in passing: those that relate to the class polarisation of party support; to the alignment of different cohorts or age groups; and to the 'two-party share' of the support of these cohorts.

Measures of class polarisation were discussed in last year's report, and the interested reader is referred there (pp. 12–15) for the background to this discussion and for the relevant time series data. Class polarisation is simply a measure of the extent to which divisions of party identity are also those of Social Class. The standard measures of this relationship show gradual secular decline over the past 20 years in the extent to which class and party are bound up with one another, to the point where the primacy of Social Class in electoral analysis has come under serious challenge (Dunleavy and Husbands, 1985). Our 1984 data also suggest that the class basis of party politics is far weaker than in the past, although there is some apparent stabilisation of the downward trend when this year's figures are compared with last, largely for the reason discussed above: the revival of Labour support among skilled manual workers. But, in any event, the thesis of class dealignment has now been re-examined and questioned by Heath, Jowell and Curtice (1985).

The extent to which different age groups were disposed towards any political party was touched upon in last year's report. Again, younger voters shared a much weaker attachment to their favoured parties than that of older people, as measured by the proportion of partisans (of any party) in the various age groups, and this was more noticeable for women than men among the under 35s. Last year's report also commented that alignment to the two-party system ('two-party share') was weakest in the younger age groups and among new voters in particular. This year's findings, however, confound that judgement, for there has been a nine-point increase in the proportion of 18-24 year olds identifying (at any level of intensity) with one or other of the major parties. This is another way of expressing a considerable erosion of Alliance support among the youngest age groups.

In order to probe for factors that may explain people's attachment or otherwise to particular parties, we included a simple question this year about whether respondents saw the parties as extreme or moderate. The responses to such a question have to be treated with some caution, for it is too easy to assume that 'extremism' is seen as a negative evaluation of a party. However, the findings do suggest that this is more likely to be the case than otherwise, so we seem to be justified in taking the extreme/moderate dichotomy as an expression of how far respondents distance themselves from the party in question. While it may well be the case that the ordinary voter does not deal in the same symbolic language of politics as the professional commentator, it would nonetheless appear that 'moderation' and 'extremism' discriminate between the parties. We asked: *On the whole, would you describe the Conservative party nowadays as extreme or moderate?* We then repeated the question for the Labour party and the SDP/Liberal Alliance.

	Total %	Conservative identifiers %	Alliance identifiers %	Labour identifiers %
The Conservative party nowadays				
is extreme	48	26	66	67
is moderate	37	61	19	20
The Alliance nowadays				
is extreme	6	6	6	7
is moderate	55	59	78	50
The Labour party nowadays				
is extreme	41	60	55	17
is moderate	41	23	28	70

Overall, more respondents saw the Conservative party as extreme (48%) than saw the Labour party in those terms (41%) despite there being a strong association between support for a party and *not* seeing it as extreme. Whether the minority who saw their favoured party as extreme supported it for that reason, or despite its extremism, is a matter of importance to the solidity of that party's support. That the latter is the case can be inferred from the fact that partisans of the two major parties are more inclined to see the *other* party as extreme than are either sympathisers or residual identifiers. The Alliance alone has an image of moderation even in the eyes of its opponents, and its adherents see it overwhelmingly as 'moderate'. Even so, it should be noted (as is apparent from the distributions above) that many Conservative and Labour identifiers would not even attempt to classify the Alliance as either extreme or moderate.

As the following table shows, people under 35 were less inclined to see the two major parties as extreme than were those above that age, but it is notable that in all age groups the Conservatives were more likely than Labour to be considered extreme. This was not the case at the time of the general election (see Heath, Jowell and Curtice, 1985), and may well have been influenced by the accession of Labour's new leadership.

		Conservative party nowadays is extreme	Labour party nowadays is extreme
Men			
18–24	%	46	31
25–34	%	50	47
35–54	%	54	42
over 55	%	50	46
Women			
18–24	%	34	27
25–34	%	45	41
35–54	%	51	39
over 55	%	46	44

Political efficacy: the individual and the government

In the 1984 Report we introduced the idea of political efficacy, that is people's expectations of being able to wield effective political influence. We were particularly interested in the propensity to act, either individually or collectively, when faced with the prospect of an unjust or harmful govern-mental action. We found that this propensity was positively associated with Social Class, education and other factors, and that the choice of individual or collective avenues of protest varied in a similar way. While in Chapter 6 we discuss the relative willingness of people to protest against the actions of *central* and *local* government respectively, this chapter takes a rather different approach, examining the relative assertiveness of various social groups; it then considers the question of system efficacy: that is, belief in the ability of government to change things.

Political efficacy and activism

The rationale for our interest in this topic was fully set out in the 1984 Report, to which the interested reader is referred for further discussion (pp. 20–26). In summary, our approach was twofold: to determine the propensity of the individual to act, and to ascertain the 'influence strategy' which would be chosen in the hypothetical circumstances of being faced with some unspecified but unwelcome act on the part of government. But we made one important change this year which precludes exact comparisons between this year's results and last year's.

Last year we sought to anchor responses more firmly in actual experience by first asking respondents whether they had ever found a proposed law to be 'unjust or harmful' before going on to ask what course of action (if any) they had taken on that occasion, and then what course of action they would choose if faced with such an eventuality today. Finally, we asked which of the courses of action they judged likely to be the most effective. This year we dropped the preliminary question, with the result that some people's responses were not influenced by their recollection that they had never found anything to object to or that, if they had, they had acquiesced in it. So we are dealing now with declarations of intent rather than with reports of characteristic behaviour, and these declarations are rather higher. Our interest is in whether or not such intentions discriminate between social groups.

First, what 'influence strategies' did our respondents claim they would adopt? These fell into three categories: inaction, actions that depended on the individual for their effectiveness (personal action), and actions that depended upon the involvement of other people as well (collective action). Each of the two categories of action included *four* distinct courses, any number of which might be chosen through repeated probes on the part of the interviewer. So the answers sum to more than 100%.

Responses to the prospect of an unjust or harmful law being considered by Parliament: hypothetical and 'most effective' actions

	Would take	Most effective
	%	%
Personal action:		
Contact MP	55	43
Speak to influential person	15	4
Contact government department	9	4
Contact radio, TV or newspaper	18	16
Collective action:		
Sign petition	57	12
Raise issue in an organisation I belong to	8	2
Go on a protest or demonstration	9	6
Form a group of like-minded people	8	3
None of these	8	7

By and large, there were no very marked differences in the ranking of these several strategies. Making representations to the MP remained the most popular of the individual strategies, and signing petitions the most popular of the collective strategies. Because this relative stability in the pattern of choice co-existed with considerable inter-group differences in the *number* of choices made and in the extent to which inaction was preferred, we have expressed the overall propensity to act in terms of a simple index: the Personal Action Index (PAI) and the similarly composed Collective Action Index (CAI). Each expresses the average number of responses chosen by a given group of respondents, after taking account of non-response, and is calculated thus:

$$\frac{P - i}{n} \quad \text{or} \quad \frac{C - i}{n}$$

where P is the number of 'personal' actions mentioned, C the number of 'collective' actions, i the number of people choosing none of the courses of action offered and n the number of respondents in the group. For the sample as a whole, this produced a PAI score of 0.88 and a CAI score of 0.74, where the minimum possible score was minus one and the maximum possible score four.

Although the values of the scores themselves will not bear close comparisons with last year's results for the reasons given above, the basic pattern of responses was broadly comparable. Those with greater resources – higher status, higher income, more education – achieved higher scores, particularly in respect of personal efficacy. Among some groups however, most notably skilled manual workers, the propensity to take collective action was no less than that for personal action, while among young people it was actually greater.

The class and income associations of political efficacy are not surprising and, being broadly congruent with access to personal and collective power, they are probably a fair reflection of the degree of assertiveness and preferred modes of influence open to these different social groups. However, when we turn to examine the various age groups more complex patterns emerge, particularly among women.

Political efficacy scores by age and sex

	PAI		CAI	
	men	women	men	women
18–24	0.88	0.75	0.94	0.97
25–34	0.92	0.90	0.95	0.82
35–44	1.09	0.91	0.87	0.80
45–54	1.04	1.04	0.69	0.70
55–64	0.94	0.83	0.72	0.60
Over 65	0.85	0.51	0.61	0.37

As the table shows, *personal* efficacy has a curvilinear relationship with age, increasing into middle age and declining among the older age groups. The peak for the total sample — a score of 1.04 – was reached by both men and women in the 45–54 age group, but it tended to be lower among women than among men in other age groups, especially the oldest. The most plausible explanation of this relationship between age and efficacy is that it results from the interaction of two processes. First, as Kavanagh, in his (1980) review of *The Civic Culture* indicates, the overall level of political assertiveness is increasing with each generation, for "the traditional bonds . . . are waning, and with them the old restraints of hierarchy and deference" (p.170). Second (and this point has been largely ignored by political scientists), personal efficacy is a learned attribute, developed through the accumulation of personal resources that comes to some extent without regard to class and income. It follows that we would expect today's 18–24 year olds to be more assertive 30 years on than are today's 45–54 year olds. If we are right, the effects on the political process in Britain will be considerable.

When we turn our attention to *collective* efficacy we find a quite different, broadly linear relationship with age, the highest scores being registered by young people, and lower scores being registered as people get older. Once again, gender differences stand out. The youngest women obtained the highest scores of any group (though much the same as the youngest men), while women over the age of 65 obtained the lowest scores (much lower than older men). The lower CAI scores for older people undoubtedly reflect the more quiescent political culture within which they reached maturity, and, in the case of women, the sharper sex-role differentiation of that time. The drop among men over 65 possibly also reflects their disengagement from the labour market.

The high scores for young people may be explained partly in cultural terms, although a rather more convincing explanation is that collective action is a substitute for the deployment of personal resources, a means of 'empowerment' for those who have yet to acquire the social resources that would predispose them to personal action. But the more extreme form of the 'cultural' explanation, emphasising as it does a secular shift towards 'revolt', towards less orderly political conduct, and towards what Marsh (1977, p. 234) calls "a noisy and disrespectful participatory democracy", is hardly sustained by our data. We are after all dealing here with what are for the most part quite prosaic courses of action. Moreover, if a trend towards greater collective action does indeed emerge over time, this need not be at the expense of personal participation. Nor need it take the form of 'noisy' or disorderly collective action.

In all, a greater willingness to act with others and make use of the proliferating voluntary associations may be thought to represent an enhancement and not a diminution of 'civility' – a blend of activism and acceptance, assertion and acquiescence – of which Almond and Verba (1963) wrote, and which, in the collective sphere, has not hitherto been a strong feature of British as compared with American political life. On the other hand, a rising collective action score, interpreted out of context, might equally well indicate an increasing taste for the politics of gesture.

We are left with three possible interpretations of these findings. The first is that 'civility' is indeed increasing, as evidenced by rising PAI scores; this interpretation posits a process of political learning whereby personal action tends to displace collective action. The second is that 'youth' is the cutting edge of political protest; this interpretation supposes that high CAI scores will be maintained and that collective action – 'unite and fight' – will *continue* to be preferred at the expense of personal action. The third interpretation sees collective action and personal action as *equally* civil or benign, reflecting increasing political sophistication and a recognition that different modes of action are appropriate to different circumstances.

Which interpretation is preferred is, for the moment, largely a matter of taste, but we do have some supplementary evidence to set beside the data on political activism. Willingness to break the law (and the likelihood of doing so) can be seen as a further index of incivility, for civil society (it may be said) depends upon assertive acts taking place only within the law.

We included two questions which are relevant to this issue. We asked first: *In general would you say that people should obey the law without exception, or are there exceptional occasions on which people should follow their consciences even if it means breaking the law?* We followed this by asking: *Are there any circumstances in which you might break a law to which you were very strongly opposed?* Those who answered 'yes' were then asked – and encouraged by the interviewer's probing – to say what those circumstances might be.

Overall, 57% of the respondents affirmed that the law should be obeyed 'without exception' with only one per cent unable to answer the question. This commitment to law was held with little regard to Social Class, although there were interesting differences between manual and non-manual workers in Social Class III, with manual workers being less inclined to obey the law without exception than white-collar workers were. Workers in manufacturing industry (whether public or private) were also markedly less committed to observance of

the law than were those currently unemployed, perhaps reflecting the possibility of unlawful industrial action; our fieldwork took place during the 1984
miners' strike.

Party identification, and the strength of identification, had a strong association with the respective claims of law and conscience, with Conservatives being
far more strongly committed to the law than were followers of the Labour and
Alliance parties. Labour identifiers as a whole were evenly divided between law
and conscience as overriding claims, while Conservatives favoured legality by a
two to one majority. As is often the case with more marked party divisions,
partisanship intensifies this relationship: 72% of Conservative partisans would
obey the law without exception, compared with only 43% of Labour partisans.

There was also an extremely powerful association with age, or stage in the
life-cycle. For instance, while 60% of the under 25s would put exceptional
claims of conscience above those of law, the 25–34 age group is more or less
equally divided on the issue, and only around a quarter of those aged 55 and
over adopt that position.

Not surprisingly, those who are ready to promote the claims of conscience
have far higher political action scores than those who think the law is
paramount, as the following table shows. It also shows the same sort of
association between political activism and the propensity *actually* to break the
law in certain circumstances.* However, the considerable support for the
claims of conscience against those of law was not matched by any general
willingness among respondents to break the law themselves. Around two-thirds
would not envisage breaking a law to which they were strongly opposed.

Political efficacy scores by orientation to the law

	PAI	CAI
The law should be obeyed without exception	0.85	0.61
People should follow their consciences on occasion	0.93	0.91
Would not break the law	0.79	0.65
Might break a law to which strongly opposed	1.05	0.98

Again, however, there were very marked differences among the several social
groups, with lower status white-collar workers and unskilled manual workers
the most 'obedient'. Party identification also proved to have a fairly strong
association with expectations of personal law-breaking, with Conservatives
showing the expected greater degree of acceptance of unpalatable laws.
Interestingly, Conservative and Alliance *partisans* were both less willing than
less committed followers of their parties to break a law to which they were
strongly opposed. Labour partisans on the other hand, were more willing to do
so, as the following figures show.

---

*Kavanagh (1980) reports "an upsurge of more direct forms of protest and self-assertiveness in
recent years" and claims to have "uncovered an important change in the political culture . . .
there appear to be higher levels of ideology and mistrust and when these are combined there is an
enhanced potential for protest" (p. 152). The source for these conclusions is Alan Marsh's *Protest
and Political Consciousness* (1977). However, Marsh set out to investigate the roots of 'protest
potential', and his sample design deliberately over-represented young middle-class respondents.

Those considering they would break a law to which they were strongly opposed

	%
Conservative:	
partisans	22
others	30
Alliance:	
partisans	26
others	35
Labour:	
partisans	36
others	27

When the likelihood of breaking the law was analysed by age and sex, we found very strong support for obedience to unpalatable laws within the older age groups, and generally more 'obedient' attitudes among women (in virtually all age groups) compared with men.

Those considering they would break a law to which they were strongly opposed

	Men	Women
18–24	50%	31%
25–34	48%	30%
35–44	46%	29%
45–54	38%	25%
55–64	28%	11%
65 and over	13%	11%

These very strong relationships, and the apparent willingness of around half of men under 45 to break a law to which they were strongly opposed, demands that the composition of these figures be closely scrutinised. An open-ended question was used to elicit the circumstances in which respondents envisaged they might break the law, and we have coded their responses into a number of categories covering such eventualities as the protection of property or the family, the protection of trade union rights, or the protection of others being unjustly or ill-treated. The generally mundane character of many of the responses suggests that it would be dangerous to overinterpret the bald figures on willingness to break the law: although the question specified a law 'to which you were very strongly opposed', many respondents referred to hypothetical circumstances in which they felt that breaking the ordinary criminal or civil law might be justified, or to evidently minor breaches of petty laws. The following table gives the distribution of responses among the one quarter of respondents who envisaged breaking the law and could specify (codable) circumstances in which they might do so.

Taking defence issues and the protection of existing rights and liberties as the manifestation of personal willingness to engage in civil disobedience or 'political law-breaking', we found that only 32% of those who could envisage breaking the law (or nine per cent of the total sample) specified such reasons of 'principle'. Most hypothetical law-breakers envisaged themselves doing so in order to protect their own interests (or those of vulnerable third parties), suggesting that respondents found it difficult to conceptualise a hypothetical law to which they might be 'strongly opposed'. The replies to this question do not suggest a significant groundswell of 'conscience politics' in Britain, even among the least 'obedient' groups. There was certainly little support for political law-breaking among the sample as a whole and still less personal inclination to take part in it. That those who registered the highest levels of political assertiveness were also the most likely to be 'disobedient' is not unexpected. It reflects the fact, perhaps, that they regarded laws as less immutable than others do and were more inclined to act to change them. In all, reports of the death of the civic culture (Marsh, 1977; Jessop, 1974; Kavanagh, 1980) appear to have been premature.

Circumstances in which respondents might break the law
(percentages of those specifying circumstances)

	%
Protection of self, family, property or others being ill-treated	36
Protection of existing rights and liberties (including trade union rights)	28
Protest about defence issues	4
Non-observance of petty or harassing laws	19
Depends on circumstances	19

Beliefs in the effectiveness of government

Beliefs in the effectiveness of government also bear closely upon the maintenance of civility. A perception that government had lost all effectiveness would deny it legitimacy and encourage direct action and, perhaps, a Weimar-like rise of 'anti-system' parties. Equally, civic stability might require that the expectations of government be tempered by moderation, or even a resigned scepticism. There is no *a priori* reason for expecting a particular relationship between a sense of personal efficacy and a belief in government efficacy. On the one hand, those with greater personal resources might look less to government than to their private efforts to achieve their aims; they might have had more opportunity to acquaint themselves with the limits of government. We might therefore expect an inverse relationship between personal assertiveness and belief in government's ability to solve social and economic problems. On the other hand, propositions from social psychology might seem more plausible: that our views of the limits of government are a projection of our view of ourselves. Thus, quietism or fatalism in the sphere of personal action would, through anthropomorphic projection, find reflection in a sceptical view of state power. These are speculations, but insofar as they predict the direction of an association, it is the second that is supported by our data. Those groups with the lowest scores of political activism also have the lowest expectations of government: manual workers, the less well paid, and those who left school earlier (all associated subgroups).

This broad picture is based on the sum of responses to a series of questions included in the self-completion questionnaire. We introduced the question in the following way: *Some people say that British governments nowadays – of whichever party – can actually do very little to change things. Others say they can do quite a bit.* We then went on to ask, in turn, whether they thought that British governments nowadays could do 'very little' or 'quite a bit' to: keep prices down, to reduce unemployment, to improve the general standard of living or to improve the health and social services. We shall not here examine the pattern of responses to each of these propositions in turn; others should do so. But to get an overall view of how far our respondents felt government could *generally* achieve objectives of this sort, we summed the responses to form two simple categories: 'governments are rather powerless' (less than two responses of 'quite a bit'), and 'governments are rather powerful' (two or more responses of 'quite a bit').

Perceptions of governments' ability to change things

		Governments are rather powerless	Governments are rather powerful
Working class: (Social Classes III manual, IV, V)	%	34	66
Middle class: (Social Classes I, II, III non-manual)	%	19	81
Household income:			
less than £8,000 pa	%	29	71
£8,000 pa and above	%	20	80
School-leaving age:			
16 or under	%	27	73
17–18	%	19	81
19 or over	%	17	83

Differences by class, income and education were marked, but there were other differences too, among the more interesting of which were sectoral location and as always, party identification. Working in the public sector seemed to engender an understandably slightly higher rating of the efficacy of government, almost regardless of whether the work was manual or non-manual. As far as party differences are concerned, the results are indeed interesting, with Conservative identifiers expressing a greater (and probably class and income-related) expectation of the performance of government, but with no intensification by degree of partisanship. In the case of Alliance partisans, however, their response (albeit that of a small number) may reflect a low expectation of governments of the *major* parties, a construction which our question unintentionally invited

As for the sample as a whole, we find that respondents discriminated quite sharply between the four objectives, regarding some as more within government's grasp than others.

Perceptions of governments' ability to change things

		Governments are rather powerless	Governments are rather powerful
Sectoral location:			
public sector	%	23	76
private sector	%	28	72
Party identification:			
Conservative	%		
partisans	%	23	77
others	%	22	78
Alliance			
partisans	%	32	69
others	%	22	79
Labour			
partisans	%	28	72
others	%	26	73

Perceptions of governments' efficacy

		Governments can do very little	Governments can do quite a bit
To keep prices down	%	38	59
To reduce unemployment	%	46	51
To improve the general standard of living	%	30	66
To improve the health and social services	%	19	77

The overall picture is clear. The state of the health and social services, being largely determined by the resources allocated to them, is seen to lie more clearly within the government's grasp than the other objectives. Nonetheless, there is fairly substantial support for the idea that government can do much to control the level of prices, and this doubtless reflects the considerable actual reduction in the rate of inflation over the past five years. But while it is commonly argued that increased unemployment has been the cost of that achievement, respondents seemed to take a relatively pessimistic view of the intractability of unemployment, despite the overwhelming view (see Chapter 2) that reducing unemployment should be a high priority.

Intervention and the role of the state

Since 1979 the role of the state in economic and social life has been among the foremost political issues as deregulation, privatisation and a stronger emphasis on monetary policy have reversed many postwar trends. The emergence of a 'new' Conservatism, drawing much of its inspiration from Friedrich von Hayek, has created a debate about aspects of the state that have largely been taken for granted in previous decades. New pressure groups and centres of thought – the Social Policy Unit, the Adam Smith Institute – have taken their place alongside such well-established bodies as the Institute of Economic Affairs. The iconoclasts of yesterday have become today's icons. But how far is this intellectual and philosophical ferment reflected in the attitudes and values of those diverse social groups that make up the British population? We asked a number of questions that address this issue on both economic and welfare policies (including attitudes to private provision) as we sought to ascertain not only the support for or opposition to the new economic orthodoxy, but also the location among various social groups of these attitudes.

Free-market economics

Faith in market processes has long divided the supporters of the two major parties in Britain, but the polarisation has surely increased since 1979 when the present government not only eschewed statutory controls of wages and prices but also sought actively to diminish the size and influence of the public sector. If these policy stances were reflected in the population, we would expect strong and consistent support for free-market philosophies among Conservatives, strong support from Labour identifiers for market management and state intervention, and Alliance attitudes to be somewhere in between, with perhaps a closer resemblance to Conservative opinion.

We first examined attitudes to a group of explicit economic policy measures concerned with the degree of regulation of wages, prices and imports. We asked people about 'a number of policies which might help Britain's economic problems' and asked the respondents simply whether they supported or opposed them. We offered nine policies representing a range of political complexions, only some of which are discussed here.

Support for economic controls

	Support	Oppose
	%	%
Control wages by legislation	42	53
Control prices by legislation	66	30
Introducing import controls	67	27

In respect of statutory wage controls, it is worth drawing attention to the fact that the expected relationship was *not* found. There were no consistent patterns that distinguished manual from non-manual workers on this issue, nor the unemployed from the employed, nor public from private sector employees, nor the North from the South, nor even the three groups of party identifiers. Conservative and Alliance *partisans* were a little stronger in their support for wage controls, but Labour partisans were, perhaps surprisingly, no different from other Labour identifiers.

There were, however, strong relationships with income. Two-thirds of those with household incomes in excess of £12,000 pa opposed wage controls, and the proportion opposing them fell with income so that wage controls had the support of virtually half (48%) of those in the lowest income group. There was also a strong association with age. The older age groups – and younger women – were more supportive, opposition to controls being particularly intense among men under 35 (70%). All of which seems to suggest that support for wage controls depends not on philosophy or ideology but on interest. The richer and the upwardly mobile are most opposed, while the poorer and those whose earning potential might well have peaked (older workers and pensioners) are most in favour.

Support for the control of prices was greater than for the control of wages and was also more sensitive to income, class and tenure. There were also modest party differences on this issue, with 61% of Conservative identifiers and 73% of Labour identifiers supporting price controls and, as expected, Alliance identifiers lying in between at 68%. However, these differences were not amplified by partisanship, suggesting that the party differences were reflections of their class and income compositions, rather than of ideology. As with wage controls, women and older people were generally more favourable, but, perhaps surprisingly, sector position – public or private, manufacturing or non-manufacturing – had no effect on the level of support for price controls.

Support for import controls was also generally high but was particularly strong among respondents in Social Class III, whether manual or non-manual (74%). Sector position again had surprisingly little effect, although there was particularly strong support from the very small group in public sector manu-facturing and transport. Curiously, perhaps, respondents in the GLC area formed a rare bastion of free trade ideology, with the unusually high figure of 41% opposing import controls (compared with 27% of the sample as a whole). Despite the Labour party's sporadic support for import controls there were few differences between the various party identifiers, nor even between partisans.

In sum, respondents were quite strongly supportive of economic regulation although they were fairly evenly divided on wage controls. Few strong differences emerged between subgroups, except for the fact that the less well off favoured regulation to a notably greater degree than did the better off. There were surprisingly few connections with political allegiance, suggesting that, paradoxically, the respective parties are not seen as having high policy profiles on economic regulation. The divisions were more pragmatic, being principally related to the respondents' likelihood of gaining or losing from such measures.

We asked one further question which sought to address the issue of Keynesian *versus* free-market ideology – whether the government should 'set up construction projects to create more jobs'. In the event, this question proved a poor discriminator, since it had the support of 89% of the sample with scarcely any room for variation by income, class, party identification or any other variable. In this respect at least, the public as a whole is distinctly interventionist.

Finally, we turn to a more clearly polarising issue, that of state ownership. We asked: *On the whole, would you like to see more or less state ownership of industry, or about the same amount as now?* Although it was the case that relatively few respondents wished to see increases in the extent of state ownership, the support for reductions (more 'privatisation') was also fairly modest, at 36% overall, with slightly stronger support among men than women.

Not surprisingly, those employed in the private sector were more in favour of privatisation (43%) than were those employed in the public sector (34%), but the difference was not as large as might have been anticipated.

At last, however, here was an interventionist issue that proved to be a powerful discriminator along traditional class and income lines, tenure and, of course, party.

Support for a reduction in the extent of state ownership of industry

		Those wishing to see less state ownership
Social Class:		
I/II	%	50
III non-manual	%	38
III manual	%	38
IV/V	%	22
Household income:		
£12,000 and over	%	48
£8,000-11,999	%	42
£5,000-7,999	%	32
less than £5,000	%	30

As many as 60% of the self-employed wanted less state ownership, and owner occupiers were much more enthusiastic 'privatisers' than were local authority tenants. It should be emphasised, however, that the major division of opinion is between less state control and maintaining the *status quo*. In other words, the argument has shifted since 1979 from being concerned with more or less nationalisation to being concerned with more or less privatisation.

The following table shows the strong pattern of party differences, not only *between* parties, but also between partisans and others *within* the same party.

Support for a reduction in state ownership

		Those wishing to see less state ownership
Conservative:		
partisans	%	61
others	%	43
Alliance:		
partisans	%	27
others	%	35
Labour:		
partisans	%	17
others	%	22

Attitudes to the extent of state ownership have, of course, developed and hardened over many decades, and the polarisation of partisan opinion on this issue has probably been accentuated by the privatisation measures of the present government. Even so, the *status quo* is rather more popular than more privatisation, and *much* more popular than more nationalisation.

On regulation in general, we found overwhelming support for employment-creating construction projects and substantial support for other aspects of intervention. There was only minority support for free-market ideology in respect of either import or price controls. Even statutory wage regulation was rejected by only a bare majority. What is most revealing about our findings, however, is that attitudes to these issues (except, notably, to state ownership) clearly depend more on pragmatic and materialistic criteria than on ideological disposition or doctrine.

Welfarism

The basic framework of the welfare state has enjoyed bi-partisan support since its inception in the period of postwar reconstruction. Latterly there have been indications of a divergence of more than marginal significance. Ministers have launched fundamental reviews of the structure of benefits, hailed with hyperbole as a 'new Beveridge'. At the same time, more emphatic encouragement has been given to private health schemes and to private education. These changes of emphasis in explicit policy are, however, likely to be eclipsed in significance by the possible consequences for health, welfare and education of present policies on public expenditure. That a pledge had to be made during the last election campaign that the NHS was 'safe' in Conservative hands was, perhaps, a sign of public concern that limits on expenditure could lead to a deterioration in the standard of the health services. Such concern spelled political dangers. But although there are arguments about how the 'real' level of health expenditure has fared under the present administration, there is no argument about the fact that the government's long-term goal is to hold down or reduce public expenditure in order to reduce taxes.

To what extent are these broad objectives supported? And by whom? To address this issue fully would require a chapter in itself. At this stage we can only review some of the more notable findings in respect of a range of questions covering social expenditure priorities, benefit levels, selectivity and the trade-off between service standards and taxation.

This last issue may conveniently be considered first for it helps to establish the parameters of opinion among respondents and the extent to which they are eager to achieve the benefits of lower taxation. We asked: *Suppose the government had to choose between these three options . . . which do you think it should choose?* and the options offered were: 'reduce taxes and spend less on health, education and social benefits'; 'keep taxes and spending on these services at the same level as now'; and 'increase taxes and spend more on health, education and social benefits'.

The overall figures are remarkable: *only five per cent of the sample supported reductions in services even when linked to tax cuts.* A year earlier the figure had been nine per cent. There was negligible support for this option throughout all social groups. Even among Conservative partisans it ran no higher than seven per cent.

The real division of opinion is confined to the more limited choice between keeping things as they are, and expanding the services by increasing taxation.

While it is true that Conservative *partisans* were the group most strongly in favour of the *status quo*, more than a fifth of them, and a quarter of all Conservatives, favoured increased taxation and services, compared with about one half of all Alliance and Labour identifiers.

This question also appeared to tap a range of class-based attitudes to the welfare state. While the differences between manual and non-manual workers were not as great as might be expected, and while the differences between the income groups were also small, the variations according to *self-rated* class were very large. Sectoral location also had a strong influence, probably via a mix of interest and image.

Choices between tax cuts and social spending

		Reduce taxes and expenditure	Maintain taxes and expenditure	Increase taxes and expenditure
Self-rated social class:				
middle class	%	5	61	28
working class	%	6	47	43
Sectoral location:				
private sector	%	4	57	35
public sector	%	4	43	51

Relating social expenditure options to levels of taxation forces respondents to make trade-offs although we did not, of course, postulate any *particular* tax-rate effects or extent of expenditure. An element of trade-off also intervenes when people are asked to choose priorities for increased government expenditure from a substantial list. Respondents were presented with 10 areas of public expenditure: education, defence, health, housing, public transport, roads, police and prisons, social security benefits, help for industry and overseas aid. They were asked which of them, if any, would be their *highest priority for extra spending*. In the event, the responses were so highly clustered – that is, the sample as a whole was so substantially in agreement – that the pattern of choice for the less popular options will not sustain analysis. As the table below shows, defence, roads, police and prisons, overseas aid and public transport were each given first *or* second priority by only six per cent or fewer of respondents.

Taking just the two most strongly supported areas for increased expenditure, health and education, we find some quite complex patterns. Support for increased health expenditure was remarkably stable throughout the sample, varying by only a few percentage points by age group, by income group (only four percentage points across the whole sample), and by Social Class (with some lessening of support in Social Classes I and II). There was a weak association with party identification, and Alliance identifiers as a whole were marginally the strongest supporters of increased health expenditure; Conservative *partisans* were the weakest, but in this respect they differed from Conservatives as a group. Support for greater investment in the NHS thus ran at very high levels throughout the sample and showed a considerable increase over the previous year. (In 1983 37% of respondents named health as their first priority for increased expenditure; in 1984 51% did so.)

Priorities for extra public expenditure

	First priority	Second priority
	%	%
Health	51	25
Education	20	29
Help for industry	10	10
Housing	6	12
Social security	7	8
Police and prisons	1	5
Defence	3	3
Roads	1	3
Overseas aid	*	1
Public transport	*	1

Although increased educational expenditure also enjoyed strong support overall, it was highly sensitive to a number of factors. Party differences were not great, but once again Alliance identifiers were the strongest and Conservatives the weakest on this issue. Nor were class differences great, but there were strong income and age group effects. As on other issues, support seemed fairly closely linked to material interest: those respondents at the point in the life-cycle where they might have children at school or college were the most strongly in favour. Also, people who had had more experience of education were more likely than their counterparts to favour extra expenditure on education, which may explain why men were, for almost all age groups, rather more in favour of such expenditure than women were.

Support for extra expenditure on education

		Those favouring increased expenditure
Age group:		
18-24	%	47
25-34	%	68
35-54	%	57
55 and over	%	33
Household income:		
under £5,000	%	37
£5,000-7,999	%	52
£8,000-11,999	%	59
£12,000 and over	%	59
School-leaving age:		
under 16	%	46
17-18	%	56
19 and over	%	62

We then asked respondents to indicate their first and second priorities for extra spending on a range of *social benefits* which we identified for them: retirement pensions, child benefits, benefits for the unemployed, benefits for disabled people, and benefits for single parents. Retirement benefits and disablement benefits were strongly favoured over unemployment benefits, with little support for child or single parent benefits. There are signs here of discrimination based on the imputed culpability of the potential recipients with strongest support for the relief of conditions which are seen as universal (age) or the result of fate (disability).

Once again, attitudes seemed clearly to be interest-laden. For instance, the groups most strongly in favour of increasing unemployment benefit were the unemployed themselves and those in the 18-24 age group for whom it was the first priority by a considerable margin. It then reappeared as a concern among men aged 45-54 but not notably among women of that age.

Similarly, support for retirement pensions was fairly low in the youngest age group and rapidly acquired increasing priority with age in a manner reminiscent of the well-known retirement policy advertisements. Support for disability benefits was also quite strongly age-related and was strongest among elderly people. Support for child benefits, by contrast, was highest among respondents under the age of 34, but declined rapidly thereafter. Support for single parent benefits was not only age-related in the expected direction, but was also stronger among women than men in all age groups. Indeed, among young (18-24) women, it was the second most important priority after unemployment benefit.

So much for priorities for future expenditure. But what of attitudes to the present level of and take-up of particular benefits? As we have seen there was little diversity between the various party or class groupings on expenditure *priorities*. But on the issue of the *level* of unemployment benefit we found great divergence. Overall, by a margin of about two to one, the sample thought that unemployment benefit levels were too low rather than too high, a pattern that held irrespective of a respondent's income group, even though manual workers were much more likely than non-manual workers to take this view. And over 70% of the unemployed themselves (compared, say, with only 37% of retired people) thought so too. There was also, in general, a strong association of that judgement with youth. Party identification and the degree of partisanship

Attitudes to the level of unemployment benefit

		Too low	Too high
Conservative:			
partisans	%	27	45
others	%	41	31
Alliance:			
partisans	%	53	23
others	%	53	28
Labour:			
partisans	%	67	19
others	%	64	21

produced even clearer subgroup differences, with Conservative partisans not only being sharply differentiated from other identifiers with that party, but also being alone within the sample in giving more support to the proposition that benefits were too high than *vice versa*.

As was the case last year, we included several questions on attitudes to the National Health Service and to possible changes in its structure. Respondents, particularly the richer and better-off ones, were strongly supportive of the NHS and its present structure. As might be expected, the people who most strongly opposed a 'selective' NHS were those who might be *excluded* by selectivity. So on this issue too, principle seems to be subordinate to pragmatism.

The welfare state therefore seems to stand on secure foundations so far as the patterns of public opinion are concerned. True, there are here, as elsewhere, diverse publics and many opinions. But the issue that divided people was not reduction *versus* expansion, but the relative merits of maintenance or expansion. There were sharp divisions on some issues such as benefit levels, but they did not seem to reflect themselves in attitudes to public expenditure. Circumstance, not ideology, shapes attitudes most directly. Still, there was little sign of public support for expenditure cuts, even if they were to bring promised tax reductions.

Greater priority was given to public services than might have been expected, particularly from among the middle classes, which suggests that these services were indeed seen as a national, and not as a class or sectional resource. (We must remember, however, that the middle classes are major beneficiaries of these resources.) Our findings thus reveal a remarkable gulf between the aspirations and rhetoric of the present administration and the concerns and priorities of most people – including here most Conservatives. The apparent appeal of tax and expenditure cuts will surely not be sustained if the consequences are perceived as further cuts in public services. On these issues then, the Alliance and the Labour party seem to be ploughing fertile ground.

Class and income equality

This year, as last, we asked a series of questions about perceptions of present and future inequality: between men and women, between white and black. The responses in terms of sex and race discrimination were not very different from those obtained in the first round of these surveys and were discussed at length by Colin Airey in the 1984 Report (pp.122-136). This year it is worth dwelling briefly on the question of class and income inequalities, in order to ascertain how far the different social groups agree on the prospects for and the desirability of greater equality in Britain.

Turning first to social class, we asked about the extent to which respondents thought a person's social class affected his or her opportunities in Britain today. We also asked whether they thought the position had changed for the better or worse in the last 10 years, and whether it was likely to change for the better or worse within the next 10 years.

In summary, around two-thirds of respondents attributed considerable influence to social class and about the same proportion felt that things had not improved (or got worse) in the last 10 years and would continue to be no better for the next 10 years. Overall then, the strong impression was one of relative stasis in the class system, an impression borne out by the very small proportions who believed themselves to have experienced personal social mobility.

The proportion of people who thought that social class affected people's opportunities was remarkably stable across all Social Classes and most other subgroups. The greatest variation occurred in the *extent* to which different groups thought that class was influential. Manual workers and people who rated themselves as 'working class' were more likely to say that class affected opportunities 'a great deal', as were tenants of local authority or new town housing. Labour identifiers, and Labour partisans in particular, also registered very much stronger class perceptions than Conservative or Alliance identifiers did.

Degree to which social class affects opportunities in Britain today

		A great deal	Quite a lot	Not very much	Not at all
Tenure:					
owner occupiers	%	22	40	30	5
public sector tenants	%	32	34	24	6
Party identification:					
Conservative					
partisans	%	19	37	36	6
others	%	20	41	32	5
Alliance					
partisans	%	18	38	39	3
others	%	16	51	29	3
Labour					
partisans	%	37	38	17	4
others	%	30	36	25	6

The figures above are notable for the differences in the perceptions of Labour partisans from those of *both* Conservative and Alliance partisans, whose responses were almost indistinguishable. These partisan divisions also carried over into judgements of the extent to which the influence of class on opportunities had diminished: only 21% of Labour partisans thought class less important now, as against 40% of Conservative partisans and 48% of Alliance partisans.

Expectations about future changes in the impact of class bore a very strong relationship to Social Class itself and, once again, to party identification. Alliance identifiers seemed particularly optimistic about change and fluidity in the class structure; almost half of Alliance partisans, for instance, expected class to be less important in 10 years time, compared with one third of Conservative partisans and one fifth of Labour partisans.

Interpretations of the past and projections into the future surely reflect the life experience of the individual and we would on that account expect to find such perceptions themselves to be rooted in class location. And, given the

extent to which British politics have been a matter of class alignment in both
social base and symbolism, the associations with party confirm and endorse
perceptions of the class basis of society. But what of generation? The
experience of class, and the colouring given to it in retrospect and prospect
might well be thought to be a matter of generation or at least of age. But it was
not, or not very much. While it is true that women under 45 were less inclined
to attribute 'a great deal' of influence to class, women generally were more
pessimistic than men about fluidity in the class structure. So far as age is
concerned, however, there was only a gentle curvilinear relationship, with both
men and women in the middle of the life-cycle (25-54) being more likely to
believe that the impact of class had diminished. In other respects the old, the
middle aged and the young had remarkably similar perceptions on this issue.

Turning from social class in general to the more tangible issue of pay
inequality, we asked all those respondents who were currently in work:
*Thinking of the highest and the lowest paid people at your place of work, how
would you describe the gap between their pay, as far as you know?* and we
offered a five-point rating from 'much too big a gap' to 'much too small a gap'.
The answers to this question will clearly be shaped by actual circumstances, but
for the larger social groups it was also intended to serve as a useful indication of
egalitarianism.

In the event, very few respondents (four per cent) regarded their income
differentials at work as either 'too small' or 'much too small'. Around one half
thought they were 'about right'. But there were some marked variations, with
skilled manual workers and younger people the most critical. There was not,
then, a straight relationship with class, and only a modest one with income.
That the perception of pay inequality is more a matter of symbolism than
material circumstance is however suggested by the association with party
identification and the intensification of that association by partisanship: in
effect it is not pay, but inequality itself that appears to be the issue here.

**Gap between lowest paid and highest paid in the workplace
by party identification**

		Much too big/ too big	About right	Much too small/ too small
Conservative:				
partisans	%	28	63	4
others	%	35	50	4
Alliance:				
partisans	%	34	54	9
others	%	29	58	–
Labour:				
partisans	%	51	35	4
others	%	44	39	3

In response to a more general question asked of *all* respondents about whether
the gap in Britain between those with high incomes and those with low incomes
was 'too large', 'about right', or 'too small', partisan divisions again outweighed

class or income divisions. These findings confirm that people's views on such redistributive matters appear to depend more on philosophy than on circumstance. Unlike the response to public expenditure matters, and more like the responses to questions of state ownership, public attitudes here seem to be infused with symbolic overtones. On this issue, however, *unlike* the state ownership issue, those identifying with the Alliance showed an almost identical level of commitment to those identifying with Labour. Only *partisan* Conservatives seem to inhabit a distinctive location.

**Gap between those with high and low incomes generally
by party identification**

		Too large	About right	Too small
Conservative:				
partisans	%	57	37	2
others	%	70	22	4
Alliance:				
partisans	%	84	11	3
others	%	86	12	–
Labour:				
partisans	%	85	7	6
others	%	83	10	3

Conclusion

This chapter has revealed some of the shades of opinion within the population as they relate to such large topics as partisanship, participation, expectations of the state, and various forms of inequality. It will be for others to go beyond these mere glimpses and to explore, by a fuller use of the dataset and by multivariate techniques, the constellation of views and interests that constitute contemporary Britain. What pointers can we offer?

First, that politics *matters*. Since the publication of Abrams and Rose's *Must Labour Lose?* (1960), far too much attention has been devoted to mechanistic analyses of the social bases of party support and to the electoral significance of social and occupational change. Whether the underlying process is one of 'dealignment' or 'realignment' will become clear enough in time; meanwhile, this survey (like its predecessor) points up the significance of the strength of the individual's attachment to party. The previous pages show time and again that partisanship is a powerful discriminator of attitudes to major public issues; it is also a useful guide to the extent to which an issue is politicised at all. And, while partisan commitment perpetuates polarised and adversarial politics (for there are few partisans of the centre), it also invites us to reinstate the individual as a political actor and to redirect our attention to long-neglected issues of political psychology.

Second, just as 'the end of ideology' was prematurely announced, so too was 'the decline of the civic culture'. There is little support in our data for the torrent of literature in the past decade which has sought to demonstrate that

Britain is 'ungovernable', that 'deference' is dead, that political 'demands' outweigh the support given to our institutions, and that formal political parties are 'structurally incapable' of accommodating the range of conflicts presented to them. On the contrary, the values of civility which were celebrated by Almond and Verba in 1963, rigorously (and rightly) questioned by the critics, and fully reassessed in *The Civic Culture Revisited* (Almond and Verba, 1980), seem to be alive and well. The 'old restraints of hierarchy and deference' may indeed have waned but the civic culture is better founded on the spirit of pragmatism and tolerance for which there is ample evidence in our findings.

Third, it must be borne continually in mind that this is a country of distinct publics and diverse opinions. Some of these powerful distinctions – like the interaction of age and gender – are subtle. Others – such as the differences between various party identifiers – are often obscured by larger aggregations. Some deserve attention for their public importance: the gulf between ordinary Conservatives and their leaders, for instance, which is recorded in this and other chapters must surely sound a warning for the present government.

So the opportunities for further rewarding analyses are considerable. The cursory analysis we have been able to undertake so far already reveals a great diversity of sub-cultures – a variety of shades of opinion – only a very few of which have been referred to in this chapter. Yet in too many reports of public opinion the tacit assumption is still made that 'the British public' has a single mind; a simple majority is taken to mean an overwhelming endorsement or rejection of one policy or another. It is as if the rules of British electoral representation – the 'winner takes all' system and the absence of proportional representation – are applied to social policy analysis with similar rigidity.

The strongest argument for this series, therefore, is that it enables variations in attitudes and values to be illuminated and to be measured over time. In this respect it probably provides a more reliable and discriminating yardstick of social difference and social change than does the selective and over-interpreted public record. Future historians may well have cause to thank our sponsors for that.

References

ABRAMS, M. and ROSE, R., *Must Labour Lose?* Penguin, Harmondsworth (1960).

ALMOND, G. A. and VERBA, S., *The Civic Culture*, Princeton University Press, Princeton N. J. (1963).

ALMOND, G. A. and VERBA, S. (eds.), *The Civic Culture Revisited*, Little, Brown and Co., Boston (1980).

DUNLEAVY, P and HUSBANDS, C. T., *British Democracy at the Crossroads: Voting and Party Competition in the 1980s*, George Allen & Unwin, London (1985).

HEATH, A., JOWELL, R. and CURTICE, J., *How Britain Votes*, Pergamon, Oxford (forthcoming, 1985).

JESSOP, B., *Traditionalism, Conservatism and British Political Culture*, George Allen & Unwin, London (1974).

JOWELL, R. and AIREY, C. (eds.), *British Social Attitudes: The 1984 Report*, Gower, Aldershot (1984).

KAVANAGH, D. 'Political Culture in Great Britain: The Decline of the Civic Culture' in Almond, G. A. and Verba, S. (eds.), *The Civic Culture Revisited*, Little, Brown and Co., Boston (1980).
MARSH, A., *Protest and Political Consciousness*, Sage Publications, London (1977).

2 Prices, incomes and consumer issues

*Gerald Goodhardt**

In this chapter we examine some of the issues that face people in their capacity as consumers and employees. The society we live in is often referred to as a 'consumer society', reflecting the power that consumers are said to wield in shaping the economy and determining the products and services which are provided for them. Whereas the providers of goods and services go to great lengths, via the standard procedures of market research, to find out the views and opinions of consumers about their products, we are rather more interested in the perceptions of people about the state of the economy in general and about its likely progress or otherwise. Public perceptions are often self-fulfilling, affecting the way that people behave and, as a result, affecting general consumption patterns and responses. Economic expectations and attitudes are therefore important and we sought to examine them in the context of income levels, perceived levels of inflation and unemployment, and various putative remedies. These were some of the economic background issues against which we assessed consumer issues more generally.

Overall expectations

The fight against inflation has been the major preoccupation of the present government. Despite all assurances, however, the British public does not seem to have been convinced that it is now under control. In answer to the question *In a year from now, do you expect prices generally to have gone up, to have*

---

* Sir John E. Cohen Professor of Consumer Studies at The City University Business School.

stayed the same, or to have gone down?, 83% said they expected them to go up. When questioned further the full breakdown of answers was:

	1983	1984
	%	%
In a year from now expect prices:		
to have gone up by a lot	24	31
to have gone up by a little	56	52
to have stayed the same	12	13
to have gone down by a little	5	3
to have gone down by a lot	1	*

The question in the 1983 survey was phrased slightly differently which could perhaps account for part of the difference. However, there is certainly no evidence that people were any more sanguine about prices in 1984 than they were in 1983. This was in some contrast to expectations about unemployment where although more than half the respondents still thought it would rise in the coming year, the answers were nevertheless more optimistic than a year earlier.

	1983	1984
	%	%
In a year from now expect unemployment:		
to have gone up by a lot	31	25
to have gone up by a little	37	31
to have stayed the same	17	31
to have gone down by a little	12	11
to have gone down by a lot	1	1

People in work were generally fairly sanguine about unemployment, while the unemployed themselves were even more pessimistic than they were a year earlier. Around half of them expected unemployment to go up a lot.

Of course, there are few people alive in Britain today who have ever experienced a time of falling prices. It is probably the case that the best that people hope for in prices is that they should remain stable, whilst on unemployment the expectation that it will stay the same can be seen as a pessimistic view. It is therefore not too unexpected that people still thought, as they did a year earlier, that the government should give higher priority to keeping down unemployment than to keeping down inflation by a ratio of nearly three to one. However, when respondents were asked *Which do you think is of most concern to you and your family . . . inflation or unemployment?* the answers were somewhat different, as the following figures show:

	Should be top priority	Of most concern
	%	%
Keeping down inflation	26	52
Keeping down unemployment	69	44

These answers place in better perspective the public's priorities. A very strong priority was attached to the reduction of unemployment as a national goal, but, from a personal viewpoint, inflation was a more serious threat to most people, particularly to those on fixed incomes such as the retired who are not in the labour market, and to people in managerial or professional occupations for whom the fear of unemployment is less immediate. On the other hand, the young were particularly likely to opt for unemployment as top priority, as were people living in the North as opposed to those in the South, and, of course, the unemployed themselves (see **Tables 2.5 and 2.6**).

What, though, did people mean by prices going up *a little* or *a lot?* Those who said they expected prices to increase were asked to say by how much they expected them to go up in the next 12 months. People on the whole find it very difficult to give numerical answers to questions of this kind, so in order to provide some sort of frame of reference respondents were told: *over the last 12 months prices went up by about 5p in the £, that is by 5%.* Answers were accepted either as a percentage or as pence in the pound, and – in view of the prompt we had given – we expected a clustering of replies around five per cent.

As it turned out 48% of those who thought prices would go up (or 40% of the total sample) thought the rate of increase would stay at five per cent. Of the others by far the majority thought prices would rise faster than in the past rather than slower. Even among those who expected prices to go up by only a little, one in four expected the rise to be greater than in the previous year.

	Total	Those who expected some rise in prices	Those who expected prices to rise a little	Those who expected prices to rise a lot
Expected annual rate of inflation:	%	%	%	%
1 to 4%	7	8	11	4
5%	40	48	59	30
6 to 10%	29	35	24	54
11% or more	2	3	*	7
Don't know	5	6	6	5

To the seven per cent who expected prices to increase less than the previous year we should add the 17% who did not expect prices to increase at all. The result is that only one in four of the sample expected the overall inflation picture to improve. The lower one's income the more pessimistic one is about prospects for inflation. (See **Table 2.1**.)

Of course, price inflation is just one of the factors affecting the standard of living. The other is household income and we asked respondents how they felt their household's income had fared compared with prices over the previous year, and how they expected it to compare in the year ahead.

	Over last year or so %	In the year ahead %
Household income has (will):		
fallen (fall) behind prices	46	43
kept (keep) up with prices	44	45
gone (go) up by more than prices	8	8

Only one in twelve felt they were better off in real terms than they had been, compared with nearly half who thought they were worse off. Expectations for the future were very similar. A cross-tabulation of these two questions showed that 71% expected the next year to continue the trend of the past (i.e. they gave corresponding answers to the two questions), while 12% thought things would get better and 12% thought they would get worse. The higher their income the more likely they were to believe that it had kept up. As many as 70% of those with incomes under £5,000 per annum believed that price rises had outstripped their income growth.

Despite this generally rather pessimistic view about prices it is surprising, but perhaps a typically British response, that to another question relating to household income, 24% claimed to be 'living comfortably' and 50% to be 'coping' on their present income. Of the remaining respondents 18% were finding it 'difficult' and only eight per cent finding it 'very difficult'. However, among the retired, the unemployed and those on low incomes, the difficulties were very much more evident.

Ability to manage on present income

	Total	Retired	Unemployed	Income of below £5,000 pa
	%	%	%	%
Living comfortably	24	16	9	9
Coping	50	51	32	42
Finding it difficult	18	25	34	30
Finding it very difficult	8	7	23	18

We now go on to examine each of these topics of prices and income in rather more detail.

Relative price changes

We asked respondents to consider the extent to which various prices had risen over the past few years. In the self-completion questionnaire we presented them with a dozen goods and services and asked them to say for each item whether they thought it had gone up more, the same, or less than the 'average' rise in prices over the past few years.

The final column below shows the actual increase in prices over the preceding five years. The figure for house prices comes from the Building Societies Association and for the TV licence from the BBC. All other figures are based on the closest appropriate item in the Retail Price Index. (There are some difficulties here. For example, the RPI does not separate fresh from canned fruit or vegetables.)

The first thing to strike one about this table is that extremely few people were prepared to say that something had gone up less than the average. Indeed the great majority of people were not prepared to admit that *any* of the twelve items were below average in inflation. It happens that only four out of the 12 items actually rose below the average level over the previous five years. (The question referred to *the past few years* and we have taken actual changes over five years; however, the relative position would not be very different if we had looked at the last three years.) Also the question form may have been slightly leading in that the preamble referred only to some things rising *faster* than others. Nevertheless the answers do seem to indicate that people have difficulty relating the prices of individual items to the abstract concept of an average price or average price rise.

	Has gone up in price:			Actual percentage increase in price March 1979 to March 1984
	more than average	same as average	less than average	
	%	%	%	%
Petrol	80	14	2	116
Electricity	78	18	2	84
British Rail fares	67	23	2	76
House prices	65	27	4	53
Your local rates	63	30	2	117
Rents	60	32	3	116
The television licence	58	34	4	84
Bus fares	58	31	6	81
Postal charges	56	37	4	85
Clothes	44	47	6	18
Fresh fruit and vegetables	40	50	7	54
Electrical products for the home	38	43	14	18
Average (12 items)	59	32	5	(all item RPI 64)

It is tempting to interpret people's answers to this question as their perceptions of individual price rises, not relative to an actual average price rise but in relation to a level of inflation which in some sense they are resigned to or have come to accept. On this interpretation one might say that for clothes, fresh fruit and vegetables, and electrical products the majority of respondents believed that the increases were in line with what might be expected, while for petrol almost everyone believed the price rise had been out of line. The overall average figure of 59% who thought the 12 items had gone up 'more than average' can be seen as a sort of measure of dissatisfaction with the level of prices. It is, of course, common for people's perceptions of reality to be coloured by what they think ought to be.

If we look now at the way the sample as a whole ordered the 12 items, the ranking by and large reflects what has actually been happening, but there are one or two interesting differences. For example both rates and rents have been rising at as fast a pace as any other item in the list throughout the last five years but are ranked fifth and sixth by the sample. On the other hand rail and bus fares have marched more or less in step with each other (and with the RPI) over the whole period but are ranked third and eighth by the sample. Here it is likely that the absolute level of prices as well as their rate of change had an effect on perceptions.

Before looking at individual differences between different demographic subgroups let us pursue the suggestion that the average percentage over the 12 items can be regarded as a dissatisfaction measure and see how that varies by subgroup.

Those who believed items had increased in price 'more than average' over the past few years

	Responses averaged over 12 items
All respondents	59
Sex	
Male	56
Female	62
Age	
18-24	54
25-34	51
35-54	57
55+	67
Region	
Scotland	64
North	60
Midlands	59
Wales	55
South	57
GLC	57
Social Class	
I and II	52
III Non-manual	58
III Manual	60
IV and V	64
Party Identification	
Conservative	56
Alliance	56
Labour	64
Household Income	
Under £5,000	68
£5,000-£7,999	60
£8,000-£11,999	55
£12,000+	49

The biggest gradient was, not surprisingly, that with household income where the better off were less likely to think the items had gone up in price 'more than average'. There were similarly anticipated differences by party identification, Social Class, and to some extent by region although these regional differences should be treated with caution because of clustering. The age breakdown suggests that older people, particularly those over 55, seemed to have the most difficulty in coming to terms with inflation. The small difference between men and women was also in the expected direction. These figures all give support to the view that the answers were reflecting something more than straightforward estimates of what had happened.

These general differences between the subgroups make it difficult to interpret the results for *individual* items in terms of subgroup variations. In this chapter we can draw attention only to the larger and more obvious differences. For example rent and house price rises seemed to be comparatively more a matter of concern for the youngest and oldest age groups. The same was true for petrol, while postal charges were more of a problem for the over 35s.

Perhaps the most interesting contrasts were the regional ones. Scotland, the North and Wales were least worried by rail fares. House prices were more often thought to be rising faster in London and Scotland. Bus fares and to a lesser extent rates were two of the items to show a difference between London and the South, but in opposite directions.

	Have gone up more than average		
	All areas	London	South
	%	%	%
Local rates	63	68	54
Bus fares	58	40	68

Attitudes to income levels

Respondents were asked to provide details of their own incomes and, perhaps more importantly from the point of view of consumer attitudes, they were asked to evaluate their income in terms of their own expectations.

Virtually all of those interviewed believed themselves to be in the middle or low income bands; only two per cent claimed to be on a high income. These self-assessments were broadly related to their reported household income.

		Household income per annum			
	Total	Under £5,000	£5,000-£7,999	£8,000-£11,999	£12,000 and over
Self-assessment of income level	%	%	%	%	%
High income	2	–	1	1	7
Middle income	48	18	44	74	79
Low income	50	82	55	26	14

There was a marked difference in income self-assessment between age groups, regions, employment status groups, Social Classes and party identifiers. A profile of the low income group compared with those placing themselves in middle or high income bands is given below. It shows that those whose self-assessed income was low were more likely to be from the oldest age groups (particularly those who had retired), to be unemployed, to be from manual Social Classes, to be from Scotland or the North, from cities, and to be Labour party identifiers. There was, of course, considerable overlap between these groups.

| | Self-assigned income group | |
	Low income	Middle or high income
	%	%
Sex		
Male	46	48
Female	54	52
Age		
18-24 years	15	12
25-34 years	13	25
35-54 years	22	41
55 years and over	50	22
Region		
Scotland and the North	42	33
Other regions	58	67
Urbanisation		
Metropolitan areas	40	30
Non-metropolitan areas	60	70
Employment status		
Unemployed	9	4
Employee	34	59
Self-employed	2	8
Retired	26	8
Other not working	29	21
Social Class		
I and II	12	29
III Non-manual	19	27
III Manual	23	22
IV and V	30	16
Party identification		
Conservative	29	48
Alliance	13	14
Labour	44	26

Despite the fact that, on this evidence, half of the population believed themselves to be on a low income, we have seen that three out of four of those interviewed reported that they were coping with, or living comfortably on, their present income.

Respondents were also asked the question:

> *Thinking of income levels generally in Britain today, would you say that the gap between those with high incomes and those with low incomes is too large, about right or too small?*

Three out of four of those interviewed believed that the gap was too large, a view which extended across ages, Social Classes and party identification with only minor variations. Even among those on incomes of £12,000 and over, 69% thought the gap was too large. These results were similar to those obtained a year previously.

	Social Class			Party identification		
I/II	III Non-manual	III Manual	IV/V	Conservative	Alliance	Labour
%	%	%	%	%	%	%
Gap is too large						
68	76	81	80	62	86	85

Employees were also asked a more specific question about pay levels within their own place of work:

> *Thinking of the highest and the lowest paid people at your place of work, how would you describe the gap between their pay, as far as you know?*

The choices offered and the distribution of responses, were:

	%
Much too big a gap	15
Too big	23
About right	49
Too small	3
Much too small	1
Don't know/not answered	9

A higher proportion of those working in the public sector (46%) than those working in private manufacturing (36%) or private non-manufacturing (30%) thought that the distribution of income at their workplace was inequitable, in that there was too big a gap.

The source of these differences in attitudes between private and public sector employees was partially explained by responses to a question which asked employees to judge their *own* pay as low or high for the jobs they did. Public sector employees were slightly more likely than others to be dissatisfied with their pay but not on a sufficient scale to explain the magnitude of differences described above.

Not surprisingly, perhaps, it was the groups at the two ends of the age distribution – the youngest group and those aged 55 years and over – who expressed most disquiet about their own pay levels, and manual workers were more dissatisfied than white-collar workers were.

	Own pay regarded as very low
	%
18-24 years	16
25-34 years	8
35-54 years	9
55 years and over	13
Manual employees	14
Non-manual employees	7

We have already mentioned the polarisation between those who felt that their own personal incomes were slipping backwards in real terms and those who felt they were keeping pace with inflation. As we expected, a substantial proportion of the former group were to be found among the unemployed and retired.

Household income has:	Total	Unemployed	Retired
	%	%	%
fallen behind prices in past year	46	64	60
will fall behind prices in coming year	43	57	54

An additional, more tightly focused question was asked of employees:

If you stay in this job would you expect your wages or salary over the coming year to . . .

	%
. . . rise by more than the cost of living,	13
rise by the same as the cost of living,	47
rise by less than the cost of living,	26
or not to rise at all?	10

It is at this point that we can see a further polarisation emerging – this time within the youngest age group. We have already noted that the young were as concerned as the oldest age group about their pay levels, and we will go on to show that the young were very concerned with unemployment levels and their future prospects. Nevertheless, for those in employment, two-thirds of those aged 18-24 believed that their pay would at least keep up with inflation (16% believed it would exceed it) compared with only 50% of the oldest age group. This is not surprising. Young workers expect their earnings to rise more quickly than others in the labour market; their main fear is, however, whether the employment market will sustain them in the future.

Policies for economic recovery

Having discussed attitudes to prices, unemployment and incomes, we now deal with people's overall assessment of Britain's economic condition and possible remedies. We asked, as we had done a year earlier:

Looking ahead over the next year, do you think Britain's general industrial performance will improve, stay much the same, or decline?

	1983	1984
	%	%
Improve a lot	5	4
Improve a little	39	34
Stay much the same	34	41
Decline a little	13	11
Decline a lot	4	4

The distribution for the two years was similar, except for the (perhaps inexorable) trickle away from optimistic forecasts. As with attitudes towards the level of unemployment, public acceptance of (or resignation about)

Britain's modest industrial performance seemed to be growing. But whereas only 38% of the sample as a whole expected an improvement, a majority (51%) of those earning over £12,000 per year, and the same proportion of the self-employed, took this view. In contrast, only about a third of the unemployed believed there would be an improvement.

In addition, as we had done a year earlier, we presented nine economic policies to respondents and asked them to indicate their support or opposition to each. The two years' figures are presented alongside each other in the table below. As will be seen, the order has not changed much. The biggest change in the figures was the increased support in 1984 for cuts in defence expenditure, caused in large part by the growing preference among younger people for this policy (see Chapters 4 and 6). It is a policy that now attracts majority support.

Support for economic policies

	1983 %	1984 %
Government to set up construction projects to create more jobs	89	89
Introduce import controls	72	67
Control prices by legislation	70	66
Increase government subsidies for private industry	64	60
Government incentives to encourage job-sharing or splitting	61	60
Reduce government spending on defence	44	51
Control of wages by legislation	48	42
Devaluation of the pound	16	13
Reduce the level of government spending on health and education	13	11

Satisfaction with services

We now leave strictly economic matters and turn our attention to the service provided by a number of organisations and institutions. The question in the self-completion questionnaire was:

Listed below are a number of organisations or services. From what you know or have heard about each one, can you say whether you are generally satisfied or not satisfied with the service that each one provides.

The aim of the question was not so much to elicit overall but comparative measures of satisfaction, particularly over time. The answers were, in rank order of satisfaction:

	Satisfied	Not satisfied
	%	%
Local doctor	84	13
Banks	82	13
The telephone service	80	16
The police	79	17
Independent TV and radio	76	21
The postal service	75	22
The BBC	66	30
The press	62	34
The civil service	53	42
British Rail	52	42
Local government	49	47
Average (11 items)	69	27

In the 1983 survey we had asked a somewhat different question. Respondents then were asked to say for each of a slightly different list of institutions whether they thought it was 'well run' or 'not well run'. The results for the seven institutions which appeared in both lists were as follows:

	Well run (1983)	Satisfied (1984)
	%	%
Banks	90	82
The police	77	79
Independent TV and radio	74	76
The BBC	72	66
The press	53	62
The civil service	43	53
Local government	35	49

The two sets of answers thus ranked these institutions in the same order. Any differences between the two sets of figures may be due in part to the passage of time but more likely to the different questions. It is tempting to derive some entertainment from the fact that the banks and the BBC did better on 'well run' (for their own benefit?) than on 'satisfied' (for the public's benefit?), while the opposite was true for the press, the civil service and local government! However, as we have said, the main value of both of these questions comes from internal comparisons of subgroups and from trends over time.

If we take the overall average over the 11 items as a general satisfaction measure (i.e. 69% for the whole sample) then, unlike the relative price change figures in the previous section, there was surprisingly little variation between the demographic subgroups. This overall stability makes it easier to pick out individual figures and contrasts between the differing levels of satisfaction for individual items by different subgroups. For example, 74% were satisfied with the press in Scotland compared with 62% nationally, and 58% with local government in both Scotland and Wales compared with 49% nationally – see also Chapter 6. There was the anticipated trend with age in satisfaction with the police from 75% among the 18-24s to 83% among the over 55s. But why was there an opposite trend for the postal service from 83% down to 71%? Perhaps older respondents can remember a time when the postal service was better! One of the biggest contrasts was between 86% satisfaction with the police among Conservative identifiers and 73% among Labour identifiers. Our fieldwork took place near to the beginning of the miners' strike so the gap could have widened later in 1984. Perhaps the most interesting comparison is between the BBC and Independent broadcasting.

	Satisfied with the BBC	Satisfied with Independent TV and radio	Difference
	%	%	
All respondents	66	76	10
Sex			
Male	64	73	9
Female	68	78	10
Age			
18-24	74	87	13
24-34	62	78	16
35-54	71	79	8
55+	60	67	7
Region			
Scotland	62	76	14
North	59	75	16
Midlands	65	73	8
Wales	65	80	15
South	72	76	4
GLC	72	76	4
Social Class			
I and II	74	73	−1
III Non-manual	74	80	6
III Manual	58	74	16
IV and V	56	75	19
Party identification			
Conservative	70	75	5
Alliance	75	76	1
Labour	60	75	15
Household income			
Under £5,000	57	71	14
£5,000-£7,999	62	79	17
£8,000-£11,999	71	78	7
£12,000+	78	78	–

The figures for the BBC faithfully reflected the pattern of its middle class, home counties stereotype. While this was to be expected, the surprising feature was that the working-class, northern image for Independent broadcasting did not come through. Indeed, apart from a marked trend with age, the satisfaction with Independent broadcasting was remarkably even across all other sub groups.

The mass media

We touched on attitudes to the broadcasting media in our 'satisfaction' question, but we also asked:

> *Can you tell me where you usually get most of your news about what's going on in Britain today: is it from the newspapers, or radio, or television, or where?*

This question is very similar (but not identical) to one which has been asked by the Roper Organisation in a series of surveys in the USA which started in 1959 and is carried out about every two years. The main differences in the American question were that they referred to news about what was going on in 'the world' (so much for American insularity!) and that they included 'magazines' and 'talking to people' among the suggested sources. The latest available figures are for the December 1982 survey which were virtually identical to those obtained two years earlier.

	USA 1982	Britain 1984
	%	%
Main source(s) of news		
Television	65	61
Newspapers	44	20
Radio	18	15

The similarity of the figures for the broadcast media is almost too good to be true; the difference in the figures for newspapers is largely due to the multiple answers allowed in the American survey.

Respondents were also asked whether they normally read any daily morning newspaper at least three times a week. Twenty-eight per cent said they did not (compared with 23% in 1983). Those who claimed to read a paper regularly were asked which paper it was. We can therefore analyse the question on source of news by which newspaper people read, as follows:

	All respondents	No regular newspaper	Any newspaper	Telegraph, Guardian, Times or Financial Times	Express or Mail	Mirror, Sun or Star
	%	%	%	%	%	%
Main source						
Television	61	76	59	32	62	65
Newspapers	20	3	30	57	28	24
Radio	15	23	15	25	14	14

Regular readers of: spans the "No regular newspaper", "Any newspaper", "Telegraph, Guardian, Times or Financial Times", "Express or Mail", and "Mirror, Sun or Star" columns.

Only the readers of the four 'quality' dailies seemed to use their newspapers as a source of news to a greater extent than the average American did (ignoring the multi-coding of the American data). The 'middlebrow' Express and Mail fared little better than the 'popular' tabloids in this respect. Our classification into quality papers, middlebrow ones and popular ones is for illustration only.

Others may wish to classify them differently for further analysis (see, for instance, Chapter 4).

We also asked a version of another Roper question on the relative credibility of the media. Our question was asked only of those who claimed to read a regular daily newspaper. Suppose, we asked respondents, they saw or heard conflicting or different reports of the same news story on radio, television and in their newspaper, which of the three versions would they be most likely to believe? The American question was asked of everybody and referred to 'radio, television, the magazines and the newspapers' (without naming any specific newspaper as we did). Nevertheless the comparison is still of interest and would seem to be rather disparaging of the usefulness and credibility of British newspapers compared with their American counterparts.

	USA 1982	Britain 1984 (Regular newspaper readers)
Most believable source of news	%	%
Television	53	57
Newspaper(s)	22	15
Radio	6	15
Magazines	8	(not asked)
Don't know/not answered	11	12

If the question had been asked of all respondents in Britain the number citing newspapers would probably have been even lower than the 15% shown above. Further analysis by which newspapers they read served only to reinforce the poor showing of the middlebrow and popular press.

		Regular readers of:		
	Any newspaper	Telegraph, Guardian, Times or Financial Times	Express or Mail	Mirror, Sun or Star
	%	%	%	%
Most believable source of news				
Television	57	30	59	66
Newspaper	15	35	13	11
Radio	15	20	16	13
Don't know/not answered	12	16	12	11

2.1 ECONOMIC EXPECTATIONS: INFLATION (Q16 a) by sex, age and household income

BASE: ALL RESPONDENTS

In a year from now, do you expect prices generally to have gone up, to have stayed the same, or to have gone down?

	WEIGHTED BASE	SEX MALE	SEX FEMALE	AGE 18-24	AGE 25-34	AGE 35-54	AGE 55+	AGE NO INF.	HOUSEHOLD INCOME UNDER £5000	£5000-£7999	£8000-£11999	£12000+	NO INF.
UNWEIGHTED BASE	1675	780	895	217	309	525	610	14	510	374	302	285	204
WEIGHTED BASE	1645	775	871	214	311	517	590	14	493	377	292	281	201
UP BY A LOT	513 31%	194 25%	319 37%	73 34%	94 30%	149 29%	194 33%	3	212 43%	149 39%	67 23%	38 14%	47 23%
UP BY A LITTLE	851 52%	429 55%	422 48%	103 48%	171 55%	282 55%	287 49%	8	214 43%	175 46%	165 56%	184 66%	112 56%
STAYED THE SAME	211 13%	111 14%	100 11%	33 16%	41 13%	63 12%	73 12%	1	43 9%	42 11%	53 18%	46 16%	26 13%
DOWN BY A LITTLE	42 3%	25 3%	17 2%	2 1%	4 1%	15 3%	21 4%	1	13 3%	9 2%	7 2%	9 3%	4 2%
DOWN BY A LOT	3 0%	2 0%	1 0%	1 0%	1 0%	1 0%	0 0%	0	0 0%	0 0%	0 0%	0 0%	3 1%
DON'T KNOW	24 1%	13 2%	12 1%	2 1%	1 0%	6 1%	15 3%	0	11 2%	2 1%	0 0%	4 1%	7 4%
NOT ANSWERED	1 0%	1 0%	0 0%	0 0%	0 0%	0 0%	0 0%	1	0 0%	0 0%	0 0%	0 0%	1 1%

2.2 ECONOMIC EXPECTATIONS: INFLATION (Q16 a) by employment status

BASE: ALL RESPONDENTS

In a year from now, do you expect prices generally to have gone up, to have stayed the same, or to have gone down?

	WEIGHTED BASE	TOTAL IN PAID WORK	SUBTOTAL: MANUAL	SUBTOTAL: NON-MANUAL	NOT WORKING: RETIRED	NOT WORKING: UNEMPLOYED	NOT WORKING: LOOKING AFTER HOME	OTHER/NO INF.
UNWEIGHTED BASE	1675	863	425	438	294	106	312	100
WEIGHTED BASE	1645	845	410	435	284	102	307	107
UP BY A LOT	513 31%	235 28%	140 34%	95 22%	78 28%	46 45%	112 37%	40 38%
UP BY A LITTLE	851 52%	467 55%	212 52%	255 59%	145 51%	43 42%	152 49%	45 42%
STAYED THE SAME	211 13%	112 13%	44 11%	68 16%	44 16%	8 8%	34 11%	12 11%
DOWN BY A LITTLE	42 3%	25 3%	11 3%	14 3%	11 4%	1 1%	3 1%	3 3%
DOWN BY A LOT	3 0%	0 0%	0 0%	0 0%	0 0%	3 3%	0 0%	0 0%
DON'T KNOW	24 1%	6 1%	3 1%	3 1%	7 2%	1 1%	6 2%	5 5%
NOT ANSWERED	1 0%	0 0%	0 0%	0 0%	0 0%	0 0%	0 0%	1 1%

2.3 ECONOMIC EXPECTATIONS: UNEMPLOYMENT (Q17) by age and region

BASE:
ALL RESPONDENTS

In a year from now, do you expect unemployment to have gone up, to have stayed the same, or to have gone down?

	WEIGHTED BASE	AGE				NO INF.	REGION							
		18-24	25-34	35-54	55+		SCOTLAND	NORTH	MID-LANDS	WALES	SOUTH	GLC	METRO POLITAN	NON-METROP
UNWEIGHTED BASE	1675	217	309	525	610	14	175	441	291	93	514	161	571	1104
WEIGHTED BASE	1645	214	311	517	590	14	177	440	282	94	495	157	576	1069
UP BY A LOT	406 25%	74 35%	78 25%	128 25%	125 21%	1	54 30%	133 30%	62 22%	24 26%	94 19%	40 25%	167 29%	240 22%
UP BY A LITTLE	503 31%	62 29%	109 35%	169 33%	155 26%	7	44 25%	122 28%	88 31%	39 41%	156 31%	54 35%	164 29%	338 32%
STAYED THE SAME	506 31%	56 26%	88 29%	160 31%	199 34%	3	50 28%	117 27%	86 30%	25 26%	188 38%	41 26%	153 27%	353 33%
DOWN BY A LITTLE	186 11%	13 6%	29 9%	54 10%	88 15%	2	23 13%	53 12%	40 14%	5 5%	50 10%	15 9%	73 13%	113 11%
DOWN BY A LOT	19 1%	4 2%	5 2%	2 0%	8 1%	0	3 2%	8 2%	4 1%	1 1%	3 1%	1 0%	8 1%	11 1%
DON'T KNOW	25 1%	4 2%	1 0%	4 1%	15 3%	0	3 2%	6 1%	3 1%	0 0%	5 1%	7 5%	10 2%	14 1%
NOT ANSWERED	1 0%	0 0%	0 0%	0 0%	0 0%	1	0 0%	0 0%	0 0%	0 0%	0 0%	0 0%	1 0%	0 0%

2.4 ECONOMIC EXPECTATIONS: UNEMPLOYMENT (Q17) by employment status

BASE:
ALL RESPONDENTS

In a year from now, do you expect unemployment to have gone up, to have stayed the same, or to have gone down?

	WEIGHTED BASE	TOTAL IN PAID WORK	SUBTOTAL: MANUAL	SUBTOTAL: NON-MANUAL	NOT WORKING: RETIRED	NOT WORKING: UNEMPLOYED	LOOKING AFTER HOME	OTHER/NO INF.
UNWEIGHTED BASE	1675	863	425	438	294	106	312	100
WEIGHTED BASE	1645	845	410	435	284	102	307	107
UP BY A LOT	406 25%	192 23%	116 28%	76 17%	55 19%	50 49%	70 23%	39 37%
UP BY A LITTLE	503 31%	276 33%	134 33%	142 33%	75 26%	22 21%	101 33%	29 27%
STAYED THE SAME	506 31%	270 32%	112 27%	158 36%	96 34%	23 22%	89 29%	27 26%
DOWN BY A LITTLE	186 11%	90 11%	39 9%	51 12%	48 17%	4 4%	37 12%	6 6%
DOWN BY A LOT	19 1%	9 1%	6 1%	4 1%	2 1%	4 4%	3 1%	1 1%
DON'T KNOW	25 1%	8 1%	3 1%	5 1%	7 2%	0 0%	7 2%	3 3%
NOT ANSWERED	1 0%	0 0%	0 0%	0 0%	0 0%	0 0%	0 0%	1 1%

2.5 GOVERNMENT'S HIGHEST ECONOMIC PRIORITY (Q18 a) by age and region

BASE: ALL RESPONDENTS

To which do you think the government should give higher priority, keeping down inflation or keeping down unemployment?

	WEIGHTED BASE	AGE 18-24	AGE 25-34	AGE 35-54	AGE 55+	AGE NO INF.	REGION SCOTLAND	REGION NORTH	REGION MID-LANDS	REGION WALES	REGION SOUTH	REGION GLC	METRO-POLITAN	NON-METROP
UNWEIGHTED BASE	1675	217	309	525	610	14	175	441	291	93	514	161	571	1104
WEIGHTED BASE	1645	214	311	517	590	14	177	440	282	94	495	157	576	1069
KEEPING DOWN INFLATION	430 / 26%	32 / 15%	84 / 27%	135 / 26%	174 / 30%	6	43 / 24%	86 / 19%	84 / 30%	26 / 28%	159 / 32%	33 / 21%	113 / 20%	317 / 30%
KEEPING DOWN UNEMPLOYMENT	1134 / 69%	173 / 81%	214 / 69%	357 / 69%	384 / 65%	7	128 / 72%	334 / 76%	186 / 66%	64 / 68%	305 / 62%	118 / 75%	440 / 76%	695 / 65%
BOTH EQUALLY/CAN'T SEPARATE	27 / 2%	4 / 2%	10 / 3%	8 / 1%	6 / 1%	0	0 / 0%	5 / 1%	2 / 1%	3 / 3%	9 / 2%	4 / 2%	9 / 2%	18 / 2%
OTHER ANSWER	9 / 1%	2 / 1%	1 / 0%	3 / 1%	3 / 1%	0	1 / 1%	2 / 0%	2 / 1%	0 / 0%	2 / 0%	2 / 1%	4 / 1%	5 / 0%
DON'T KNOW	33 / 2%	1 / 1%	1 / 0%	10 / 2%	20 / 3%	0	3 / 2%	9 / 2%	4 / 1%	1 / 1%	15 / 3%	1 / 1%	7 / 1%	26 / 2%
NOT ANSWERED	12 / 1%	2 / 1%	2 / 1%	3 / 1%	3 / 1%	1	2 / 1%	5 / 1%	0 / 0%	0 / 0%	5 / 1%	0 / 0%	4 / 1%	8 / 1%

2.6 GOVERNMENT'S HIGHEST ECONOMIC PRIORITY (Q18 a) by employment status

BASE: ALL RESPONDENTS

To which do you think the government should give higher priority, keeping down inflation or keeping down unemployment?

	WEIGHTED BASE	TOTAL IN PAID WORK	SUBTOTAL: NON-MANUAL	SUBTOTAL: MANUAL	NOT WORKING: RETIRED	NOT WORKING: UNEMPLOYED	NOT WORKING: LOOKING AFTER HOME	OTHER/NO INF.
UNWEIGHTED BASE	1675	863	438	425	294	106	312	100
WEIGHTED BASE	1645	845	435	410	284	102	307	107
KEEPING DOWN INFLATION	430 / 26%	218 / 26%	131 / 30%	87 / 21%	88 / 31%	23 / 23%	80 / 26%	21 / 20%
KEEPING DOWN UNEMPLOYMENT	1134 / 69%	586 / 69%	281 / 65%	304 / 74%	178 / 62%	76 / 75%	216 / 70%	78 / 74%
BOTH EQUALLY/CAN'T SEPARATE	27 / 2%	18 / 2%	9 / 2%	9 / 2%	5 / 2%	3 / 3%	0 / 0%	2 / 2%
OTHER ANSWER	9 / 1%	4 / 0%	4 / 1%	0 / 0%	3 / 1%	0 / 0%	2 / 1%	0 / 0%
DON'T KNOW	33 / 2%	13 / 2%	13 / 3%	0 / 0%	10 / 3%	0 / 0%	7 / 2%	4 / 4%
NOT ANSWERED	12 / 1%	7 / 1%	7 / 1%	0 / 0%	3 / 1%	0 / 0%	2 / 1%	1 / 1%

2.7 ECONOMIC PROBLEM OF GREATEST CONCERN TO RESPONDENT AND HIS/HER FAMILY (Q18 b) by age and region

BASE: ALL RESPONDENTS

Which do you think is of most concern to you and your family — inflation or unemployment?

	WEIGHTED BASE	AGE 18-24	25-34	35-54	55+	NO INF.	REGION SCOT-LAND	NORTH	MID-LANDS	WALES	SOUTH	GLC	METRO-POLITAN METRO	NON-METRO
UNWEIGHTED BASE	1675	217	309	525	610	14	175	441	291	93	514	161	571	1104
WEIGHTED BASE	1645	214	311	517	590	14	177	440	282	94	495	157	576	1069
INFLATION	849 52%	86 40%	164 53%	227 44%	364 62%	8	87 49%	217 49%	136 48%	63 66%	263 53%	85 54%	283 49%	566 53%
UNEMPLOYMENT	731 44%	120 56%	135 44%	272 53%	199 34%	4	86 48%	211 48%	137 48%	29 30%	206 42%	63 40%	275 48%	455 43%
BOTH EQUALLY, CAN'T SEPARATE	31 2%	6 3%	7 2%	11 2%	7 1%	0	1 1%	6 1%	6 2%	1 1%	12 2%	5 3%	9 2%	22 2%
NEITHER A THREAT	10 1%	0 0%	1 0%	2 0%	7 1%	0	0 0%	2 0%	1 0%	0 0%	5 1%	2 1%	4 1%	6 1%
OTHER ANSWER	2 0%	0 0%	0 0%	1 0%	1 0%	0	0 0%	0 0%	0 0%	0 0%	1 0%	0 0%	0 0%	2 0%
DONT KNOW	20 1%	2 1%	4 1%	4 1%	11 2%	1	3 2%	2 0%	3 1%	2 2%	9 2%	1 1%	4 1%	16 1%
NOT ANSWERED	3 0%	0 0%	0 0%	0 0%	2 0%	1	1 1%	2 0%	0 0%	0 0%	0 0%	0 0%	1 0%	2 0%

2.8 ECONOMIC PROBLEM OF GREATEST CONCERN TO RESPONDENT AND HIS/HER FAMILY (Q18 b) by employment status

BASE: ALL RESPONDENTS

Which do you think is of most concern to you and your family — inflation or unemployment?

	WEIGHTED BASE	TOTAL IN PAID WORK	SUBTOTAL: MANUAL	SUBTOTAL: NON-MANUAL	NOT WORKING: RETIRED	NOT WORKING: UNEMPLOYED	NOT WORKING: LOOKING AFTER HOME	OTHER/NO INF.
UNWEIGHTED BASE	1675	863	425	438	294	106	312	100
WEIGHTED BASE	1645	845	410	435	284	102	307	107
INFLATION	849 52%	405 48%	172 42%	234 54%	193 68%	26 25%	172 56%	53 49%
UNEMPLOYMENT	731 44%	406 48%	227 55%	178 41%	80 28%	75 73%	123 40%	47 44%
BOTH EQUALLY, CAN'T SEPARATE	31 2%	19 2%	7 2%	12 3%	1 1%	1 1%	4 1%	4 4%
NEITHER A THREAT	10 1%	6 1%	2 0%	4 1%	2 1%	0 0%	2 1%	0 0%
OTHER ANSWER	2 0%	1 0%	0 0%	0 0%	1 0%	0 0%	0 0%	0 0%
DONT KNOW	20 1%	9 1%	2 0%	7 2%	5 2%	0 0%	6 2%	1 1%
NOT ANSWERED	3 0%	0 0%	0 0%	0 0%	2 1%	0 0%	0 0%	1 1%

2.9 RELATIONSHIP BETWEEN PRICE INCREASES AND OWN (HOUSEHOLD) INCOME (Q24 a, b) by current standard industrial classification (SIC 1980) and age

BASE: ALL RESPONDENTS	WEIGHTED BASE	CURRENT SIC (1980)						AGE				
		PUB SECT SERV	PUB SECT M+T	PRIV SECT MAN	PRIV SECT N.MAN	WORKING BUT NO INF	NOT WORKING /N.C.	18-24	25-34	35-54	55+	NO INF
UNWEIGHTED BASE	1675	244	56	244	310	17	804	217	309	525	610	14
WEIGHTED BASE	1645	237	55	239	307	14	793	214	311	517	590	14

Looking back over the last year or so, would you say your household's income ...

HAS FALLEN BEHIND PRICES	763 46%	94 40%	29 52%	89 37%	98 32%	4	448 57%	73 34%	130 42%	218 42%	336 57%	6
HAS KEPT UP WITH PRICES	719 44%	118 50%	25 45%	120 50%	171 56%	7	278 35%	113 53%	132 43%	248 48%	220 37%	6
HAS GONE UP BY MORE THAN PRICES	128 8%	20 9%	4 4%	26 11%	33 11%	3	44 6%	17 8%	43 14%	42 8%	26 4%	1
DONT KNOW	31 2%	4 2%	0 0%	4 2%	3 1%	0	20 3%	11 5%	5 2%	8 2%	8 1%	0
NOT ANSWERED	4 0%	1 0%	0 0%	0 0%	1 0%	0	2 0%	0 0%	0 0%	2 0%	1 0%	1

Looking forward to the year ahead, do you expect your household's income ...

WILL FALL BEHIND PRICES	711 43%	101 43%	35 63%	76 32%	92 30%	2	406 51%	70 33%	111 36%	204 39%	321 54%	5
WILL KEEP UP WITH PRICES	743 45%	114 48%	18 32%	134 56%	173 56%	9	295 37%	115 54%	148 48%	260 50%	215 36%	5
WILL GO UP BY MORE THAN PRICES	124 8%	20 8%	2 4%	22 9%	36 12%	3	41 5%	20 9%	42 13%	41 8%	21 4%	1
DONT KNOW	64 4%	2 1%	1 2%	8 3%	6 2%	0	48 6%	9 4%	10 3%	11 2%	32 5%	2
NOT ANSWERED	3 0%	1 0%	0 0%	0 0%	0 0%	0	2 0%	0 0%	0 0%	1 0%	1 0%	1

2.10 RELATIONSHIP BETWEEN PRICE INCREASES AND OWN (HOUSEHOLD) INCOME (Q24 a,b) by employment status

BASE: ALL RESPONDENTS	TOTAL IN PAID WORK	SUBTOTAL: MANUAL	SUBTOTAL: NON-MANUAL	NOT WORKING: RETIRED	NOT WORKING: UNEMPLOYED	LOOKING AFTER HOME	OTHER/NO INF.
WEIGHTED BASE							
UNWEIGHTED BASE 1675	863	425	438	294	106	312	100
WEIGHTED BASE 1645	845	410	435	284	102	307	107

Looking back over the last year or so, would you say your household's income ...

	ALL RESP.	TOTAL IN PAID WORK	SUBTOTAL: MANUAL	SUBTOTAL: NON-MANUAL	NOT WORKING: RETIRED	NOT WORKING: UNEMPLOYED	LOOKING AFTER HOME	OTHER/NO INF.
HAS FALLEN BEHIND PRICES	763 46%	313 37%	179 44%	133 31%	170 60%	66 64%	161 52%	53 50%
HAS KEPT UP WITH PRICES	719 44%	438 52%	195 48%	242 56%	101 36%	25 25%	121 39%	34 32%
HAS GONE UP BY MORE THAN PRICES	128 8%	82 10%	31 8%	51 12%	10 3%	6 5%	16 5%	15 14%
DONT KNOW	31 2%	11 1%	4 1%	7 2%	3 1%	6 5%	9 3%	3 2%
NOT ANSWERED	4 0%	2 0%	0 0%	2 0%	1 0%	0 0%	0 0%	1 1%

Looking forward to the year ahead, do you expect your household's income ...

	ALL RESP.	TOTAL IN PAID WORK	SUBTOTAL: MANUAL	SUBTOTAL: NON-MANUAL	NOT WORKING: RETIRED	NOT WORKING: UNEMPLOYED	LOOKING AFTER HOME	OTHER/NO INF.
WILL FALL BEHIND PRICES	711 43%	303 36%	172 42%	132 30%	153 54%	58 57%	147 48%	49 46%
WILL KEEP UP WITH PRICES	743 45%	444 53%	197 48%	247 57%	113 40%	27 27%	121 40%	36 34%
WILL GO UP BY MORE THAN PRICES	124 8%	81 10%	33 8%	48 11%	5 2%	12 11%	18 6%	9 9%
DONT KNOW	64 4%	16 2%	9 2%	7 2%	12 4%	5 5%	20 7%	11 10%
NOT ANSWERED	3 0%	1 0%	0 0%	1 0%	1 0%	0 0%	0 0%	1 1%

2.11 BRITAIN'S ECONOMIC PROBLEMS: SUPPORT FOR AND OPPOSITION TO POLICIES (Q20) by employment status and party identification

TABLE INCLUDES ONLY THOSE WHO SUPPORT OR OPPOSE THE FOLLOWING POLICIES:

BASE: ALL RESPONDENTS	ALL RESPONDENTS	TOTAL IN PAID WORK	SUBTOTAL: MANUAL	SUBTOTAL: NON-MANUAL	NOT WORKING: RETIRED	NOT WORKING: UNEMPLOYED	NOT WORKING: LOOKING AFTER HOME	OTHER/NO INF.	TORY	LAB.	ALLIANCE	OTHER	NON-ALIGN
UNWEIGHTED BASE	1675	863	425	438	294	106	312	100	640	595	220	24	196
WEIGHTED BASE	1645	845	410	435	284	102	307	107	635	575	219	28	188
Control of wages by legislation													
SUPPORT	688 42%	299 35%	145 35%	154 35%	152 54%	40 39%	140 46%	56 52%	281 44%	238 41%	89 41%	10	70 37%
OPPOSE	879 53%	522 62%	251 61%	271 62%	111 39%	59 57%	143 47%	44 41%	329 52%	313 54%	118 54%	18	101 54%
Control of prices by legislation													
SUPPORT	1088 66%	541 64%	281 69%	259 60%	200 70%	70 69%	204 67%	73 69%	390 61%	417 73%	148 68%	17	115 61%
OPPOSE	493 30%	283 33%	118 29%	165 38%	66 23%	29 28%	86 28%	29 27%	223 35%	140 24%	63 29%	9	58 31%
Reducing the level of Government spending on health and education													
SUPPORT	185 11%	93 11%	42 10%	52 12%	37 13%	12 11%	33 11%	11 10%	88 14%	53 9%	17 8%	4	23 12%
OPPOSE	1430 87%	744 88%	365 89%	378 87%	238 84%	87 85%	268 87%	92 86%	532 84%	512 89%	201 92%	24	160 85%
Introducing import controls													
SUPPORT	1105 67%	583 69%	290 71%	293 67%	179 63%	65 63%	194 63%	83 78%	416 66%	401 70%	152 69%	20	116 62%
OPPOSE	436 27%	232 27%	105 26%	127 29%	78 27%	31 30%	79 26%	16 15%	182 29%	142 25%	58 26%	5	49 26%
Increasing Government subsidies for private industry													
SUPPORT	988 60%	544 64%	272 66%	272 63%	155 55%	62 60%	177 58%	50 47%	424 67%	325 57%	126 58%	15	98 52%
OPPOSE	536 33%	267 32%	118 29%	149 34%	98 34%	37 36%	92 30%	43 40%	176 28%	208 36%	81 37%	14	58 31%
Devaluation of the pound													
SUPPORT	207 13%	110 13%	60 15%	50 12%	32 11%	17 17%	35 11%	13 12%	65 10%	97 17%	24 11%	7	14 8%
OPPOSE	1212 74%	644 76%	306 75%	337 77%	201 71%	67 66%	220 72%	80 75%	492 77%	406 71%	165 75%	20	130 69%
Reducing Government spending on defence													
SUPPORT	845 51%	448 53%	217 53%	232 53%	128 45%	59 58%	159 52%	52 48%	247 39%	363 63%	127 58%	21	86 46%
OPPOSE	737 45%	376 44%	183 45%	193 44%	143 50%	40 39%	132 43%	46 43%	368 58%	193 34%	85 39%	7	83 44%
Government incentives to encourage job sharing or splitting													
SUPPORT	994 60%	491 58%	225 55%	266 61%	175 61%	66 65%	205 67%	57 53%	393 62%	338 59%	143 66%	18	101 54%
OPPOSE	567 34%	329 39%	172 42%	156 36%	90 32%	34 33%	73 24%	42 39%	212 33%	211 37%	67 31%	10	66 35%
Government to set up construction projects to create more jobs													
SUPPORT	1464 89%	748 89%	359 87%	389 89%	252 89%	95 93%	273 89%	95 89%	541 85%	528 92%	205 94%	28	161 86%
OPPOSE	138 8%	88 10%	45 11%	43 10%	19 7%	4 4%	22 7%	5 4%	78 12%	33 6%	9 4%	0	17 9%

PARTY I.D. (columns TORY, LAB., ALLIANCE, OTHER, NON-ALIGN)

3 Sex roles and gender issues

Sharon Witherspoon*

Following the publication of the 1984 Report, much interest was expressed in the findings on household divisions of labour (Jowell and Airey, 1984, pp.133-135). Almost simultaneously, the Department of Employment and OPCS published the results of their authoritative and influential *Women and Employment Survey* – WES (Martin and Roberts, 1984).

We had planned to include a much-expanded module on women's issues in our 1984 questionnaire which could then be repeated in future years to monitor changes, particularly in the relationship between domestic work and paid employment as they come under increasing scrutiny by employees, employers and government alike. Now we had a model in the shape of WES on which to base some of our questions. Our questionnaire focused then on the different experiences and attitudes of men and women in paid work, on attitudes towards women's household responsibilities, and on more general assessments of women's rights and sexual equality. We will not report here on all sex-related differences in the dataset.

Our module was able to replicate some items from WES, the fieldwork for which took place in 1980. It would, we felt, be interesting to see if any measurable change in some of the attitudinal questions had occurred in the four years between the two surveys. In the following pages, comparisons are therefore made, but it must be appreciated that the two surveys are not based on fully comparable samples, nor do they use exactly the same classifications on a number of important variables. In particular, they differ in their definitions of part-time employment. For various reasons, we use 10 hours per week as a lower limit in classifying people as being in paid work, and thus exclude a number of people (particularly women) employed part-time. Thus, we cannot

* Researcher, Social and Community Planning Research

always tell how much of the difference between the two surveys is attributable to the passage of time and how much to the different definitions employed. In any event, our data reveal nine per cent fewer women in part-time employment than does WES, balanced by nine per cent more women who are economically inactive.

For those interested in terminology, we should note here that in general we use the phrase 'sex roles' rather than 'gender' to refer to women's and men's different social and cultural roles, rather than their biological differences. The analytical distinction is, in any case, empirically conflated. But see Reid and Wormald (1982, pp.1-2) for a useful discussion on terminology.

Houseworking

The domestic division of labour

Our questionnaire included a number of items about past and future labour market participation by women. Before discussing work outside the home, however, we return to the questions on the domestic division of labour that we referred to last year, and report on the omission we promised in 1984 to rectify.

As we had done last time, we asked married men and women (and those living as married) which partner performed various domestic tasks in their household; this year we then asked all respondents, both married and unmarried, who they thought *ought* to do the various chores. Once again we found that the domestic division of labour is remarkably unequal. Women were largely responsible for the day-to-day care and maintenance of the home, with men assuming major responsibilities only for repairs of household equipment.

This is not to say there was absolute uniformity either between tasks or between different types of household. As Pahl found in his 1981 study of the Isle of Sheppey, the employment status of the wife did indeed affect whether married women performed tasks traditionally associated with women at home (Pahl, 1984). Not that women working full-time outside the home had an egalitarian division of domestic work: they were merely somewhat less unequal. And women with part-time jobs outside the home had a particularly unequal division of labour, partly reflecting the fact that many women who worked part-time also had young children. In the table below, we show only those tasks in which full-time women employees did have an advantage over part-time women.

Households with young children displayed an inegalitarian pattern, with wives more likely to do most of the tasks, although men in such households were also slightly more likely than average to do some traditionally 'non-male' tasks like household shopping and the evening dishes. Another interesting pattern to emerge was that control over the organisation of household money was more likely to fall to the woman if she worked full-time – according to her report at least. (Men reported that if their wives worked full-time, organisation of money was more likely to be shared.)

In addition to being affected by the employment status of the wife and the presence of young children, the allocation of household tasks seemed to change over the life-cycle; some tasks showed strong age effects. Shopping and

		Full-time working women %	Part-time working women %
Household shopping:	Mainly man	4	4
	Mainly woman	52	64
	Shared equally	43	32
Preparation of evening meal:	Mainly man	11	4
	Mainly woman	61	79
	Shared equally	26	15
Household cleaning:	Mainly man	6	1
	Mainly woman	61	83
	Shared equally	33	15
Washing and ironing:	Mainly man	4	–
	Mainly woman	81	95
	Shared equally	14	5
Repairs of household equipment:	Mainly man	83	74
	Mainly woman	5	13
	Shared equally	12	11

cleaning in particular were more likely to be shared when both partners were retired, although even among older respondents, cleaning remained a task largely done by women. This too is consistent with Pahl's findings (Pahl, 1984, p.273).

Although these subgroup differences emerged from answers given by both men and women respondents, subtle but consistent differences were apparent between the reports of men and women about the sharing of household tasks. Broadly, men appeared to overstate slightly the extent to which tasks were shared. For instance, we asked respondents to say who looked after the children when they were ill; as the primary carers in this situation women are often held back from a strong labour market commitment while their children are young. Men were much more likely than women to report that they shared this task.

Who looks after child(ren) when they are sick?

	Reported by men %	Reported by women %
Mainly the man	2	–
Mainly the woman	56	70
Shared equally	42	29

This was certainly the largest difference in reporting between men and women, but small differences emerged on many other items. Men seemed to exaggerate their participation most in respect of those tasks in which men actually do play a larger role. However, in respect of traditionally more 'female' tasks, such as making the evening meal, doing household cleaning or doing the washing and ironing, there was no discrepancy in reporting.

Our data on this subject can provide only a crude approximation of actual household divisions of labour. The way we group our answers may also affect interpretations. We could make the statement, for instance, that 21% of the married respondents reported a 'strong traditionalistic' division of labour, in which it was mainly the woman who did the shopping, made the evening meal, did the evening dishes, the household cleaning and the washing and ironing. Simply by omitting the evening dishes from that summary, we cause that proportion to rise to 40% of married respondents reporting a traditional division of labour. As Pahl has shown, multivariate analysis is needed to model the conditions under which traditional divisions of labour are more or less likely. Martin and Roberts also provide useful warnings about the interpretation of such task-based models and point to the likely over estimate of sharing contained in already depressingly unequal answers. (Pahl, 1984; Martin and Roberts, 1984, p.100.)

More sophisticated modelling cannot, however, hide the extent to which women have primary responsibility for home and children. Further on in the questionnaire, we asked all respondents who was the person mainly responsible for general domestic duties in their household. Eighty-seven per cent of married women said that they were mainly responsible, and seven per cent said that they shared responsibility with their spouse; 75% of married men said their spouse was mainly responsible, and 14% said they shared. When asked who was mainly responsible for the general care of the children in the household, 76% of married women with children said they were mainly responsible, and 14% said that they shared childcare; 72% of married men with children said their spouse was mainly responsible, and 21% said childcare was shared.

In view of the prevalence of this inegalitarian division of domestic labour (confirmed in both our surveys to date), we were looking forward to seeing the pattern of responses to the question about who *should* do the various household tasks. We added this question, which was clearly missing from the previous year's survey, asking married and cohabiting couples – as well as the unmarried – what division of tasks they thought ought to obtain. Here married men and women gave remarkably similar answers, in both cases favouring a more equal division of labour than actually existed. But the answers from both sexes were still far from egalitarian.

Ideals were clearly tempered by current experience, as married men and women were less egalitarian (even prescriptively) than either the formerly married or the never married. Nevertheless, it is striking to compare the opinions of how household tasks should be divided with how they actually were divided. Since the answers given by men and women were relatively similar, the table below concentrates on differences by marital status rather than sex.

The patterns are remarkably consistent. If one concentrates only (for simplicity) on the 'shared equally' rows, there is always a difference between what happens and what 'should' happen; moreover is always in the same direction. There is also always a similar difference between the married and the never married respondents in their view of what should happen. The divorced or separated (not shown here) gave responses between those given by the currently and never married. Part of the explanation for these differences lies in greater egalitarianism (or lesser inegalitarianism) of younger respondents; for

		Married 'does' %	Married 'should do' %	Never married 'should do' %
Household shopping:	Mainly man	6	*	*
	Mainly woman	54	35	31
	Shared equally	39	62	68
Preparation of evening meal:	Mainly man	5	1	1
	Mainly woman	77	61	49
	Shared equally	16	35	49
Evening dishes:	Mainly man	18	12	13
	Mainly woman	37	21	15
	Shared equally	41	64	71
Household cleaning:	Mainly man	3	*	1
	Mainly woman	72	51	42
	Shared equally	23	45	56
Washing and ironing:	Mainly man	1	*	*
	Mainly woman	88	77	68
	Shared equally	9	21	30
Repairs of household equipment:	Mainly man	83	79	74
	Mainly woman	6	2	*
	Shared equally	8	17	24
Organisation of household money and bills:	Mainly man	32	23	19
	Mainly woman	38	15	16
	Shared equally	28	58	63

instance, widowed respondents (predominantly older women) favoured a more inegalitarian prescriptive pattern than did currently married respondents.

There is, of course, much further analysis to be done. For instance, are the differences between present and preferred allocations attributable to a few married respondents answering in a more egalitarian fashion on most items, or to most married respondents answering in a more egalitarian fashion on a few items? We do not currently know.

Even so, we can see from the analyses we have already carried out that married women working full-time not only had markedly more egalitarian attitudes than other married women to the preferred allocation of tasks; they were also more likely to prefer an egalitarian division of labour than the never married women. Those women who most felt the burden of juggling household and employment responsibilities seemed to be most dissatisfied with the traditional domestic division of labour. This is not to say, however, that full-time houseworkers were uniformly satisfied with present arrangements.

Aspirations of houseworkers

In order to ascertain the labour market aspirations of those women who did not have paid work outside the home, we asked questions of all women who were currently engaged in 'looking after the home'. About a third of the women in our sample described this as their main economic activity. Some of them might have preferred to describe themselves as retired, but interviewers were instructed that the 'retired' code should apply only to those who had worked in the years immediately prior to reaching normal retirement age. In fact, of those women 'looking after the home', about a quarter gave as their main reason for not working in a paid job that they were too old to work; almost all of these women were indeed over retirement age. Most younger women gave as their reason for not having a paid job that they were looking after the home or children, or that they preferred to look after the home and family.

Work outside the home was strongly associated with age. Over half of the women aged under 35 had had a paid job in the five years prior to the survey; this figure fell to under 30% for women aged 35 or over.

We asked all women who were not in paid work how likely they were to look for a paid job in the next five years. This was not intended to be a predictor of behaviour, and certainly not a predictor of their likelihood of actually finding work; it was simply a crude measure of attitudes toward future labour market participation. Again there were strong age-related differences, which might be related to generational differences in attitude: older women might, for instance, have been more fully committed to their role as houseworkers. Or the differences might be related to differences in expectation: older women, many of whom had been out of the labour market for a long time, might believe that their chances of returning to work in present circumstances were very poor and not worth attempting.

	Houseworkers	
	Aged 18-34	Aged 35-59
	%	%
Likelihood of looking for paid job in next five years:		
Will look for full-time job	13	5
Will look for part-time job	58	33
Will not look for job	26	55

Although nearly three-quarters of the younger women planned to look for a paid job, the vast majority wanted a part-time job. This remains the most popular strategy among women for mixing domestic and employment responsibilities, and, since it coincides with the growth in labour market demands for part-time staff, we can expect the debate over labour market stratification and component-waged work to continue.

Women and work

Employment status and occupational segregation

Women in Britain continue to work outside the home in significant numbers, with over half of all the women aged 18-59 in our sample in paid work, even with our relatively strict definition of what constitutes paid employment.

Economic activity of women aged 18-59

	%
Full-time paid work	36
Part-time paid work	18
Unemployed	5
Total economically active:	59
Economically inactive:	39
Full-time students:	2

The well-documented effect of the life-cycle is evident in our survey, with full-time employment highest in the youngest age groups, who were more likely to be single and childless, and lowest for married women over the age of 29 with young dependent children. 73% of women who had never married were employed full-time, compared with only 10% of women whose youngest child was under five years. Multivariate analysis of WES suggests that the presence of a young child in the household has a larger effect on women's employment than does marital status *per se*. See for instance, Joshi (1984); Dex (1984).

We went on to ask employees about aspects of their work. We wanted to see whether men and women had different occupational profiles, and to examine the extent of occupational segregation. We used a question from the 1980 WES survey, but were able to compare the responses for women and men employees directly rather than to compare women and their husbands, as in WES.

Occupational segregation occurs both because men and women are concentrated in different industries and different occupations (vertical segregation) and because women tend to be employed in less skilled, and less well paid jobs than men within the same occupations (horizontal segregation). (See Hakim, 1979, 1981; Martin and Roberts, 1984; Reid and Wormald, 1982). We followed Martin and Roberts in asking men and women employees whether there were members of the opposite sex doing the same sort of work as themselves at their workplace.

This question provides a measure of occupational segregation expressed as a proportion of employees who experience it, rather than a measure of segregation in occupations or establishments. It is known, for instance, that women are disproportionately found in a restricted number of occupations; Martin and Roberts (1984, p.23) report that while three of the 18 government (OPCS) occupational orders accounted for 69% of women's jobs in 1980, the three orders with the highest proportions of men's jobs accounted for only 43% of men's jobs.

We found that women employees, particularly part-time employees, did indeed experience high levels of segregation, with fewer than half reporting that there were any men doing the same sort of work at their workplace. But what is often overlooked is that, although women employees are occupationally segregated, men are in veritable occupational isolation.

As can be seen, men were only about half as likely as women to work with members of the opposite sex. It is clear that many women are occupationally

	All men employees %	All women employees %	Women full-time %	Women part-time %
Works with own sex only	72	51	45	64
Works with both sexes	27	47	54	33
Works alone/only person doing that job	*	2	1	2

segregated because their jobs tend to be lower paid and less attractive than men's jobs. However, given that many male 'skilled' manual jobs require little more skill than driving a car (Blackburn and Mann, 1979) it is unlikely that all those who were occupationally segregated were so because of absolute skill levels. We shall come later in the chapter to the possible attitudinal factors which underlie this segregation when we look at sex-stereotyped images of different occupations.

Although our sample size is too small to show separate analyses of Standard Industrial Classification by sex, it is clear that the pattern identified in WES obtains, with women in manufacturing more likely than those in service industries to work with women only. Women in semi-skilled and unskilled jobs (Social Classes IV and V) were the most likely to be segregated occupationally, followed by those in clerical and sales jobs (Social Class III non-manual). This pattern does not hold for men, where it was the skilled manual employees who were most likely to work with men only. For both men and women, occupational segregation at the workplace was lower in non-manual jobs than in manual jobs, but even there men were more segregated at work than women were, as the following table shows.

	Social Class							
	Male employees				Female employees			
	I/II	III non-manual	III manual	IV/V	I/II	III non-manual	III manual*	IV/V
	%	%	%	%	%	%	%	%
Respondent works with:								
Own sex only	58	56	87	74	23	58		69
Both sexes	41	44	13	27	77	41		28

* Base too small to percentage.

It is important to mention the debate about the classification of women's occupations here, since the occupational classifications in common use (and to which we have referred) were all developed mainly with reference to a male-dominated labour market. The distribution of occupational segregation shows that women tend to work in different occupations from men, but it also suggests that these occupations have different social ranking and rewards from 'male' occupations in the same social class. Moreover occupational groupings that are female-dominated tend to be allocated to fewer social classes even when they span many levels of training, pay, supervisory responsibility and prestige. (For instance, nurses with high levels of professional training are in the same Social Class as nursing auxiliaries.) The literature on this problem is growing and there have already been several attempts to devise a classification that takes more account of women's occupations; some other schemes seek to classify housework as an occupation or social class *sui generis*, and some seek to abandon occupationally-defined social class altogether. For the moment, however, we are locked into existing classifications, since none of these newer schemes have yet been completed or adopted widely. We have therefore continued to use Registrar General's Social Class, and Socio-Economic Group (SEG). We do, however, classify women according to their *own* occupations, not to those of putative 'heads of household'. We also collect information routinely on spouse's occupation for married or cohabiting respondents, whether male or female.

Job stereotyping

Our question on occupational segregation was followed by one on job stereotyping, also asked in WES, but for which we are able directly to compare the responses of men and women. We asked all employees whether they thought of their work as mainly men's work, mainly women's work, or work that either men or women do. We found that men were significantly more likely to describe their work as mainly men's work than women were to describe theirs as mainly women's work. If men employees (nearly all of whom worked full-time) are compared with full-time women employees, the contrast is even starker. If we take the description 'work that either do' as an indicator of a job that is likely to be better paid and of higher status, then full-time women employees were more likely to be in better-paid jobs than were part-time women employees.

	Men employees	Women employees	Women full-time	Women part-time
Work is:	%	%	%	%
Mainly men's work	49	1	2	–
Mainly women's work	–	36	32	45
Work that either do	50	63	67	55

As was found in WES, it seems that men and women had different reasons for describing their work as they did. Of the women who described their jobs as mainly women's work, 42% were in non-manual jobs (such as sales or clerical work), and 36% were in semi-skilled or unskilled manual jobs – probably the very jobs identified by Martin and Roberts as those that women felt men would *not* be prepared to do. Reasons given in 1980 for thinking of these jobs as women's work tended to be that such jobs are generally associated with low pay, and required 'typically female' personal skills and a greater toleration of boredom. Of the men who described their jobs as mainly men's work, 57% were in skilled manual jobs, and 21% were in semi-skilled or unskilled jobs. These are the types of jobs that the WES sample of husbands was more likely to feel that women *could* not do for reasons of heavy physical demands, unpleasant working conditions and the need for appropriate (apprenticeship-type) training (Martin and Roberts, 1984).

In the future rounds of this survey we intend to include a follow-up question on respondents' reasons for gender labelling of jobs, in view of the fact that both the nature and number of 'male preserves' are changing in response to changes in Britain's industrial structure.

Attitudes towards pay

Despite their different labour market positions, men and women did not vary much in their evaluations of their pay, or in their pay expectations for the coming year. We asked all employees the following question about their present level of pay:

> *How would you describe the wages or salary you are paid for the job you do – on the low side, reasonable, or on the high side?* [If described as low] *Very low or a bit low?*

Pay for the job is:	Men	Women
	%	%
Very low	10	11
A bit low	32	28
Reasonable	52	58
On the high side	5	2

The similarities of these marginal distributions do, however, conceal some differences. For instance, women in clerical and sales jobs (Social Class III non-manual) appeared to be the most satisfied group – more so than any other male or female category. And women in semi-skilled and unskilled manual jobs were much more likely than men in these categories to be satisfied with their wages (59% compared with 41%). Ironically, these are among the lowest paid workers, particularly since many women in these occupations are part-time employees.

When we turned to pay *expectations* in the coming year, we found that women employees were less likely than men to believe that their wages or salary would rise by more than the cost of living, and were more likely to believe that it would not rise at all.

Over the next year pay will:	Men	Women
	%	%
Rise by more than the cost of living	16	9
Rise by the same as the cost of living	47	48
Rise by less than the cost of living	26	26
Not rise at all	7	13

Here the different occupational roles of women were certainly important in producing the overall differences between men and women. There were interesting contrasts between men and women in similar occupational categories and employment sectors.

Pay expectations by non-manual/manual occupations

	Men non-manual	Women non-manual	Men manual	Women manual
Pay will:	%	%	%	%
Rise by more than the cost of living	23	12	11	4
Rise by the same as the cost of living	48	50	46	42
Rise by less than the cost of living	24	25	28	30
Not rise at all	3	10	10	18

Pay expectations by employment sector

	Men private sector	Women private sector	Men public sector	Women public sector
Pay will:	%	%	%	%
Rise by more than the cost of living	21	8	5	9
Rise by the same as the cost of living	51	47	40	49
Rise by less than the cost of living	17	21	45	33
Not rise at all	9	19	5	6

The first table above shows that men in non-manual occupations were the most likely to anticipate high pay increases. Women in non-manual occupations were only as optimistic as men in manual occupations, while women in manual jobs were the least optimistic of all.

From the second table it is clear that men and women do very different jobs within the public and private sectors; while women in the public sector were on the whole rather more optimistic than men in the public sector about pay, the opposite was true in the private sector. Indeed, men in the private sector were particularly optimistic about pay increases; about a fifth expected to receive an increase greater than the cost of living. Contrast their situation with women in the private sector, who were particularly pessimistic, with nearly a fifth believing they would get no increase at all.

A large part of the explanation for these differences may be found in the different expectations of part-time as compared with full-time employees.

	Full-time male	Full-time female	Part-time female
Pay will:	%	%	%
Rise by more than the cost of living	16	11	5
Rise by the same as the cost of living	48	48	47
Rise by less than the cost of living	26	29	21
Not rise at all	7	10	20

While the distribution for full-time men and women employees was very similar, part-time women were markedly more pessimistic. Since part-timers form a larger proportion of manual women workers (60%) than of non-manual (22%), this probably accounts for much of the difference in pay expectations within manual occupations and within the private sector.

Job commitment

We then went on to explore employees' expectations about staying with or leaving their current employers; if they expected to leave within the next year we asked them why. We were interested to discover the extent to which men and women would give different reasons for wanting to leave their current employers. Among the categories on the showcard of possible reasons for leaving one's job was one to do with looking after the home, children or a relative. Respondents were invited to give as many reasons as they wished for leaving. Here our findings showed little difference between men and women. Working women were no more likely than men to leave their jobs, and – if they did plan to leave – they saw themselves as likely to leave for much the same reasons.

	Men	Women
	%	%
Unlikely to leave job:	75	73
Likely to leave – total:	25	27
Reasons given:		
To work for another employer	12	12
Will be made redundant	5	5
To look after home/children/relatives	–	4
To retire	3	3
To work as self-employed	3	1
Other answer	4	4

These responses do not, of course, capture the actual reasons for women leaving work over a life-cycle, which, according to Martin and Roberts (1984, p.140), are very frequently for 'domestic' reasons (including job changes made to follow a husband or fit in with a husband's career). Yet, even over the life-cycle, the WES survey also found that, in more than half of departures made, women employees went directly to another employer. What our findings reveal of women currently in employment is that a large majority expected to continue to work over the next year, and among those who expected to leave, many more expected to do so to work for another employer than to look after a home or family.

As a further indication of labour market commitment, we asked all employees two hypothetical questions. The first question was:

> Suppose you lost your job for one reason or another, would you start looking for another job, would you wait for several months or longer before you started looking, or would you decide not to look for another job?

Men and women employees showed a small but significant difference here. Working women were slightly more likely than working men to say they would not look for another job, but this was highly correlated with age. Only women over the age of 45 showed a significantly greater likelihood than men of the same age to decide not to look for another job. As can be seen from the summary table below, full-time men and women employees gave much the same responses. Women working part-time were, however, less likely than others to say they would start looking for another job immediately.

	Full-time men	Full-time women	Part-time women
If lost job:	%	%	%
Would start looking immediately	91	90	71
Would wait several months	4	3	9
Would decide not to look	5	6	21

An obvious reason for the difference between full-time and part-time workers is that part-time workers may not be so financially dependent on their work. Many are married, and married women were much less likely than the never married to look for an alternative job immediately. But this may partly be an age effect, the never married respondents being younger. Nonetheless, there was no such difference in replies made by married and never married men. Even so, among women, the differences between the married and never married were not as large as the differences between full-time and part-time workers. This suggests, as we would expect, that marital status *per se* is not as important as financial dependence in determining one's attachment to paid work. Moreover, part-time women workers tend to have more constraining domestic responsibilities, such as young children, which will certainly affect their labour market commitment.

The second question asked in order to examine labour market commitment was more hypothetical; it was meant as a partial measure of an intrinsic attachment to work.

> If without having to work, you had what you would regard as a reasonable living income, do you think you would still prefer to have a paid job, or wouldn't you bother?*

Although each person's answer will inevitably depend on how he or she interprets the phrase 'a reasonable living income', we were trying with this question to elicit an attachment to work that was to some extent divorced from financial need.

As before, age mattered here, particularly in the case of women, with older women showing the least preference for keeping a job. There were also significant differences between full-time and part-time women workers; once again, the responses of full-time women employees were similar to those of full-time men employees. The full distribution of answers can be seen in **Table 3.5.** In summary, nearly three-quarters of full-time men employees would prefer a paid job even if they did not need one financially, compared with over

---

* The EEC-sponsored Eurobarometers asked a similar question in 1978 and 1983 and showed similar differences between men and women. But the differences in question wording between their survey and ours clearly has an effect on the question marginals. (See EEC 1979; 1984.)

two-thirds of full-time women employees, and only half of part-time women employees.

Reasons for working

To pursue the possible reasons why women and men work, we followed WES in asking men and women employees to choose from a showcard the items which best described their reasons for working. Such lists have been used before to distinguish underlying 'work-orientations' of different groups of (usually male) workers. But as Blackburn and Mann (1979) point out, the existence of deep-seated psychological orientations to work is neither implied nor measured by this sort of question. We added an item to our list ('for a change from children or housework'), as this response came up relatively frequently during piloting of the questionnaire, but otherwise the question we asked was the same as WES. The aim in using the WES list was to present items that would distinguish between men and women, as well as allow for other types of analysis. (For instance there were marked differences in reasons given by employees and the self-employed.) As might be expected given the under-representation of part-time women employees discussed earlier, the distri-bution of the reasons given by women for working was more nearly like the pattern reported of full-time women workers in 1980. Nevertheless, there were interesting differences in the reasons given by men and women. Since respon-dents could give as many reasons as they wished, answers sum to more than 100%.

	Men	Women
Reasons for working:	%	%
Need money for basic essentials	81	58
To earn money to buy extras	32	43
To earn money of my own	21	38
Enjoy working	45	59
Working is the normal thing to do	46	21
To follow my career	30	26
For the company of other people	16	36
For a change from the children/housework	1	11

Although women were much less likely than men to say they worked because they needed money for essentials, this reason was nonetheless given by nearly three-fifths of working women. We recognise that the distinction between 'essentials' and 'extras' is problematical and will depend on an individual's or a society's implicit definition of necessity and luxury. Moreover as Martin and Roberts (1984, p.68) said: "We have no way of knowing . . . whether the women who said they worked to earn money for 'extras' were in fact meeting basic needs too . . . some people's basic needs are other people's extras." In any event, altogether 80% of women said they were working to provide *either* essentials or extras, a striking confirmation of the financial importance of women's earnings.

The differences between men's and women's reasons for working, as shown in the table above, were very large. The only item that men and women were more or less equally likely to choose is the one on career-building. In all other respects the contrasts were more striking than the similarities.

Majorities of both men and women workers said that they worked to make money for essentials, but men were much more likely than women were to see that reason as the *sine qua non* of their working lives. Women chose that motive for working as frequently as they chose the motive of enjoyment.

Men were also more than twice as likely as women to say that working was the 'normal' thing to do. 'Normal' here was clearly interpreted as continuous employment until retirement. Women on the other hand were more than twice as likely as men to choose the 'social' reason for working. Only one in ten working women, however, and almost no men, chose the reason that working is an escape route from housework and child-rearing. As we have noted, for men it would hardly be an escape since they are not the major participants in housework anyway.

As **Table 3.6** shows, there were also significant age differences which the totals above do not reveal. Younger working women (aged 18-24) gave similar responses to those of younger men. They were, for instance, almost as likely as men to say they worked because working is the normal thing to do and were *more* likely (than men of the same age) to say they worked in order to earn money for essentials. Over half of both younger men and younger women said they worked to earn money of their own, reflecting the fact that many in this age group live with their parents and wish to be financially independent.

Older working women were significantly less likely than older men to say they worked because working was the normal thing to do, or to say they worked in order to buy essentials. They were more likely than other women to say they worked for 'extras' or for company or as a change from housework.

Age, though, was closely related to other factors which influenced the choice of reasons for working, notably full-time or part-time employment.

Reasons for working:	Men full-time %	Women full-time %	Women part-time %
Need money for basic essentials	81	61	52
To earn money to buy extras	32	38	54
To earn money of my own	21	42	32
Enjoy working	45	62	53
Working is the normal thing to do	46	26	11
To follow my career	30	33	11
For the company of other people	16	35	37
For a change from children/housework	1	8	17

Women working full-time were more likely than those working part-time to say they worked in order to buy essentials, although still not as likely as full-time male employees. It now becomes apparent too that the career-builders among women were confined largely to full-time employees. Full-time women workers were also much more likely than their part-time counterparts to regard working as the normal thing to do. More surprisingly, perhaps, they were also more likely than either part-time working women or than men to say they enjoyed working.

Occupational differences were also illuminating. In general women showed more differences between social classes than did men. Non-manual women employees were more likely than their manual counterparts to regard working as the normal thing to do, and particularly likely to say they enjoyed their work. Indeed they were also more likely than non-manual men employees (68% to 57%) to choose this reason, a difference not found between men and women manual workers. This discrepancy may be related partly to the association between full-time employment and non-manual occupations for women, but it may also be due to the large numbers of non-manual women employees who are in the 'caring professions', and who might be expected to have higher levels of intrinsic attachment to their work. Women manual workers were, not surprisingly, particularly likely to choose reasons for working that related to money rather than social factors or enjoyment. In other words, non-manual women workers seemed to express greater intrinsic attachment to work than their male counterparts, while women manual employees were more like men manual employees.

Finally, while few differences emerged among men – except for apparently age-dependent responses – according to whether or not they were married, there were clear differences between married and unmarried women in their reasons for working. As might be expected, the principal difference was that married women were much more likely than unmarried ones to say they worked to buy extras. This response was anticipated not only because many married women, although contributing vital finances, are less reliant than unmarried women on their own income to buy necessities, but also because some may be reluctant to admit they are working for necessities (see Martin and Roberts, 1984, p.69).

We followed the question on reasons for working by asking respondents to choose a 'main' reason for working, and the pattern of responses was subject to the same influences discussed above: there were marked differences by social class, age and marital status, especially among women. The totals for men and women were as follows:

Main reason for working:	Men %		Women %	
Need money for basic essentials	71	} 73	50	} 65
To earn money to buy extras	2		15	
To earn money of my own	4		8	
Enjoy working	7		13	
Working is the normal thing to do	9		2	
To follow my career	5		8	
For the company of other people	*		2	
For a change from the children/housework	–		1	

Women working in manual occupations were more likely to mention financial need as their main reason for working, and women in general were more likely than men to mention enjoyment of work as their main reason. But even among married women, the preponderance of financial factors was marked.

Main reason for working:	Married men %		Married women %	
Need money for basic essentials	79	⎫	46	⎫
To earn money to buy extras	1	⎬ 81	23	⎬ 75
To earn money of my own	*	⎭	6	⎭

We have so far referred only to the reasons that people themselves gave for working. But we wanted also to discover general attitudes towards married women working. Had we elicited such attitudes, say, in the 1950s or earlier we would almost certainly have discovered a censoriousness towards married women abandoning the housework and children. What are attitudes now? To what extent do people see the trade-off that many married women have to make? To shed some light on this we included a question with the same list of reasons for working as we had given employees to choose from, and asked all respondents to choose the reasons they thought applied to why married women work. We realised that we were posing a difficult problem: in order to answer the question, respondents had both to stereotype married women (compared with other people) and to generalise (among all married women).

In the event, few respondents (fewer than two per cent) gave responses other than those on the showcards. Instead they seemed to react to the difficulty by choosing more items as reasons for work than did the employees themselves. (On average each respondent chose 3.2 items when asked about married

Reasons for working:	Reason given when asked about married women		Actual reasons given by married women employees
	men %	women %	%
Need money for basic essentials	59	68	53
To earn money to buy extras	74	69	52
To earn money of their own	48	43	36
Enjoy working	26	30	60
Working is the normal thing to do	7	6	13
To follow a career	30	30	23
For the company of other people	36	40	37
For a change from children/ housework	37	44	15

women, compared with an average of 2.8 items chosen by employees when asked to name their own reasons.)

An interesting finding was that, although both men and women recognised the importance of financial factors, women of all age groups were more likely than all but the youngest men to say that married women worked in order to earn money for essentials; men were more likely to say that married women worked for extras or for financial independence. Even so, the generalisations about married women and work exceeded the reality by a large margin in respect of financial factors, and fell short of reality by a large margin in respect of enjoyment. Both men and women overestimated the apparent importance of a change from children and housework.

Another finding seems to bear upon the relationship that is felt to exist between paid employment and financial independence. Compare the responses given by women who were themselves in paid work with women who were not employed and whose work was looking after the house.

Reasons for married women working:	Women in paid work %	Houseworkers %
Need money for basic essentials	73	65
To earn money to buy extras	72	69
To earn money of their own	52	37
Enjoy working	25	28
Working is the normal thing to do	5	5
To follow a career	24	35
For the company of other people	44	38
For a change from children/housework	49	42

Women who were employees were not only more likely to believe that married women work for reasons of financial need but were also more likely to mention the need for money of their own (in fact they mentioned this more often than did married women workers when discussing their own reasons); the effect is not wholly reducible to the greater propensity of younger women to choose this reason. Women in paid work, then, seemed to be giving greater importance to the relative financial independence that paid employment might bring to married women, and were possibly more aware of the uncertainties and restrictions related to married women's financial dependence.

Women's issues: egalitarianism and traditionalism

In addition to asking about men's and women's attitudes to work and domestic matters, we included several questions on attitudes to women's rights and to legislation offering protection to women. We also included items designed to measure egalitarianism and traditionalism in respect of women's roles.

Equal opportunities legislation and discrimination

As was generally found in WES, there was overwhelming support among both men and women for all the major provisions of the equal opportunity legislation of the 1970s.

Instead of using an 'importance' rating (as was used in WES) we tried to incorporate a more direct measure of "attitudes towards the value propositions underlying the legislative provisions" (Martin and Roberts, 1984, p.182). Interestingly, despite the change in the scale, the ranking of statements by those who supported them was identical to that revealed in 1980 by WES. More support was given to items to do with 'universal' equal opportunities provision, and somewhat less to work-related rights which lie at the heart of a sex-linked division of labour.

Provisions:	Support %	Oppose %
The opportunity for boys and girls to study the same subjects at school	96	2
Laws giving men and women equal pay for equal work	93	5
The right to six weeks' maternity pay if a woman has been in her job for two years	88	8
Laws making it illegal to treat men and women differently at work	81	14
The right for a woman to return to her job within six months of having a baby	77	18

The high level of support for equal opportunities legislation is also reflected in answers given to a more general question about sex discrimination legislation.

There is a law in Britain against sex discrimination, that is against giving unfair preference to men – or to women – in employment, pay and so on. Do you generally support or oppose the idea of a law for this purpose?

	1983 %	1984 %
Support	76	80
Oppose	22	17

Moreover, there is some evidence that the wording of our question may have led to an *understatement* of support for sex discrimination legislation.*

The wording was, however, apparently not a problem for all respondents, as the answers to this question were highly correlated with answers given in response to other items related to equal opportunities.

---

* See Chapter 7 on the panel study. SCPR's Survey Methods Centre has also carried out further methodological work which involved taping about 100 Social Attitudes interviews. This work too reveals the difficulty some respondents had in identifying opposition to sex discrimination with support for anti-discrimination legislation. (See Sykes, forthcoming.)

Women and men were equally likely to support the idea of laws against sex discrimination, and there were few subgroup differences, other than those related to income and education, as reported last year (Jowell and Airey, 1984, p.135).

Divorce legislation and maintenance provision

A recent change in one traditional legal protection for women, ostensibly in the direction of greater sex equality, was the passage of the Matrimonial and Family Proceedings Act of 1984. This Act aimed to implement a clean financial break at the end of a marriage, encouraging women to become economically independent of their former spouse.

Our findings show that both men and women were aware of the difficulty that married women face in attaining financial independence when they have specialised in the role of full-time houseworker. In the 1984 Report we described the findings of a series of questions about maintenance payments to wives in the event of a divorce. We framed these questions in respect of a hypothetical couple, with both partners aged 35 and working. We then varied one element of the situation – the presence or not of dependent children – to see how this element affected attitudes.

We found, as we expected, that judgements about such a complex matter were inevitably sensitive to the context presented. In our 1984 questionnaire, therefore, we again varied the elements of the situation. Once again we held age constant (but at 45 rather than 35 to make the later variations more plausible). But this time we also held constant the *absence* of dependent children. Instead we varied the wife's working history.

Comparing the 1983 responses to the item that postulated no dependent children with the 1984 data, we can see that the change in age *by itself* appears to make little difference. Most of the difference can be accounted for by a shift towards 'qualified' responses.

	1983	1984
Should the man make maintenance payments to support the wife?	%	%
Yes	10	13
No	86	79
Qualified response	1	6

Women of all age groups, especially older women, were more likely to think that the man should make maintenance payments to the wife, but the differences were not large. In general an overwhelming majority of all subgroups seemed to oppose maintenance payments when there were no dependent children involved. But here is a good example of the extent to which a single question can mislead. We followed this question by one which made explicit a dimension mentioned by some of those who had qualified their initial responses to our first question. We asked:

> *Consider a similar couple, also aged about 45 with no children at home. They are both working at the time of the divorce, but the woman's earnings are much lower than the man's.*
>
> *In your opinion should the man make maintenance payments to support the wife?*

	Men	Women
	%	%
Yes	41	47
No	47	42
Qualified response	11	8

Again there was a small difference in the responses given by men and women, although in the youngest age group, men's and women's responses were almost identical.

Most important, however, was the very large shift in attitudes occasioned by the new information provided. The ability of a formerly-married woman to support herself was clearly seen to be relevant to maintenance provision. Is it possible that egalitarian beliefs about marriage as a joint enterprise are coming into play here? The evidence for this interpretation is strengthened when we look at responses to the third situation we presented. We asked respondents about a similar couple, but in this case the woman had *never* had a paid job outside the home. It was possible, we thought, that some people would see in this situation the caricature of the 'alimony drone'. But in answering the question, respondents appeared instead to have a more realistic and sympathetic view of the woman's future employment prospects. The answers were almost a reversal of the attitudes expressed when the wife held a paid job with unspecified earnings.

	Men	Women
Maintenance payments should be made:	%	%
Yes	70	74
No	18	17
Qualified response	10	8

Interestingly, younger women were more likely at each of the three questions to support maintenance payments than women aged 25-44. Not surprisingly, however, married women were less likely to support maintenance payments than separated, divorced or widowed women; in fact married men and women held similar views.

It is striking, though, that notwithstanding the passage of the Matrimonial and Family Proceedings Act (1984), men and women seemed to be aware of the social consequences of the sex-based division of paid work and domestic labour. In other words, women who had performed the role of houseworker and whose employment prospects were low, were accorded entitlements to part of the former family wage. The shift in responses produced by the introduction of financial and labour market considerations made it clear that people found it difficult to hold formally egalitarian beliefs (financial independence) if it meant penalising women for adhering to the traditional domestic division of labour.

Discrimination at work and occupational stereotypes

We included only one question on an aspect of sex discrimination in the labour market. We asked whether respondents felt that women were generally less likely than men to be promoted at work, even when their qualifications and experience were the same.

Over 80% of the sample believed that such discrimination occurred, divided more or less evenly between those who thought it happened 'a lot' and those who thought it happened 'a little'. Men's and women's responses were broadly the same. Older women, however, (of whom there were more in our sample than older men), were much less likely to think discrimination of this sort occurred. Moreover, current women employees were more likely to believe that such discrimination happend 'a lot' than were women looking after the home (48% compared to 35%). We did not follow up this question with others which could have asked whether women generally were thought to possess qualifications and experience comparable to men, or questions which attempted to explore attitudes towards other forms of sex discrimination at work. This question is therefore no more than one measure of perceived discrimination which may or may not correlate with others that we intend to include in future years.

We did, however, explore another important area of occupational sex-differentiation. In the self completion questionnaire we asked respondents to look at a list of 11 occupations and to categorise them as being *particularly suitable for men, particularly suitable for women*, or *suitable for both equally*. A 'principled egalitarian' should presumably have answered that all the roles were suitable for either sex to perform; but that is not necessarily the way respondents approach these subjects. When answering questions like this, many respondents are as likely to think in terms of what is rather than what ought to be. The total distributions certainly suggest that an awareness of who traditionally plays the roles exerted some influence.

	Particularly suitable for men	Particularly suitable for women	Suitable for both equally
Traditionally male occupations	%	%	%
Car mechanic	72	1	25
Bus driver	49	1	49
Police officer	49	*	49
Bank manager	39	1	58
Traditionally female occupations			
Secretary	1	60	38
Nurse	*	41	47
Political, service or newer occupations			
Member of parliament	16	*	82
Local councillor	12	1	85
Social worker	1	11	87
Family doctor/GP	10	1	87
Computer programmer	6	3	89

We cannot, of course, say exactly what features of the jobs asked about were most important to the respondent in answering the question; we do not know whether, for instance, it was the working conditions, the traditionally male skills or the manual labour involved which was responsible for the answers about the car mechanic. It is striking, however, that respondents tended to see the more professional and white-collar roles as suitable for both sexes, but that this did not apply to the job of bank manager nearly as much as it did to other white-collar jobs. We have constructed a general index of egalitarianism for this question, based on the number of jobs which respondents felt were suitable for both sexes equally. On this measure, shown in the table below, women were slightly more egalitarian than men, but this difference was greater if men and women under the age of 55 are examined separately. On all the items shown, older women were more likely than other groups to designate the job as suitable to its traditional holders.

In addition, on both the general index and with regard to many of the separate occupations, the working status of women respondents mattered, with full-time employees displaying more egalitarian views than women looking after the home. (Although this too is partly an effect of age.) Education as measured by school-leaving age was also important, with the more educated *women*, especially, displaying more egalitarian views. The figures given below are for the general index only; for more detailed figures on a selection of occupations and roles see **Tables 3.9 – 3.12**.

			1-2	3-5	6-9	10-11
Men:	aged 18-54	%	5	19	55	21
	aged 55 or over	%	8	22	52	13
Women:	aged 18-54	%	3	10	56	30
	aged 55 or over	%	12	26	49	10
Women:	all employees	%	2	10	59	27
	full-time employees	%	3	10	58	30
	looking after the home	%	10	15	49	24
Men:	finished schooling aged 18 or under	%	6	21	54	18
	finished schooling aged 19 or over	%	4	14	56	26
Women:	finished schooling aged 18 or under	%	7	17	53	21
	finished schooling aged 19 or over	%	–	7	49	43

Number of jobs suitable for men and women equally

Traditionalist views of gender roles

Not surprisingly, people who held traditionalist attitudes on occupational stereotyping also tended to hold traditionalist attitudes more generally. There is some evidence, however, that traditionalist attitudes towards women's roles are slightly less widespread than in 1980.

We included four agree/disagree statements from WES in our self-completion questionnaire, one with a significant wording change. Three of these statements were used in WES to define an underlying dimension of traditionalism; one of the statements showed a particularly high association in our survey with traditionalist responses to other questions, such as the one on occupational stereotyping. The statement was:

A husband's job is to earn the money; a wife's job is to look after the home and family.

In the case of all four statements, women, as a whole, were more likely to disagree strongly with traditionalist views and more likely to agree strongly with more egalitarian positions. As might be expected, younger women were notably less traditionalist than older women, who were in fact even more traditionalist than older men. There is some evidence that this may be partly generational, and not a life-cycle effect – that is, older women have more traditionalist attitudes not simply because they have developed them with age, but because they have retained them from their formative years. Yet by comparing our sample of 20-64 year olds with the WES sample of 16-59 year olds, thereby confining the comparison to the views of the relevant age cohort for WES, we could account only for slightly less than half of the shift in attitudes that has apparently occurred since 1980.

Women in paid employment were less likely to hold traditionalist attitudes towards women's roles than women whose main work was looking after the home. As was found in 1980, higher levels of education were also associated with less traditionalist attitudes, even allowing for the association of education with age. (Martin and Roberts, 1984, p.173; Dex, 1984.) (For marginals and further details, see **Tables 3.13 – 3.14**). Married people, especially married women, were more likely than the single to reject the view that 'most married women work only to earn money for extras rather than because they need the

WES data* and Social Attitudes data compared (women only)

Traditionalist attitudes		Agree	Neither agree nor disagree	Disagree
'In times of high unemployment married women should stay at home'				
1980: (women aged 16-59 years old)	%	35	16	49
1984: (women aged 18-59 years old)	%	27	14	58
'A husband's job is to earn the money; a wife's job is to look after the home and family'				
1980	%	46	21	33
1984	%	32	17	51
Most married women only work:				
1980: 'for pin money, they don't need a job'	%	20	14	66
1984: 'to earn money for extras rather than because they need the money'	%	42	11	47
Attitudes towards benefits of women working				
'Having a job is the best way for a woman to be an independent person'				
1980	%	67	17	16
1984	%	70	18	12

* Martin and Roberts (1984).

money', and that 'in times of high unemployment married women should stay at home'. This confirms the proposition that many households now depend on two wage-earners, to sustain their standard of living.

Whereas there has been no marked shift since 1980 in attitudes towards the benefits of work for women, it is interesting nonetheless that women in 1984 displayed notably less traditionalist attitudes towards other aspects of women's roles in the labour market. The findings from our survey and those from WES are not exactly comparable, since our sample included only women aged 18 or older, while the 1980 survey included 16 and 17 year olds. But since younger women were generally *more* egalitarian that cannot be the explanation for the significant shift in responses in the intervening years.

A sizeable minority – of about a third – still remains traditionalist on these measures. It can be seen that, in the case of the statement whose wording we changed (in response to pilot complaints that the original 1980 wording was belittling to women), we have perhaps transformed the item from being principally a measure of *attitudes* to principally a measure of *beliefs* about the reasons married women work. It appears that the disparaging phrase 'pin money' generated a different feeling from the phrase 'money for extras', since 'extras' can be important, even if not essential.

Unfortunately we cannot compare men's attitudes in 1984 with those of men in 1980 (since the WES sample was confined to husbands of the sampled women). Nonetheless it does appear that egalitarian attitudes were somewhat more widely shared by men in 1984 than they were in 1980. Or perhaps the four intervening years of recession have led to a greater appreciation of women's economic contributions to many households.

Our survey also suggests, however, that while there was widespread disapproval of formal obstacles to women's equality and of overt discrimination, there was much less evidence of attitude change in respect of the domestic division of labour which is a major cause of labour market inequality. Some real changes have been brought about by legally providing for equality of opportunity; others have been brought about by improvements in employment opportunities for part-time workers. Yet in the absence of changes in the division of domestic labour, and its perceived value, women will continue to be faced with difficulties of entry to the labour market and success within it that are not shared by men. An intriguing question remains. If, as it appears, *working* women are more likely to hold egalitarian beliefs and to be dissatisfied with the allocation of household work, is the greater participation in the labour market by women likely to presage a change on the domestic front? Or does the process work the other way around?

References

BLACKBURN, R. M. and MANN, M. *The Working Class in the Labour Market*, Macmillan, London (1979).
BRITTEN, N. and HEATH, A., 'Women, Men and Social Class' in Garmarnikow, E., Morgan, D., Purvis and J. and Taylorson, D. (eds.), *Gender, Class and Work*, Heinemann, London (1983).

BROWN, R., CURRAN, M and COUSINS, J., *Changing Attitudes to Employment?* Research Paper No.40, Department of Employment, London (1983).
DEX, S., *Women's Work Histories: an analysis of the Women and Employment Survey*, Research Paper No.46, Department of Employment, London (1984).
EEC, *European Men and Women in 1978*, EEC, Brussels (1979).
EEC, *European Men and Women in 1983*, EEC, Brussels (1984).
EQUAL OPPORTUNITIES COMMISSION, *Women and government statistics*, Research Bulletin No.4, EOC, Manchester (1980).
GOLDTHORPE, J. H., 'Women and Class Analysis : In Defence of the Conventional View', *Sociology*, vol. 17, No.4 (1983), pp.465-488.
HAKIM, C., *Occupational Segregation*, Research Paper No.9, Department of Employment, London (1979).
HAKIM, C., 'Job Segregation: trends in the 1970s', *Department of Employment Gazette*, vol. 89, no.12 (1981) pp.521-9.
JOSHI, H., *Women's participation in paid work : further analysis of the Women and Employment Survey*, Research Paper No.45, Department of Employment, London (1984).
JOWELL, R, and AIREY, C., *British Social Attitudes : The 1984 Report*, Gower, Aldershot (1984).
LAND, H., *Parity begins at home: women's and men's work in the home and its effects on their paid employment*, Equal Opportunities Commission and Social Science Research Council (1981).
MARTIN, J. and ROBERTS, C., *Women and Employment – a Lifetime Perspective*, HMSO, London (1984).
PAHL, R. E., *Divisions of Labour*, Basil Blackwell, Oxford, (1984).
REID, I. and WORMALD, E. (eds.), *Sex Differences in Britain*, Grant McIntyre, London (1982).
STANWORTH, M. 'Women and Class Analysis: A Reply to John Goldthorpe', *Sociology* vol. 18, no.2 (1984) pp.159-170.

Acknowledgements

I am grateful to Catherine Hakim, Barbara Ballard and Ed Puttick for their advice on the questionnaire. Jean Martin's and Ceridwen Roberts' *Women and Employment Survey* was an authoritative model for many of the employment-related questions. Thanks also to those within SCPR who gave invaluable advice and comments on the chapter.

3.1 DOMESTIC DIVISION OF LABOUR (Q84 i, ii, iii, iv) by sex and economic position within sex

BASE: ALL MARRIED OR LIVING AS MARRIED

Who does each of the following tasks in your household?	BASE	Male	Female	ECONOMIC POSITION: MEN†φ				ECONOMIC POSITION: WOMEN†φ				
				Full-time employee or self-employed	Part-time employee or self-employed	Retired	Other/ N.C.	Full-time employee or self-employed	Part-time employee or self-employed	Looking after the home	Retired	Other/ N.C.
UNWEIGHTED BASE	1120	542	578	377	12	98	54	136	97	252	55	37
WEIGHTED BASE	1126	552	574	378	11	95	66	130	98	251	59	35
Household shopping												
MAINLY MAN	65 6%	31 6%	34 6%	14 4%	2	10 11%	6 9%	5 4%	4 4%	16 6%	2 3%	7
MAINLY WOMAN	605 54%	289 54%	316 55%	220 58%	3	40 42%	26 40%	70 54%	63 64%	143 57%	26 44%	14
SHARED EQUALLY	438 39%	219 40%	219 38%	144 38%	7	43 45%	24 37%	53 41%	31 32%	89 36%	30 51%	14
OTHER/D.K./NA	18 2%	13 2%	5 1%	0 0%	0	2 2%	10 15%	1 1%	0 0%	3 1%	2 2%	0
Makes the evening meal												
MAINLY MAN	59 5%	32 6%	27 5%	18 5%	3	8 8%	3 5%	14 11%	4 4%	6 2%	1 2%	2
MAINLY WOMAN	862 77%	416 75%	447 78%	300 79%	9	72 76%	35 53%	82 63%	79 80%	211 84%	45 76%	29
SHARED EQUALLY	183 16%	90 16%	94 16%	58 15%	0	14 14%	18 27%	31 24%	14 14%	31 12%	13 22%	4
OTHER/D.K./NA	22 2%	15 3%	7 1%	3 1%	0	2 2%	10 15%	2 2%	2 2%	3 1%	0 0%	0
The evening dishes												
MAINLY MAN	200 18%	107 19%	94 16%	64 17%	2	30 32%	10 15%	26 20%	18 18%	29 12%	14 23%	8
MAINLY WOMAN	422 37%	187 34%	235 41%	143 38%	2	23 24%	18 27%	46 36%	33 34%	118 47%	20 34%	18
SHARED EQUALLY	458 41%	232 42%	227 39%	158 42%	6	40 42%	27 41%	52 40%	43 44%	96 38%	25 43%	9
OTHER/D.K./NA	46 4%	27 5%	18 3%	13 3%	1	2 2%	12 17%	6 4%	4 4%	8 3%	0 0%	1
The household cleaning												
MAINLY MAN	35 3%	15 3%	19 3%	6 1%	0	7 7%	3 4%	7 5%	1 1%	8 3%	2 3%	2
MAINLY WOMAN	807 72%	396 72%	412 72%	307 81%	8	47 50%	32 48%	82 63%	83 83%	186 74%	37 63%	24
SHARED EQUALLY	261 23%	126 23%	135 23%	63 17%	3	39 41%	22 32%	40 31%	14 15%	52 21%	20 34%	8
OTHER/D.K./NA	24 2%	15 3%	9 1%	1 1%	0	2 2%	10 15%	1 1%	1 1%	6 2%	0 0%	1

†, φ: refer to Appendix II for notes on tabulations

3.2 DOMESTIC DIVISION OF LABOUR (Q84 v, vi, vii) by sex and economic position within sex

BASE: ALL MARRIED OR LIVING AS MARRIED

Who does each of the following tasks in your household?	BASE	Male	Female	MEN†φ Full-time employee or self-employed	MEN†φ Part-time employee or self-employed	MEN†φ Retired	MEN†φ Other/ N.C. employed	WOMEN†φ Full-time employee or self-employed	WOMEN†φ Part-time employee or self-employed	WOMEN†φ Looking after the home	WOMEN†φ Retired	WOMEN†φ Other/ N.C.
UNWEIGHTED BASE	1120	542	578	377	12	98	54	136	97	252	55	37
WEIGHTED BASE	1126	552	574	378	11	95	66	130	98	251	59	35
The washing and ironing												
MAINLY MAN	11 1%	4 1%	7 1%	1 0%	0	3 3%	0 0%	5 4%	0 0%	1 0%	0 0%	0
MAINLY WOMAN	994 88%	477 86%	517 90%	339 90%	8	78 81%	51 77%	107 82%	92 94%	233 93%	54 91%	30
SHARED EQUALLY	100 9%	55 10%	45 8%	34 9%	3	13 13%	5 8%	17 13%	6 6%	13 5%	5 9%	5
OTHER/D.K./NA	21 2%	16 3%	5 1%	4 1%	0	2 2%	10 15%	1 1%	0 0%	4 2%	0 0%	0
Repairs the household equipment												
MAINLY MAN	932 83%	478 87%	453 79%	337 89%	11	81 85%	48 73%	109 84%	71 73%	192 76%	52 88%	29
MAINLY WOMAN	72 6%	21 4%	51 9%	14 4%	0	5 5%	2 3%	6 4%	14 15%	25 10%	5 9%	1
SHARED EQUALLY	93 8%	33 6%	60 10%	23 6%	0	7 7%	4 6%	14 11%	11 11%	28 11%	2 3%	5
OTHER/D.K./NA	29 3%	19 4%	10 2%	4 1%	0	3 3%	12 18%	1 1%	2 2%	6 2%	0 0%	1
Organises the household money and payment of bills												
MAINLY MAN	361 32%	190 34%	171 30%	142 38%	4	29 31%	14 21%	29 23%	33 34%	77 31%	21 35%	10
MAINLY WOMAN	431 38%	204 37%	227 40%	138 36%	4	33 35%	29 44%	58 45%	37 38%	93 37%	24 41%	15
SHARED EQUALLY	317 28%	145 26%	172 30%	96 25%	4	32 33%	13 20%	42 32%	28 28%	78 31%	14 24%	10
OTHER/D.K./NA	17 2%	13 2%	4 1%	2 1%	0	1 1%	10 15%	1 1%	0 0%	3 1%	0 0%	0

3.3 PRESCRIPTIVE DOMESTIC DIVISION OF LABOUR (Q85 i, ii, iii, iv) by marital status within sex, economic position within sex

How do you think the following household tasks should be shared between men and women?

BASE: ALL RESPONDENTS	BASE	MEN† Married/ living as married	MEN† Separated/ divorced/ widowed	MEN† Never married	WOMEN† Married/ living as married	WOMEN† Separated/ divorced/ widowed	WOMEN† Never married	ECON. POS. MEN†◊ Full-time	ECON. POS. MEN†◊ Part-time	ECON. POS. MEN†◊ Retired	ECON. POS. MEN†◊ Other/ N.C.	ECON. POS. WOMEN†◊ Full-time	ECON. POS. WOMEN†◊ Part-time	ECON. POS. WOMEN†◊ Retired	ECON. POS. WOMEN†◊ Looking after the home	ECON. POS. WOMEN†◊ Other/ N.C.
UNWEIGHTED BASE	1675	542	65	171	578	202	112	499	16	145	119	231	119	311	149	84
WEIGHTED BASE	1645	552	58	163	574	190	105	492	14	138	130	223	117	306	146	77
The household shopping																
MAINLY MAN	5 0%	1 0%	0 0%	0 0%	2 0%	0 0%	1 1%	2 0%	0	1 1%	3 2%	0 0%	1 1%	1 0%	2 1%	0 0%
MAINLY WOMAN	566 34%	188 34%	13 23%	42 26%	209 36%	73 39%	41 39%	163 33%	7	40 29%	33 26%	61 27%	48 41%	130 43%	64 44%	19 25%
SHARED EQUALLY	1031 63%	343 62%	41 71%	118 73%	352 61%	113 60%	64 60%	311 63%	6	94 68%	89 69%	160 72%	66 56%	167 55%	79 54%	57 74%
OTHER/D.K./NA	44 3%	21 4%	3 6%	2 1%	11 2%	4 2%	0 0%	17 3%	1	4 3%	6 5%	2 1%	2 2%	7 2%	4 3%	1 2%
The evening meal																
MAINLY MAN	12 1%	5 1%	1 1%	3 2%	2 0%	0 0%	1 1%	4 1%	1	2 1%	4 3%	2 1%	0 0%	1 0%	1 1%	1 1%
MAINLY WOMAN	944 57%	340 61%	29 50%	80 49%	343 60%	103 54%	50 48%	267 54%	9	98 71%	73 56%	83 37%	70 59%	207 68%	96 66%	39 51%
SHARED EQUALLY	634 39%	184 33%	24 42%	76 47%	215 37%	80 42%	54 51%	198 40%	3	34 24%	48 37%	138 62%	44 38%	87 29%	46 31%	34 44%
OTHER/D.K./NA	56 3%	24 4%	4 7%	4 2%	14 2%	7 3%	0 0%	23 5%	1	4 3%	5 4%	0 0%	3 2%	11 4%	3 3%	3 4%
The evening dishes																
MAINLY MAN	189 11%	70 13%	8 14%	14 9%	62 11%	13 7%	21 20%	38 8%	1	27 20%	26 20%	25 11%	22 18%	24 8%	15 10%	10 13%
MAINLY WOMAN	328 20%	114 21%	9 16%	32 20%	119 21%	44 23%	9 8%	100 20%	3	27 20%	26 20%	20 9%	15 13%	88 29%	36 25%	13 17%
SHARED EQUALLY	1080 66%	347 63%	37 64%	114 70%	378 66%	129 68%	75 71%	335 68%	9	81 59%	73 56%	176 79%	76 65%	185 60%	93 63%	53 68%
OTHER/D.K./NA	48 3%	21 4%	4 6%	4 2%	14 2%	3 1%	1 1%	18 4%	1	3 2%	5 4%	2 1%	5 4%	9 3%	3 2%	2 2%
The household cleaning																
MAINLY MAN	6 0%	2 0%	0 0%	3 1%	2 0%	0 0%	0 0%	0 0%	0	1 1%	2 2%	0 0%	0 0%	1 0%	0 0%	1 1%
MAINLY WOMAN	810 49%	266 48%	19 34%	64 39%	313 55%	98 52%	49 47%	234 48%	8	64 46%	43 33%	81 36%	79 67%	187 61%	77 53%	36 47%
SHARED EQUALLY	783 48%	264 48%	34 59%	93 57%	247 43%	89 47%	56 53%	240 49%	5	67 49%	78 60%	141 63%	36 30%	111 36%	65 45%	39 50%
OTHER/D.K./NA	46 3%	21 4%	4 7%	4 2%	12 2%	3 1%	0 0%	18 4%	1	5 4%	8 6%	1 1%	3 2%	7 2%	4 3%	2 2%

3.4 PRESCRIPTIVE DOMESTIC DIVISION OF LABOUR (Q85 v, vi, vii) by marital status within sex and economic position within sex

How do you think the following household tasks should be shared between men and women?

BASE: ALL RESPONDENTS

	BASE	MEN† Married/living as married	MEN† Separated/divorced/widowed	MEN† Never married	WOMEN† Married/living as married	WOMEN† Separated/divorced/widowed	WOMEN† Never married	ECON. MEN†φ Full-time	ECON. MEN†φ Part-time	ECON. MEN†φ Retired	ECON. MEN†φ Other/N.C.	ECON. WOMEN†φ Full-time	ECON. WOMEN†φ Part-time	ECON. WOMEN†φ Looking after the home	ECON. WOMEN†φ Retired	ECON. WOMEN†φ Other/N.C.
UNWEIGHTED BASE	1675	542	65	171	578	202	112	499	16	145	119	231	119	311	149	84
WEIGHTED BASE	1645	552	58	163	574	190	105	492	14	138	130	223	117	306	146	77
The washing and ironing																
MAINLY MAN	3 / 0%	1 / 0%	0 / 0%	1 / 1%	1 / 0%	0 / 0%	0 / 0%	2 / 0%	0	0 / 0%	0 / 0%	0 / 0%	1 / 1%	0 / 0%	0 / 0%	0 / 0%
MAINLY WOMAN	1240 / 75%	420 / 76%	40 / 70%	107 / 66%	445 / 78%	152 / 80%	76 / 72%	352 / 72%	10	112 / 81%	92 / 71%	146 / 65%	99 / 84%	249 / 81%	124 / 85%	55 / 71%
SHARED EQUALLY	361 / 22%	113 / 20%	14 / 24%	51 / 31%	119 / 21%	35 / 18%	29 / 28%	121 / 25%	3	23 / 17%	31 / 24%	76 / 34%	18 / 15%	50 / 16%	18 / 12%	21 / 28%
OTHER/D.K./NA	41 / 3%	19 / 3%	3 / 6%	4 / 2%	9 / 2%	3 / 2%	0 / 0%	17 / 3%	1	3 / 2%	7 / 5%	1 / 0%	0 / 0%	7 / 2%	4 / 3%	1 / 2%
Repair the household equipment																
MAINLY MAN	1276 / 78%	454 / 82%	43 / 75%	123 / 76%	432 / 75%	146 / 77%	76 / 72%	382 / 78%	12	120 / 86%	106 / 82%	148 / 66%	92 / 78%	241 / 79%	121 / 83%	52 / 68%
MAINLY WOMAN	26 / 2%	7 / 1%	0 / 0%	0 / 1%	5 / 1%	5 / 2%	0 / 0%	7 / 1%	0	3 / 2%	0 / 0%	4 / 2%	4 / 3%	6 / 2%	5 / 3%	2 / 2%
SHARED EQUALLY	305 / 19%	74 / 13%	11 / 19%	37 / 23%	118 / 21%	37 / 19%	28 / 27%	90 / 18%	1	13 / 9%	19 / 14%	71 / 32%	21 / 18%	52 / 17%	17 / 11%	22 / 28%
OTHER/D.K./NA	38 / 2%	17 / 3%	3 / 6%	1 / 1%	11 / 2%	2 / 1%	1 / 1%	14 / 3%		3 / 2%	5 / 4%	2 / 1%	1 / 1%	7 / 2%	4 / 3%	2 / 2%
Organise the household money and payment of bills																
MAINLY MAN	345 / 21%	129 / 23%	10 / 17%	35 / 21%	128 / 22%	27 / 14%	17 / 16%	105 / 21%	1	30 / 22%	35 / 27%	29 / 13%	28 / 24%	66 / 21%	31 / 21%	19 / 24%
MAINLY WOMAN	269 / 16%	91 / 16%	16 / 29%	26 / 16%	76 / 13%	42 / 22%	18 / 17%	81 / 17%	1	34 / 24%	17 / 13%	29 / 13%	14 / 12%	48 / 16%	35 / 24%	9 / 12%
SHARED EQUALLY	970 / 59%	308 / 56%	28 / 48%	101 / 62%	348 / 61%	117 / 62%	68 / 64%	286 / 58%	10	69 / 50%	72 / 56%	157 / 70%	72 / 62%	182 / 60%	73 / 50%	47 / 61%
OTHER/D.K./NA	62 / 4%	25 / 5%	3 / 6%	1 / 1%	22 / 4%	4 / 2%	3 / 3%	19 / 4%	2	5 / 4%	5 / 4%	5 / 4%	3 / 3%	8 / 3%	8 / 5%	2 / 3%

3.5 ATTITUDE TOWARD PAID JOB IF REASONABLE INCOME WITHOUT WORK (Q34)
by age within sex and full-time or part-time working within sex

If without having to work, you had what you would regard as a reasonable living income, do you think you would still prefer to have a paid job, or wouldn't you bother?

BASE: ALL EMPLOYEES	BASE	AGE† MEN 18-24	25-34	35-54	55+	WOMEN 18-24	25-34	35-54	55+	MEN† FULL-TIME EMPLOYEE	PART-TIME EMPLOYEE	WOMEN† FULL-TIME EMPLOYEE	PART-TIME EMPLOYEE
UNWEIGHTED BASE	778	72	115	177	77	55	70	166	43	430	12	220	115
WEIGHTED BASE	762	70	117	175	75	54	76	153	41	427	10	211	113
WOULD STILL PREFER PAID JOB	524 69%	57 82%	88 75%	124 71%	50 67%	43 80%	58 76%	91 59%	13	314 74%	5	146 69%	58 51%
WOULDN'T BOTHER	218 29%	10 14%	27 23%	45 26%	24 32%	9 16%	16 21%	58 38%	28	101 24%	5	59 28%	53 47%
DO VOLUNTARY/ SERVICE WORK	8 1%	1 1%	1 1%	1 1%	1 1%	0 0%	1 1%	3 2%	0	4 1%	0	3 1%	1 1%
OTHER ANSWER (SPECIFY)	9 1%	2 3%	2 1%	2 1%	0 0%	2 4%	1 1%	0 0%	0	6 1%	1	3 1%	0 0%
DONT KNOW	2 0%	0 0%	0 0%	1 1%	0 0%	0 0%	0 0%	1 1%	0	1 0%	0	0 0%	1 1%
NOT ANSWERED	1 0%	0 0%	0 0%	1 0%	0 0%	0 0%	0 0%	0 0%	0	1 0%	0	0 0%	0 0%

3.6 REASONS FOR WORKING (Q32 a, b)
by age within sex and non-manual/manual employment within sex

BASE: ALL EMPLOYEES

Which of the following statements best describe your own reasons for working at present?

	BASE	MEN 18-24	MEN 25-34	MEN 35-54	MEN 55+	WOMEN 18-24	WOMEN 25-34	WOMEN 35-54	WOMEN 55+	MEN† Non-manual	MEN† Manual	WOMEN† Non-manual	WOMEN† Manual
UNWEIGHTED BASE	778	72	115	177	77	55	70	166	43	172	265	221	113
WEIGHTED BASE	762	70	117	175	75	54	76	153	41	172	261	218	105
WORKING IS NORMAL THING TO DO	269 35%	28 41%	41 35%	91 52%	41 55%	17 31%	17 22%	27 18%	6	75 43%	125 48%	52 24%	16 15%
NEED MONEY FOR BASIC ESSENTIALS	542 71%	38 55%	102 87%	151 87%	61 82%	34 62%	41 55%	88 58%	23	133 77%	219 84%	120 55%	67 63%
TO EARN MONEY TO BUY EXTRAS	282 37%	28 40%	38 33%	54 31%	21 28%	16 29%	33 43%	78 51%	13	43 25%	98 38%	89 41%	52 50%
TO EARN MONEY OF MY OWN	217 28%	36 52%	19 16%	28 16%	9 12%	31 57%	33 44%	47 31%	12	34 20%	58 22%	87 40%	37 36%
FOR COMPANY OF OTHER PEOPLE	188 25%	9 13%	19 16%	26 15%	17 23%	12 23%	42 55%	55 36%	7	40 23%	31 12%	86 40%	30 29%
I ENJOY WORKING	387 51%	24 34%	54 46%	84 48%	35 47%	27 50%	52 68%	87 57%	23	98 57%	98 37%	148 68%	42 40%
TO FOLLOW MY CAREER	212 28%	31 44%	43 37%	44 25%	11 14%	21 38%	24 31%	38 25%	2	83 48%	44 17%	79 36%	4 4%
FOR A CHANGE FROM CHILDREN/HOUSEWORK	42 5%	1 1%	0	4 2%	1 2%	0	9 12%	23 15%	5	1 1%	5 2%	24 11%	13 12%
OTHER ANSWER	10 1%	0	1 1%	2 1%	2 3%	0	0	4 3%	0	4 2%	1 0%	5 2%	0 0%
DONT KNOW	0 0%	0	0	0	0	0	0	0	0	0	0	0	0
NOT ANSWERED	0 0%	0	0	0	0	0	0	0	0	0	0	0	0

And which one of these would you say is your main reason for working?

	BASE	MEN 18-24	MEN 25-34	MEN 35-54	MEN 55+	WOMEN 18-24	WOMEN 25-34	WOMEN 35-54	WOMEN 55+	MEN† Non-manual	MEN† Manual	WOMEN† Non-manual	WOMEN† Manual
WORKING IS NORMAL THING TO DO	45 6%	9 13%	3 3%	18 10%	10 13%	2 4%	1 1%	3 2%	0	15 8%	24 9%	4 2%	2 2%
NEED MONEY FOR BASIC ESSENTIALS	470 62%	29 42%	85 73%	136 78%	58 78%	22 41%	35 47%	78 51%	24	111 64%	196 75%	97 44%	63 60%
TO EARN MONEY TO BUY EXTRAS	58 8%	2 3%	2 2%	0 0%	3 4%	1 2%	15 20%	30 20%	4	4 2%	4 2%	29 13%	21 20%
TO EARN MONEY OF MY OWN	46 6%	14 20%	4 3%	1 0%	0 0%	13 24%	7 10%	4 3%	3	5 3%	14 5%	19 9%	9 8%
FOR COMPANY OF OTHER PEOPLE	8 1%	1 1%	0 0%	0 0%	0 0%	1 2%	0 0%	5 3%	1	1 0%	0 0%	6 3%	1 1%
I ENJOY WORKING	72 9%	5 7%	13 11%	11 6%	2 3%	3 6%	12 16%	20 13%	6	15 9%	15 6%	35 16%	6 6%
TO FOLLOW MY CAREER	48 6%	9 12%	7 6%	7 4%	4 5%	11 20%	4 5%	9 6%	2	18 10%	6 2%	23 11%	1 1%
FOR A CHANGE FROM CHILDREN/HOUSEWORK	4 0%	0 0%	0 0%	0 0%	0 0%	0 0%	1 1%	2 1%	1	0 0%	0 0%	1 0%	3 2%
OTHER ANSWER	6 1%	0 0%	0 0%	2 1%	3 4%	0 0%	0 0%	1 1%	0	3 2%	0 0%	3 1%	0 0%
DONT KNOW	2 0%	0 0%	2 2%	1 1%	1 1%	0 0%	1 1%	1 1%	0	1 1%	1 0%	0 0%	0 0%
NOT ANSWERED	4 0%	1 1%	1 1%	1 1%	1 1%	2 2%	1 1%	2 1%	0	1 1%	2 1%	0 0%	0 0%

3.7 REASONS FOR MARRIED WOMEN WORKING (Q83 a, b) by marital status within sex and economic position within sex

BASE: ALL RESPONDENTS	BASE	MEN+ Married living as married	MEN+ Separated/divorced/widowed	MEN+ Never married	WOMEN: Married living as married	WOMEN: Separated/divorced/widowed	WOMEN: Never married	ECON MEN+ Full-time	Part-time	Retire	Other/N.C.	ECON WOMEN: Full-time	Part-time	Looking after the home	Retire	Other/N.C.
Which of the following statements best describe the reasons why many married women work?																
UNWEIGHTED BASE	1675	542	65	171	578	202	112	499	16	145	119	231	119	311	149	84
WEIGHTED BASE	1645	552	58	163	574	190	105	492	14	138	130	223	117	306	146	77
WORKING IS NORMAL THING TO DO	106 6%	24 4%	7 11%	22 13%	36 6%	10 5%	7 7%	25 5%	1	11 8%	16 13%	11 5%	9 8%	14 5%	9 6%	10 13%
NEED MONEY FOR BASIC ESSENTIALS	1050 64%	319 58%	37 63%	99 61%	401 70%	131 69%	63 60%	279 57%	9	79 57%	88 68%	160 72%	89 76%	200 65%	99 67%	47 61%
TO EARN MONEY TO BUY EXTRAS	1174 71%	423 77%	39 68%	111 68%	412 72%	125 66%	64 61%	375 76%	11	101 73%	84 65%	163 73%	82 70%	211 69%	92 63%	51 66%
TO EARN MONEY OF THEIR OWN	790 48%	274 50%	30 52%	69 42%	250 44%	79 42%	48 45%	245 50%	8	56 41%	63 48%	119 53%	58 49%	113 37%	54 37%	33 43%
FOR COMPANY OF OTHER PEOPLE	625 38%	190 34%	30 52%	57 35%	233 41%	71 37%	43 41%	188 38%	5	38 28%	46 36%	98 44%	53 45%	117 38%	50 35%	30 38%
THEY ENJOY WORKING	459 28%	140 25%	18 32%	43 26%	174 30%	63 33%	22 21%	111 23%	5	35 25%	51 39%	53 24%	32 27%	87 28%	58 40%	29 37%
TO FOLLOW A CAREER	489 30%	163 30%	19 33%	48 30%	184 32%	45 24%	30 28%	140 28%	7	47 34%	37 28%	50 23%	31 27%	108 35%	44 30%	25 32%
FOR A CHANGE FROM CHILDREN/HOUSEWORK	670 41%	204 37%	21 37%	64 40%	262 46%	70 37%	49 47%	199 40%	9	42 30%	40 31%	109 49%	59 50%	128 42%	49 34%	36 46%
OTHER ANSWER	8 0%	3 1%	3	2	2	1	1 1%	3 1%	0	1 1%	1 1%	1 0%	1 1%	2	0	0
DONT KNOW	11 1%	4 1%	0	3 1%	1 0%	2 1%	2 2%	2 0%	0	2 1%	1 1%	0	2 2%	2 1%	1 1%	0
NOT ANSWERED	9 1%	2 0%	0	0	2 0%	2 1%	0	1 0%	0	2 1%	1 1%	0	2 2%	1 0%	1 1%	3 3%
And which one of these would you say is generally the main reason why married women work?																
WORKING IS NORMAL THING TO DO	10 1%	0 0%	0	1 1%	6 1%	3 2%	0	0 0%	0	1 1%	0 0%	0 0%	1 1%	5 2%	1 1%	1 1%
NEED MONEY FOR BASIC ESSENTIALS	739 45%	220 40%	23 40%	68 42%	294 51%	93 49%	40 38%	193 39%	6	56 41%	56 43%	120 54%	62 53%	136 44%	75 52%	33 43%
TO EARN MONEY TO BUY EXTRAS	582 35%	225 41%	20 35%	56 35%	187 33%	60 32%	33 32%	201 41%	4	39 30%	68 53%	68 30%	35 30%	107 35%	44 30%	26 34%
TO EARN MONEY OF THEIR OWN	132 8%	43 8%	10 16%	14 9%	32 6%	19 10%	15 14%	46 9%	3	9 7%	9 7%	22 10%	11 9%	20 7%	9 6%	5 6%
FOR COMPANY OF OTHER PEOPLE	33 2%	15 3%	1	0	10 2%	4 2%	3 3%	11 2%	0	3 2%	2 2%	6 3%	1 1%	8 3%	4 2%	2 3%
THEY ENJOY WORKING	28 2%	15 3%	5	0 0%	7 1%	5 3%	4 4%	6 1%	1	12 9%	2 2%	8 3%	1 1%	8 3%	3 2%	2 3%
TO FOLLOW A CAREER	29 2%	9 2%	1	5 3%	10 2%	4 2%	4 4%	9 2%	0	3 1%	3 2%	8 3%	1 1%	8 3%	3 2%	1 1%
FOR A CHANGE FROM CHILDREN/HOUSEWORK	56 3%	15 3%	3 4%	9 5%	20 4%	3 2%	7 7%	16 3%	0	3 2%	8 6%	5 2%	3 3%	14 5%	4 3%	5 6%
OTHER ANSWER	4 0%	0 0%	0	0	0 0%	0	0	0 0%	0	1 0%	0 0%	0 0%	0 0%	1 0%	0	0
DONT KNOW	20 1%	2 0%	0	5 3%	5 1%	2 1%	3 3%	7 1%	1	2 1%	1 1%	2 1%	2 2%	3 1%	2 2%	0
NOT ANSWERED	12 1%	2 0%	2 2%	0	4 1%	0	0	1 0%	0	2 1%	2 2%	0 0%	1 1%	2 1%	1 1%	3 3%

3.8 MAINTENANCE PAYMENTS AFTER DIVORCE (Q79 a, b, c)
by marital status within sex and economic position within sex

In each of the following situations should the man make maintenance payments to support the wife?

BASE: ALL RESPONDENTS

Base (Unweighted / Weighted counts)

	ALL	MEN Married/ living as married	MEN Separated/ divorced/ widowed	MEN Never married	WOMEN Married/ living as married	WOMEN Separated/ divorced/ widowed	WOMEN Never married	MEN† Full-time	MEN† Part-time	MEN† Retire/N.C.	MEN† Other/N.C.	WOMEN† Full-time	WOMEN† Part-time	WOMEN† Retire/N.C.	WOMEN† Other/N.C.	WOMEN† Looking after the home
UNWEIGHTED BASE	1675	542	65	171	578	202	112	499	16	145	119	311	231	119	149	84
WEIGHTED BASE	1645	552	58	163	574	190	105	492	14	138	130	306	223	117	146	77

Q79a. Consider a married couple, both aged about 45, with no children at home. They are both working at the time of the divorce.

	ALL	MEN Mar	MEN Sep	MEN Nev	WOM Mar	WOM Sep	WOM Nev	MEN FT	MEN PT	MEN Ret	MEN Oth	WOM FT	WOM PT	WOM Ret	WOM Oth	WOM Look
UNQUALIFIED YES	222 / 13%	63 / 11%	7 / 12%	21 / 13%	64 / 11%	44 / 23%	23 / 22%	57 / 11%	1 / 7%	27 / 19%	6 / 5%	54 / 18%	27 / 12%	11 / 9%	24 / 16%	15 / 20%
UNQUALIFIED NO	1307 / 79%	453 / 82%	45 / 77%	134 / 82%	469 / 82%	129 / 68%	77 / 73%	430 / 87%	11 / 79%	93 / 67%	98 / 75%	231 / 75%	189 / 85%	96 / 82%	101 / 69%	58 / 75%
DEPENDS ON GUILTY PARTY	32 / 2%	8 / 1%	4 / 7%	2 / 1%	13 / 2%	5 / 3%	1 / 1%	6 / 1%	0 / 0%	5 / 3%	3 / 2%	4 / 1%	3 / 1%	3 / 3%	5 / 3%	0 / 0%
DEPENDS ON CIRCUMSTANCES	26 / 2%	11 / 2%	1 / 2%	0 / 0%	9 / 2%	3 / 2%	2 / 1%	7 / 1%	0 / 0%	3 / 3%	3 / 2%	3 / 1%	3 / 1%	2 / 1%	4 / 3%	0 / 0%
DEPENDS ON INCOME/WEALTH	17 / 1%	9 / 2%	0 / 0%	1 / 0%	2 / 0%	4 / 2%	1 / 1%	7 / 1%	0 / 0%	2 / 1%	2 / 1%	2 / 1%	1 / 0%	2 / 2%	3 / 2%	0 / 0%
OTHER/D.K./NA	41 / 3%	8 / 1%	1 / 2%	4 / 3%	17 / 3%	5 / 3%	2 / 2%	6 / 1%	2 / 0%	6 / 3%	6 / 3%	9 / 3%	3 / 2%	3 / 3%	9 / 3%	4 / 5%

Q79b. Consider a similar couple, also aged about 45 with no children at home. They are both working at the time of the divorce, but the woman's earnings are much lower than the man's.

	ALL	MEN Mar	MEN Sep	MEN Nev	WOM Mar	WOM Sep	WOM Nev	MEN FT	MEN PT	MEN Ret	MEN Oth	WOM FT	WOM PT	WOM Ret	WOM Oth	WOM Look
UNQUALIFIED YES	727 / 44%	225 / 41%	19 / 32%	71 / 43%	263 / 46%	94 / 49%	57 / 54%	182 / 37%	5 / 36%	66 / 48%	60 / 48%	148 / 48%	92 / 41%	59 / 50%	66 / 45%	41 / 53%
UNQUALIFIED NO	728 / 44%	260 / 47%	26 / 45%	77 / 47%	252 / 44%	74 / 39%	38 / 36%	258 / 52%	5 / 37%	52 / 40%	47 / 36%	135 / 44%	107 / 48%	45 / 38%	52 / 36%	28 / 36%
DEPENDS ON GUILTY PARTY	53 / 3%	18 / 3%	2 / 3%	5 / 3%	16 / 3%	4 / 2%	4 / 3%	16 / 3%	1 / 1%	8 / 6%	4 / 3%	4 / 1%	6 / 3%	4 / 4%	6 / 5%	1 / 1%
DEPENDS ON CIRCUMSTANCES	51 / 3%	18 / 3%	1 / 1%	2 / 1%	21 / 4%	6 / 3%	3 / 2%	14 / 3%	0 / 0%	6 / 4%	3 / 2%	5 / 1%	9 / 4%	3 / 3%	7 / 5%	1 / 2%
DEPENDS ON INCOME/WEALTH	21 / 1%	8 / 1%	1 / 1%	2 / 1%	7 / 1%	2 / 1%	1 / 1%	5 / 1%	0 / 0%	3 / 2%	2 / 1%	4 / 1%	3 / 1%	1 / 1%	2 / 1%	1 / 1%
OTHER/D.K./NA	66 / 4%	24 / 4%	4 / 7%	6 / 4%	15 / 3%	10 / 5%	3 / 3%	17 / 3%	1 / 0%	9 / 7%	15 / 5%	10 / 3%	6 / 3%	5 / 5%	9 / 5%	5 / 6%

Q79c. Finally, consider another couple, also aged about 45 with no children at home. The man is working at the time of the divorce, but the woman has never worked in a paid job outside the home.

	ALL	MEN Mar	MEN Sep	MEN Nev	WOM Mar	WOM Sep	WOM Nev	MEN FT	MEN PT	MEN Ret	MEN Oth	WOM FT	WOM PT	WOM Ret	WOM Oth	WOM Look
UNQUALIFIED YES	1187 / 72%	396 / 72%	36 / 62%	113 / 70%	423 / 74%	136 / 72%	82 / 78%	333 / 68%	10 / 71%	108 / 78%	94 / 72%	224 / 73%	153 / 69%	83 / 71%	116 / 80%	65 / 84%
UNQUALIFIED NO	287 / 17%	96 / 17%	9 / 16%	36 / 22%	107 / 19%	23 / 12%	16 / 15%	98 / 20%	3 / 0%	16 / 12%	24 / 18%	62 / 20%	40 / 18%	24 / 20%	13 / 9%	8 / 10%
DEPENDS ON GUILTY PARTY	56 / 3%	15 / 3%	5 / 9%	8 / 5%	14 / 2%	13 / 7%	2 / 1%	19 / 4%	0 / 0%	5 / 3%	4 / 3%	8 / 2%	12 / 5%	4 / 3%	8 / 4%	0 / 0%
DEPENDS ON CIRCUMSTANCES	45 / 3%	26 / 5%	1 / 2%	2 / 1%	9 / 2%	5 / 3%	3 / 3%	24 / 5%	0 / 0%	3 / 2%	3 / 2%	7 / 2%	7 / 3%	2 / 2%	3 / 1%	3 / 1%
DEPENDS ON INCOME/WEALTH	7 / 0%	4 / 1%	1 / 1%	0 / 0%	2 / 0%	0 / 0%	0 / 0%	2 / 0%	0 / 0%	1 / 1%	1 / 1%	1 / 1%	1 / 0%	0 / 0%	0 / 0%	0 / 0%
OTHER/D.K./NA	64 / 4%	16 / 3%	6 / 10%	5 / 3%	20 / 3%	12 / 6%	2 / 3%	16 / 3%	1 / 0%	5 / 3%	4 / 3%	4 / 1%	11 / 5%	4 / 3%	6 / 4%	4 / 6%

3.9 OCCUPATIONAL STEREOTYPING (Q219)
by age within sex and school leaving age within sex

BASE: THOSE RETURNING SELF-COMPLETION

	BASE	AGE† MEN				AGE† WOMEN				SCHOOL LEAVING AGE† MEN			SCHOOL LEAVING AGE† WOMEN		
		18-24	25-34	35-54	55+	18-24	25-34	35-54	55+	16 or under	17-18	19 or over	16 or under	17-18	19 or over
UNWEIGHTED BASE	1562	105	141	224	256	99	158	276	294	567	88	55	637	119	62
WEIGHTED BASE	1522	101	142	225	245	101	153	261	287	558	85	54	618	114	61

General index of egalitarianism: number of jobs suitable for both men and women equally.

	BASE	18-24	25-34	35-54	55+	18-24	25-34	35-54	55+	16 or under	17-18	19 or over	16 or under	17-18	19 or over
1 - 2 JOBS SUITABLE FOR BOTH MEN AND WOMEN EQUALLY	91 6%	5 4%	6 4%	11 5%	19 8%	2 1%	3 2%	13 5%	33 11%	36 6%	1 1%	2 4%	47 8%	4 4%	0 0%
3 - 5 JOBS SUITABLE FOR BOTH MEN AND WOMEN EQUALLY	275 18%	23 22%	25 18%	42 19%	56 23%	13 13%	14 9%	24 9%	74 26%	114 20%	21 25%	8 14%	105 17%	16 14%	4 7%
6 - 9 JOBS SUITABLE FOR BOTH MEN AND WOMEN EQUALLY	813 53%	50 49%	73 52%	134 59%	127 52%	57 56%	90 58%	141 54%	139 48%	297 53%	48 56%	30 56%	324 52%	67 59%	30 49%
10 - 11 JOBS SUITABLE FOR BOTH MEN AND WOMEN EQUALLY	316 21%	22 22%	37 26%	38 17%	33 13%	28 28%	45 30%	81 31%	28 10%	100 18%	14 17%	14 26%	126 20%	27 24%	26 43%
DONT KNOW	1 0%	0 0%	0 0%	0 0%	0 0%	1 1%	1 1%	0 0%	0 0%	0 0%	0 0%	0 0%	0 0%	0 0%	1 2%
NOT ANSWERED	10 1%	1 1%	0 0%	0 0%	4 1%	1 1%	1 0%	1 0%	4 1%	3 1%	1 1%	0 0%	6 1%	0 0%	0 0%

Do you think the following jobs are suitable for men only, women only, or for both equally?

Social worker

	BASE	18-24	25-34	35-54	55+	18-24	25-34	35-54	55+	16 or under	17-18	19 or over	16 or under	17-18	19 or over
PARTICULARLY SUITABLE FOR MEN	10 1%	2 2%	1 1%	0 0%	2 1%	2 2%	1 1%	0 0%	1 1%	4 1%	1 1%	0 0%	4 1%	2 2%	0 0%
PARTICULARLY SUITABLE FOR WOMEN	163 11%	11 11%	16 11%	32 14%	33 14%	14 14%	13 8%	12 5%	32 11%	68 12%	15 17%	8 15%	58 9%	10 9%	1 2%
SUITABLE FOR BOTH EQUALLY	1322 87%	86 86%	123 87%	190 84%	202 83%	84 84%	137 89%	245 94%	245 86%	473 85%	69 81%	46 85%	546 88%	101 89%	59 97%
DONT KNOW	1 0%	0 0%	0 0%	0 0%	0 0%	0 0%	0 0%	0 0%	0 0%	0 0%	0 0%	0 0%	0 0%	0 0%	0 0%
NOT ANSWERED	26 2%	2 2%	2 2%	2 1%	8 3%	1 1%	3 2%	2 1%	6 2%	13 2%	1 1%	0 0%	10 2%	1 1%	0 0%

Police officer

	BASE	18-24	25-34	35-54	55+	18-24	25-34	35-54	55+	16 or under	17-18	19 or over	16 or under	17-18	19 or over
PARTICULARLY SUITABLE FOR MEN	748 49%	45 45%	78 55%	112 50%	140 57%	42 42%	58 38%	94 36%	176 61%	286 51%	52 61%	27 50%	294 48%	50 44%	21 35%
PARTICULARLY SUITABLE FOR WOMEN	5 0%	2 1%	1 1%	1 0%	0 0%	0 0%	1 0%	1 1%	0 0%	3 1%	0 0%	0 0%	0 0%	0 0%	0 0%
SUITABLE FOR BOTH EQUALLY	745 49%	53 53%	60 43%	110 49%	97 40%	58 57%	94 61%	163 63%	103 36%	257 46%	32 38%	27 50%	312 50%	63 56%	39 64%
DONT KNOW	1 0%	0 0%	0 0%	0 0%	0 0%	0 0%	0 0%	0 0%	0 0%	0 0%	0 0%	0 0%	0 0%	0 0%	0 0%
NOT ANSWERED	25 2%	1 1%	2 1%	1 1%	8 3%	1 1%	1 0%	4 2%	7 2%	12 2%	1 1%	0 0%	12 2%	0 0%	0 0%

3.10 OCCUPATIONAL STEREOTYPING (Q219)
by age within sex and school leaving age within sex

Do you think the following jobs are suitable for men only, women only, or for both equally?

BASE: THOSE RETURNING SELF-COMPLETION

	BASE	AGE† MEN 18-24	25-34	35-54	55+	AGE† WOMEN 18-24	25-34	35-54	55+	SCHOOL LEAVING AGE† MEN 16 or under	17-18	19 or over	SCHOOL LEAVING AGE† WOMEN 16 or under	17-18	19 or over
UNWEIGHTED BASE	1562	105	141	224	256	99	158	276	294	567	88	55	637	119	62
WEIGHTED BASE	1522	101	142	225	245	101	153	261	287	558	85	54	618	114	61
Secretary															
PARTICULARLY SUITABLE FOR MEN	11 / 1%	3 / 3%	3 / 2%	2 / 1%	2 / 1%	0 / 0%	1 / 1%	0 / 0%	0 / 0%	9 / 2%	1 / 1%	0 / 0%	0 / 0%	0 / 0%	0 / 0%
PARTICULARLY SUITABLE FOR WOMEN	911 / 60%	69 / 69%	83 / 59%	153 / 68%	142 / 58%	59 / 59%	96 / 62%	141 / 54%	163 / 57%	350 / 63%	55 / 65%	35 / 65%	362 / 58%	67 / 59%	23 / 38%
SUITABLE FOR BOTH EQUALLY	572 / 38%	27 / 27%	54 / 38%	67 / 30%	92 / 37%	40 / 40%	54 / 35%	118 / 45%	115 / 40%	185 / 33%	28 / 33%	19 / 35%	244 / 39%	46 / 40%	37 / 60%
DONT KNOW	2 / 0%	0 / 0%	0 / 0%	0 / 0%	1 / 0%	0 / 0%	0 / 0%	0 / 0%	1 / 0%	1 / 0%	0 / 0%	0 / 0%	0 / 0%	0 / 0%	0 / 0%
NOT ANSWERED	27 / 2%	2 / 1%	2 / 1%	3 / 1%	9 / 3%	1 / 1%	3 / 2%	0 / 0%	8 / 3%	14 / 2%	1 / 1%	0 / 0%	11 / 2%	1 / 1%	0 / 0%
Car mechanic															
PARTICULARLY SUITABLE FOR MEN	1103 / 72%	72 / 72%	93 / 65%	175 / 78%	194 / 79%	64 / 63%	95 / 62%	172 / 66%	230 / 80%	420 / 75%	64 / 75%	39 / 73%	439 / 71%	82 / 73%	36 / 59%
PARTICULARLY SUITABLE FOR WOMEN	12 / 1%	1 / 1%	2 / 1%	3 / 1%	1 / 0%	2 / 2%	0 / 0%	1 / 0%	3 / 1%	6 / 1%	1 / 1%	0 / 0%	4 / 1%	1 / 1%	0 / 0%
SUITABLE FOR BOTH EQUALLY	378 / 25%	26 / 25%	46 / 33%	45 / 20%	43 / 18%	34 / 34%	56 / 37%	84 / 32%	42 / 15%	123 / 22%	20 / 24%	15 / 27%	158 / 26%	29 / 26%	24 / 39%
DONT KNOW	1 / 0%	0 / 0%	0 / 0%	0 / 0%	0 / 0%	0 / 0%	0 / 0%	0 / 0%	0 / 0%	0 / 0%	0 / 0%	0 / 0%	0 / 0%	0 / 0%	0 / 0%
NOT ANSWERED	29 / 2%	2 / 1%	1 / 0%	2 / 1%	8 / 3%	1 / 1%	2 / 1%	4 / 2%	11 / 4%	10 / 2%	1 / 1%	0 / 0%	17 / 3%	1 / 1%	1 / 2%
Nurse															
PARTICULARLY SUITABLE FOR MEN	4 / 0%	0 / 0%	0 / 0%	1 / 0%	1 / 0%	0 / 0%	1 / 1%	1 / 0%	0 / 0%	2 / 0%	0 / 0%	0 / 0%	2 / 0%	0 / 0%	0 / 0%
PARTICULARLY SUITABLE FOR WOMEN	625 / 41%	50 / 49%	63 / 44%	112 / 50%	126 / 51%	50 / 50%	39 / 25%	75 / 29%	132 / 46%	265 / 47%	51 / 60%	25 / 47%	209 / 34%	46 / 40%	17 / 27%
SUITABLE FOR BOTH EQUALLY	861 / 57%	50 / 49%	76 / 54%	108 / 48%	108 / 44%	75 / 75%	111 / 72%	182 / 70%	147 / 51%	274 / 49%	33 / 39%	29 / 53%	396 / 64%	67 / 59%	43 / 71%
DONT KNOW	3 / 0%	0 / 0%	0 / 0%	2 / 1%	0 / 0%	0 / 0%	0 / 0%	0 / 0%	1 / 0%	2 / 0%	0 / 0%	0 / 0%	0 / 0%	0 / 0%	1 / 2%
NOT ANSWERED	29 / 2%	2 / 1%	3 / 2%	2 / 1%	11 / 4%	1 / 1%	3 / 2%	3 / 1%	7 / 2%	16 / 3%	1 / 1%	0 / 0%	12 / 2%	1 / 1%	0 / 0%

3.11 OCCUPATIONAL STEREOTYPING (Q219)
by age within sex and school leaving age within sex

Do you think the following jobs are suitable for men only, women only, or for both equally?

BASE: THOSE RETURNING SELF-COMPLETION

	BASE	AGE† MEN 18-24	MEN 25-34	MEN 35-54	MEN 55+	AGE† WOMEN 18-24	WOMEN 25-34	WOMEN 35-54	WOMEN 55+	SCHOOL LEAVING AGE† MEN 16 or under	MEN 17-18	MEN 19 or over	WOMEN 16 or under	WOMEN 17-18	WOMEN 19 or over
UNWEIGHTED BASE	1562	105	141	224	256	99	158	276	294	567	88	55	637	119	62
WEIGHTED BASE	1522	101	142	225	245	101	153	261	287	558	85	54	618	114	61

Computer programmer

	BASE	MEN 18-24	MEN 25-34	MEN 35-54	MEN 55+	WOMEN 18-24	WOMEN 25-34	WOMEN 35-54	WOMEN 55+	MEN 16 or under	MEN 17-18	MEN 19 or over	WOMEN 16 or under	WOMEN 17-18	WOMEN 19 or over
PARTICULARLY SUITABLE FOR MEN	85 6%	4 3%	4 3%	3 1%	13 5%	4 4%	5 3%	13 5%	38 13%	22 4%	0 0%	2 2%	56 9%	4 4%	1 2%
PARTICULARLY SUITABLE FOR WOMEN	42 3%	2 2%	2 1%	6 3%	14 6%	1 1%	1 1%	3 1%	15 5%	21 4%	1 1%	0 0%	17 3%	3 2%	0 0%
SUITABLE FOR BOTH EQUALLY	1355 89%	94 93%	133 94%	213 95%	207 84%	95 95%	146 95%	241 93%	218 76%	497 89%	83 98%	53 98%	526 85%	107 94%	59 97%
DONT KNOW	7 0%	0 0%	0 0%	0 0%	2 1%	0 0%	0 0%	1 0%	4 1%	2 0%	0 0%	0 0%	4 1%	0 0%	1 2%
NOT ANSWERED	34 2%	2 1%	3 2%	3 1%	10 4%	1 1%	2 1%	3 1%	12 4%	16 3%	0 0%	0 0%	16 3%	0 0%	0 0%

Bus driver

	BASE	MEN 18-24	MEN 25-34	MEN 35-54	MEN 55+	WOMEN 18-24	WOMEN 25-34	WOMEN 35-54	WOMEN 55+	MEN 16 or under	MEN 17-18	MEN 19 or over	WOMEN 16 or under	WOMEN 17-18	WOMEN 19 or over
PARTICULARLY SUITABLE FOR MEN	742 49%	41 41%	41 29%	104 46%	146 59%	31 31%	51 33%	111 43%	213 74%	259 46%	48 56%	20 37%	340 55%	48 42%	18 29%
PARTICULARLY SUITABLE FOR WOMEN	9 1%	1 1%	2 1%	1 0%	1 1%	1 1%	0 0%	2 1%	2 1%	3 1%	0 0%	0 0%	5 1%	0 0%	0 0%
SUITABLE FOR BOTH EQUALLY	741 49%	57 57%	96 67%	116 52%	90 37%	68 68%	101 66%	146 56%	64 22%	278 50%	37 43%	34 63%	263 43%	64 57%	42 70%
DONT KNOW	2 0%	0 0%	0 0%	0 0%	0 0%	0 0%	0 0%	0 0%	1 0%	1 0%	0 0%	0 0%	0 0%	0 0%	0 1%
NOT ANSWERED	28 2%	2 1%	3 2%	4 2%	9 3%	1 1%	2 1%	2 1%	7 2%	16 3%	1 1%	0 0%	10 2%	1 1%	1 2%

Bank manager

	BASE	MEN 18-24	MEN 25-34	MEN 35-54	MEN 55+	WOMEN 18-24	WOMEN 25-34	WOMEN 35-54	WOMEN 55+	MEN 16 or under	MEN 17-18	MEN 19 or over	WOMEN 16 or under	WOMEN 17-18	WOMEN 19 or over
PARTICULARLY SUITABLE FOR MEN	595 39%	32 32%	37 26%	76 34%	123 50%	30 29%	43 28%	79 30%	170 60%	221 40%	32 38%	10 19%	278 45%	33 29%	13 21%
PARTICULARLY SUITABLE FOR WOMEN	11 1%	2 2%	1 0%	2 1%	3 1%	1 1%	0 0%	1 0%	2 1%	6 1%	0 0%	0 0%	4 1%	0 0%	0 0%
SUITABLE FOR BOTH EQUALLY (O)	882 58%	65 65%	101 71%	144 64%	110 45%	69 69%	109 71%	178 68%	103 36%	313 56%	52 61%	44 81%	322 52%	79 70%	47 78%
DONT KNOW	3 0%	0 0%	0 0%	0 0%	1 0%	0 0%	0 0%	0 0%	2 1%	2 0%	0 0%	0 0%	1 0%	0 0%	1 2%
NOT ANSWERED	32 2%	2 1%	3 2%	4 2%	9 3%	1 1%	2 1%	3 1%	10 3%	16 3%	1 1%	0 0%	13 2%	1 1%	0 0%

3.12 OCCUPATIONAL STEREOTYPING (Q219)
by age within sex and school leaving age within sex

Do you think the following jobs are suitable for men only, women only, or for both equally?

BASE: THOSE RETURNING SELF-COMPLETION

	BASE	AGE† MEN 18-24	25-34	35-54	55+	WOMEN 18-24	25-34	35-54	55+	SCHOOL LEAVING AGE† MEN 16 or under	17-18	19 or over	WOMEN 16 or under	17-18	19 or over
UNWEIGHTED BASE	1562	105	141	224	256	99	158	276	294	567	88	55	637	119	62
WEIGHTED BASE	1522	101	142	225	245	101	153	261	287	558	85	54	618	114	61

Family doctor/GP

	BASE	MEN 18-24	25-34	35-54	55+	WOMEN 18-24	25-34	35-54	55+	MEN 16 or under	17-18	19 or over	WOMEN 16 or under	17-18	19 or over
PARTICULARLY SUITABLE FOR MEN	156 10%	14 14%	7 5%	17 8%	35 14%	1 1%	7 5%	14 5%	58 20%	65 12%	3 4%	3 7%	73 12%	8 7%	2 3%
PARTICULARLY SUITABLE FOR WOMEN	22 1%	2 2%	1 0%	0 0%	3 1%	2 2%	1 1%	3 1%	11 4%	4 1%	0 0%	0 0%	16 3%	1 1%	0 0%
SUITABLE FOR BOTH EQUALLY	1318 87%	84 83%	133 94%	205 91%	199 81%	97 97%	145 94%	242 93%	209 73%	475 85%	81 95%	50 93%	518 84%	105 92%	58 95%
DONT KNOW	1 0%	0 0%		0 0%	0 0%	0 0%	0 0%	0 0%	0 0%	0 0%	0 0%	0 0%	0 0%	0 0%	0 0%
NOT ANSWERED	25 2%	1 1%	2 1%	3 1%	9 4%	1 1%	1 0%	3 1%	8 3%	13 2%	1 1%	0 0%	11 2%	0 0%	0 0%

Local councillor

	BASE	MEN 18-24	25-34	35-54	55+	WOMEN 18-24	25-34	35-54	55+	MEN 16 or under	17-18	19 or over	WOMEN 16 or under	17-18	19 or over
PARTICULARLY SUITABLE FOR MEN	187 12%	14 14%	8 6%	20 9%	30 12%	20 20%	9 6%	19 7%	64 22%	65 12%	5 5%	3 6%	104 17%	6 6%	0 0%
PARTICULARLY SUITABLE FOR WOMEN	11 1%	2 2%	1 0%	2 1%	3 1%	1 1%	1 1%	2 1%	1 0%	5 1%	0 0%	0 0%	4 1%	1 1%	0 0%
SUITABLE FOR BOTH EQUALLY	1290 85%	83 83%	130 91%	200 89%	203 83%	79 79%	141 92%	236 91%	212 74%	470 84%	80 93%	51 94%	496 80%	105 93%	60 98%
DONT KNOW	3 0%	0 0%	0 0%	0 0%	1 0%	0 0%	0 0%	0 0%	2 1%	1 0%	0 0%	0 0%	1 0%	0 0%	0 0%
NOT ANSWERED	31 2%	2 1%	3 2%	4 2%	9 3%	1 1%	3 2%	3 1%	8 3%	16 3%	1 1%	0 0%	13 2%	1 1%	0 0%

Member of Parliament

	BASE	MEN 18-24	25-34	35-54	55+	WOMEN 18-24	25-34	35-54	55+	MEN 16 or under	17-18	19 or over	WOMEN 16 or under	17-18	19 or over
PARTICULARLY SUITABLE FOR MEN	241 16%	13 13%	17 12%	28 13%	48 20%	21 21%	11 7%	23 9%	76 27%	97 17%	7 8%	3 6%	122 20%	8 7%	0 0%
PARTICULARLY SUITABLE FOR WOMEN	7 0%	1 1%	1 0%	1 0%	2 1%	1 1%	0 0%	1 0%	1 0%	3 0%	0 0%	0 0%	4 1%	0 0%	0 0%
SUITABLE FOR BOTH EQUALLY	1241 82%	85 84%	121 85%	193 86%	187 76%	78 77%	140 91%	232 89%	199 69%	442 76%	78 91%	51 94%	478 77%	104 91%	60 98%
DONT KNOW	2 0%	0 0%	0 0%	0 0%	1 0%	0 0%	0 0%	0 0%	2 1%	2 0%	0 0%	0 0%	1 0%	0 0%	1 2%
NOT ANSWERED	32 2%	2 1%	3 2%	4 2%	9 3%	1 1%	3 2%	3 1%	9 3%	16 3%	1 1%	0 0%	14 2%	1 1%	0 0%

3.13 TRADITIONALISM AND WOMEN'S ROLE IN SOCIETY (Q220)
by age within sex and school leaving age within sex

BASE: THOSE RETURNING SELF-COMPLETION

	BASE	AGE† MEN				AGE† WOMEN				SCHOOL LEAVING AGE† MEN			SCHOOL LEAVING AGE† WOMEN		
		18-24	25-34	35-54	55+	18-24	25-34	35-54	55+	16 or under	17-18	19 or over	16 or under	17-18	19 or over
UNWEIGHTED BASE	1562	105	141	224	256	99	158	276	294	567	88	55	637	119	62
WEIGHTED BASE	1522	101	142	225	245	101	153	261	287	558	85	54	618	114	61

Do you agree or disagree with the following statements?

Having a job is the best way for a woman to be an independent person.

	BASE	18-24	25-34	35-54	55+	18-24	25-34	35-54	55+	16 or under	17-18	19 or over	16 or under	17-18	19 or over
AGREE STRONGLY	462 30%	24 24%	31 22%	68 30%	73 30%	44 43%	41 27%	96 37%	84 29%	155 28%	19 23%	17 32%	197 32%	40 35%	23 38%
JUST AGREE	544 36%	39 38%	58 41%	68 30%	92 38%	32 32%	60 39%	82 32%	108 38%	201 36%	34 40%	22 40%	234 38%	35 31%	11 18%
NEITHER AGREE NOR DISAGREE	337 22%	30 30%	39 28%	60 26%	57 23%	18 18%	27 18%	48 18%	57 20%	150 27%	25 29%	5 9%	110 18%	16 14%	21 35%
JUST DISAGREE	99 7%	7 7%	9 6%	17 7%	11 5%	3 3%	15 9%	20 7%	18 6%	28 5%	10 12%	5 9%	42 7%	12 10%	2 3%
DISAGREE STRONGLY	58 4%	1 1%	3 2%	9 4%	8 3%	3 3%	11 7%	14 5%	10 3%	16 3%	1 1%	3 6%	22 3%	11 10%	4 7%
DONT KNOW	1 0%	0%	0%	0%	0%	0%	0%	0%	0%	0%	0%	1%	0%	0%	0%
NOT ANSWERED	22 1%	2 1%	1 0%	3 1%	4 1%	1 1%	2 1%	2 1%	11 4%	8 1%	0%	0%	14 2%	0%	0%

Most married women work only to earn money for extras rather than because they need the money.

	BASE	18-24	25-34	35-54	55+	18-24	25-34	35-54	55+	16 or under	17-18	19 or over	16 or under	17-18	19 or over
AGREE STRONGLY	244 16%	10 10%	18 12%	39 17%	56 23%	8 8%	17 11%	37 14%	60 21%	106 19%	10 12%	5 9%	104 17%	10 9%	6 10%
JUST AGREE	457 30%	33 33%	38 26%	60 27%	87 35%	29 29%	48 32%	72 28%	83 29%	181 33%	23 27%	8 15%	189 31%	33 29%	11 18%
NEITHER AGREE NOR DISAGREE	201 13%	25 25%	24 17%	33 15%	27 11%	14 15%	14 9%	26 10%	35 12%	84 15%	12 14%	8 15%	63 10%	16 14%	10 16%
JUST DISAGREE	331 22%	17 17%	40 28%	56 25%	42 17%	24 24%	26 17%	59 23%	65 23%	105 19%	28 32%	19 35%	113 18%	38 33%	18 30%
DISAGREE STRONGLY	270 18%	15 15%	22 15%	35 16%	27 11%	24 24%	46 30%	65 25%	35 12%	75 14%	11 13%	12 22%	137 22%	17 15%	16 26%
DONT KNOW	0%	0%	0%	0%	0%	0%	0%	0%	0%	0%	0%	0%	0%	0%	0%
NOT ANSWERED	19 1%	1 0%	1 0%	1 0%	5 2%	0%	1 1%	2 1%	3 1%	6 1%	0%	0%	12 2%	0%	0%

A husband's job is to earn the money; a wife's job is to look after the home and family.

	BASE	18-24	25-34	35-54	55+	18-24	25-34	35-54	55+	16 or under	17-18	19 or over	16 or under	17-18	19 or over
AGREE STRONGLY	353 23%	13 13%	20 14%	33 14%	111 45%	13 13%	10 6%	39 15%	114 40%	158 28%	11 13%	7 13%	155 25%	13 12%	8 13%
JUST AGREE	299 20%	14 14%	27 19%	49 22%	52 21%	13 13%	26 17%	49 19%	66 23%	118 21%	15 18%	6 11%	128 21%	20 18%	6 10%
NEITHER AGREE NOR DISAGREE	284 19%	23 23%	23 16%	59 26%	37 15%	17 17%	24 16%	44 17%	53 19%	106 19%	26 31%	7 13%	117 19%	18 16%	4 7%
JUST DISAGREE	237 16%	21 20%	31 22%	36 16%	24 10%	22 21%	35 23%	45 17%	21 7%	79 14%	16 19%	12 23%	81 13%	21 19%	18 29%
DISAGREE STRONGLY	334 22%	29 29%	40 28%	46 20%	18 7%	35 35%	59 39%	83 32%	23 8%	91 16%	16 19%	21 39%	127 21%	39 35%	25 41%
DONT KNOW	1 0%	0%	0%	0%	0%	0%	0%	0%	0%	0%	0%	0%	0%	0%	0%
NOT ANSWERED	16 1%	1 0%	1 0%	2 1%	1 0%	0%	0%	1 0%	1 0%	5 1%	0%	0%	11 2%	0%	0%

3.14 TRADITIONALISM AND WOMEN'S ROLE IN SOCIETY (Q220)
by age within sex and school leaving age within sex

Do you agree or disagree with the following statements?

| | | AGE† | | | | | | | | SCHOOL LEAVING AGE† | | | | | |
| | | MEN | | | | WOMEN | | | | MEN | | | WOMEN | | |
BASE: THOSE RETURNING SELF-COMPLETION	BASE	18-24	25-34	35-54	55+	18-24	25-34	35-54	55+	16 or under	17-18	19 or over	16 or under	17-18	19 or over
UNWEIGHTED BASE	1562	105	141	224	256	99	158	276	294	567	88	55	637	119	62
WEIGHTED BASE	1522	101	142	225	245	101	153	261	287	558	85	54	618	114	61

Women should be paid the same as men for doing the same work.

	BASE	18-24	25-34	35-54	55+	18-24	25-34	35-54	55+	16 or under	17-18	19 or over	16 or under	17-18	19 or over
AGREE STRONGLY	1029 68%	67 66%	92 65%	149 66%	151 62%	83 82%	123 80%	196 75%	165 58%	350 63%	52 61%	43 81%	420 68%	82 72%	53 88%
JUST AGREE	351 23%	25 25%	35 25%	57 25%	68 28%	14 14%	22 14%	51 20%	72 25%	149 27%	27 31%	9 16%	137 22%	20 17%	6 9%
NEITHER AGREE NOR DISAGREE	65 4%	4 4%	10 7%	6 2%	6 2%	1 1%	3 2%	7 2%	20 7%	29 5%	4 5%	0 0%	25 4%	7 6%	0 0%
JUST DISAGREE	35 2%	1 1%	1 1%	8 3%	6 2%	0 0%	3 2%	4 1%	13 5%	14 3%	1 1%	0 0%	16 3%	2 2%	1 2%
DISAGREE STRONGLY	24 2%	3 3%	1 1%	0 0%	3 1%	2 2%	2 1%	2 1%	8 3%	9 2%	0 0%	1 2%	11 2%	4 3%	0 0%
DONT KNOW	1 0%	0 0%	0 0%	0 0%	0 0%	0 0%	0 0%	0 0%	0 0%	0 0%	1 1%	0 0%	0 0%	0 0%	0 0%
NOT ANSWERED	17 1%	1 0%	2 1%	2 1%	3 1%	1 1%	1 0%	1 0%	8 3%	6 1%	0 0%	1 1%	9 1%	0 0%	1 2%

In times of high unemployment married women should stay at home.

	BASE	18-24	25-34	35-54	55+	18-24	25-34	35-54	55+	16 or under	17-18	19 or over	16 or under	17-18	19 or over
AGREE STRONGLY	275 18%	7 7%	12 9%	36 16%	75 31%	9 9%	16 10%	35 14%	84 29%	118 21%	7 8%	5 9%	126 20%	14 13%	4 7%
JUST AGREE	260 17%	14 14%	16 11%	34 15%	54 22%	7 6%	18 12%	39 15%	75 26%	98 18%	13 15%	4 7%	118 19%	20 18%	5 8%
NEITHER AGREE NOR DISAGREE	266 17%	25 25%	31 22%	39 18%	44 18%	11 11%	23 15%	38 15%	53 18%	113 20%	10 12%	8 16%	92 15%	21 18%	13 21%
JUST DISAGREE	314 21%	21 21%	37 26%	54 24%	40 16%	32 32%	33 22%	55 21%	40 14%	105 19%	29 34%	14 26%	114 18%	27 24%	15 24%
DISAGREE STRONGLY	390 26%	32 32%	45 32%	59 26%	30 12%	41 41%	61 40%	92 35%	28 10%	117 21%	25 29%	22 41%	160 26%	31 27%	24 39%
DONT KNOW	1 0%	0 0%	0 0%	0 0%	1 0%	0 0%	0 0%	0 0%	0 0%	0 0%	1 1%	0 0%	0 0%	0 0%	0 0%
NOT ANSWERED	16 1%	0 0%	1 1%	3 1%	2 1%	1 1%	2 1%	2 1%	6 2%	6 1%	0 0%	1 1%	9 1%	0 0%	2 2%

4 Attitudes to defence and international affairs

*Paul Whiteley**

Defence and international affairs have generally been regarded as secondary electoral issues by students of public opinion. In their 1963 survey of the British electorate, Butler and Stokes (1974, p. 297) found that only seven per cent of the electorate regarded international affairs and defence as the most important issues facing the government. Thus these issues appeared to be far less salient than domestic issues concerning the economy and social welfare. In subsequent surveys of the electorate as part of the British Election Study Series, Butler and Stokes, and later Särlvik and Crewe, dropped any questions to do with defence and international politics, apart from the question of British membership of the European Economic Community. This reflected their judgement of the apparent lack of significance of these issues for voters.

However, in the 1983 General Election, defence, and more specifically nuclear weapons, came to the forefront during the campaign. For instance the BBC/Gallup eve-of-poll survey in 1983 showed that defence was the second most important issue of the election, after unemployment; some 35% of respondents mentioned defence and nuclear weapons in reply to an open-ended question in the survey about the most important issues facing the country (Whiteley, 1984). The major post-election study in the British Election Study Series (Heath, Jowell and Curtice, 1985, forthcoming), confirms the relative importance of defence in the 1983 election campaign.

The purpose of this chapter is to explore the nature of public attitudes towards defence and international affairs, with respect to Britain's role, its perceived influence, its alliances and its options.

* Lecturer in Politics, University of Bristol.

Britain as a world power

The self-completion questionnaire contained two questions to provide insights into attitudes towards Britain's role in world affairs. The first asked respondents to compare Britain's influence on world events with that of a range of other countries (excluding – amongst others – Russia and the USA). Although not all European countries were listed, the responses suggest that in the European arena only West Germany was considered as having more influence on world events than Britain – and then only marginally. And in comparison with other leading countries such as China, Canada and Australia, Britain's political standing (according to the British public) was relatively high.

Perceptions of countries' influence on world events

		Less than Britain	About the same	More than Britain
West Germany	%	10	56	27
France	%	19	58	16
Canada	%	31	50	10
Australia	%	37	47	7
China	%	42	22	27
Israel	%	50	21	20
East Germany	%	50	25	14
India	%	73	14	4

These views about world influence were fairly consistently held across the sample. The main factor associated with variations in opinions was party identification. Labour identifiers in the sample consistently rated Britain lower, but not by a substantial margin, than Alliance identifiers did; while Conservative identifiers generally accorded Britain the highest relative influence.

Percentages who believed each country had *less* influence than Britain

	Conservative identifiers	Alliance identifiers	Labour identifiers
	%	%	%
West Germany	11	10	9
France	24	20	14
Canada	36	39	25
Australia	44	43	31
China	50	41	33
Israel	53	52	48
East Germany	59	59	39
India	77	77	70

The second measure we elicited about Britain's international standing was derived from respondents' level of agreement (57% overall) with the statement we offered that *the days when Britain was an important world power are over*. Although the young and Conservative identifiers were less likely than other subgroups to agree with the statement, there was – in all the subgroups we identified – a clear margin of agreement over disagreement.

The days when Britain was an important world power are over

	Total	Age				Party identification		
		18-24	25-34	35-54	55+	Conservative	Alliance	Labour
	%	%	%	%	%	%	%	%
Agree strongly *or* just agree	57	49	49	59	61	48	59	63
Disagree strongly *or* just disagree	26	21	29	27	23	35	26	16

These two sets of results suggest a widespread recognition of Britain's role as one among several second-tier nations in its potential for influencing world events. Implicit in the data was the dominance of the two superpowers. Among the second-tier nations, however, Britain was seen to have an influential – and perhaps overstated – role.

Britain's comparative standard of living

Despite its perceived importance as a political force in the world, compared with other European countries, questions about standards of living revealed doubts about Britain's place in the world. Whereas most people regarded countries like West Germany, Canada and Australia as no more influential than Britain in international circles, those countries were thought by sizeable majorities to enjoy a standard of living higher than Britain's. On the other hand, in the case of France and Japan a majority felt that these countries' standards of living were the same or lower than Britain's. These attitudes did not closely reflect the reality according to recent World Bank figures on Gross National Product.

	GNP per capita in 1982* ($ in 1982 prices)	percentage who thought each country had a higher standard of living than Britain %
West Germany	12,460	66
France	11,680	26
Canada	11,320	65
Australia	11,140	52
Japan	10,080	38
Britain	9,660	–

* Source: World Development Report 1984, World Bank.

Six countries were compared with Britain in the self-completion questionnaire, and in only one instance (East Germany, for which World Bank data are unavailable) was the majority view that Britain's standard of living was higher. Moreover, even in the case of West Germany, Canada and Australia, sizeable minorities held the view that their standard of living was no higher than Britain's. Opinions about standards of living seem to lag behind actual standards of living, since many people's perceptions now seem to reflect the reality of the 1950s and early 1960s insofar, that is, as 'reality' coincides with GNP per capita.

People's views on standards of living were affected by their occupations, income, school-leaving age and Social Class, but differences in attitudes between social groups were not large. The youngest age group (18-24 years) expressed a generally more favourable view than other respondents of Britain's relative standard of living, especially compared to West Germany, Canada and France; reflecting perhaps less knowledge on their part of the differences in industrial growth rates during the 1960s and 1970s. Yet, as we have noted, the young were also more optimistic about Britain's power in the world.

Perceptions of countries' standards of living

	Total	Those aged 18-24 years
Higher than Britain:	%	%
West Germany	66	58
Canada	65	58
Australia	52	54
Japan	38	38
France	26	19
East Germany	12	17

As a measure, in part, of people's concern about the relative state of Britain's economy, we asked respondents how much they agreed or disagreed with the view that *British people should try to buy British goods even when they have to pay a bit more for them.*

British people should try to buy British goods even when they have to pay a bit more for them

	Total	Social Class				Age			
		I/II	III non-manual	III manual	IV/V	18-24	25-34	35-54	55+
	%	%	%	%	%	%	%	%	%
Agree strongly	36	29	36	38	44	26	27	33	49
Agree	30	33	32	28	24	29	31	29	30
Neither agree nor disagree	14	14	12	14	15	19	17	15	9
Disagree	13	15	15	14	8	15	18	15	7
Disagree strongly	6	8	5	6	6	11	7	8	3

Nearly two-thirds of the sample agreed with this statement, compared with less than one-fifth who disagreed. Views, however, differed markedly between Social Classes and age groups, with the higher Social Classes and younger age groups being less inclined to protect British industry by this means. Even though older respondents and those working in less skilled occupations tended to be much less well off, they were much more likely to agree strongly that people ought to pay more to buy British.

Britain's alliances

As the answers to preceding questions demonstrate, there was relative optimism about Britain's international influence as a second-tier power, and a more cautious mood about Britain's international economic standing. We now move on to people's views about Britain's present international alliances and about the links it should develop with other countries.

The question on British membership of the EEC is particularly interesting because it provides insights into some of the factors which influence public opinion over time. As the table below illustrates, attitudes towards Britain's membership of the EEC have fluctuated widely over the years (though the important effect of question wording on responses to this question is well documented; see, for instance, Jowell and Hoinville, 1976).

Opinion on British Membership of the EEC*

Britain should:	1963	1966	1970	1974	Referendum vote Great Britain (1975)	1983	1984
	%	%	%	%	%	%	%
go in/remain in	32	33	54	50	68	53	48
stay out/withdraw	29	32	17	46	32	42	45
no opinion/don't know	39	35	29	4	–	5	6

In the 1960s when there was relatively lukewarm support for membership, many voters had no opinion on the question at all. However, by the mid-1970s, when the Heath government had already negotiated British entry, and the Labour opposition supported membership in principle but challenged its terms of entry, opinion had become more polarised, most people having made up their minds one way or the other. The high watermark of support was reached at the time of the referendum in 1975 when British membership received 2:1 endorsement from those who voted (Butler and Sloman, 1980, p. 211). At that time the political elites in the Conservative and Liberal parties, together with the media, supported continued membership, and Labour was split. From then onwards support for membership declined, though not at a uniform rate. The unfavourable publicity surrounding the issue of Britain's budgetary contributions, together with damaging rows about harmonisation of community policies and the burden of the Common Agricultural Policy have subsequently shifted opinion away from support for the EEC. Our results showed a roughly

* Sources: Särlvik, Crewe, Alt and Fox (1976); Jowell and Airey (1984).

even division between support for and opposition to the EEC. The gap was three per cent (in favour) compared with 11% a year previously.

These trends in public attitudes to the EEC suggest that two major factors have been at work in influencing opinion. Firstly, there is the position taken up by opinion leaders, principally the leaders of the main political parties. When nearly all supported membership, as at the time of the referendum, the balance of public opinion was strongly in its favour. When party leaders were more divided, as they had been a year earlier, in 1974, public opinion was more divided. The second major factor is external events associated with the issue, and their coverage by the media. When publicity for the EEC was very favourable, as in 1975, so too was public opinion; when publicity was adverse, something broadly true since 1979, support for continued membership declined.

The continued influence of party identification can be seen in comparing the 1983 and 1984 Social Attitudes data. Whereas the intervening General Election campaign did not significantly change the opinions of Conservative and Alliance identifiers, it appears to have had a marked effect on Labour identifiers, particularly Labour partisans, among whom support for continued membership of the EEC dropped substantially – despite a relaxation in Labour's 'official' opposition to membership since the election.

Support for Britain remaining in EEC

	Total	Conservative		Alliance		Labour	
		partisans	others	partisans	others	partisans	others
	%	%	%	%	%	%	%
1983	53	72	57	59	56	39	35
1984	48	70	61	54	48	25	34

Support also varied by Social Class and education, variables which are themselves obviously related. Over two-thirds of Social Classes I and II supported continued membership of the EEC, compared with only one third of Social Classes IV and V (see **Table 4.1**). As we show below, level of education attained, as measured by school-leaving age, also made a clear difference to level of support.

Membership of the EEC

	Total	School-leaving age		
		16 or under	17-18	19 or over
	%	%	%	%
Britain should continue to be a member	48	42	61	77
Britain should withdraw	45	51	32	17

There was much greater public support (79%) for Britain's continued membership of NATO, with no change in the level of support since 1983. Moreover, although the level of support differed according to party identification, there were clear majorities for NATO within each party: 88% support among Conservatives, 86% among Alliance identifiers, and 70% among Labour identifiers. (For detailed breakdowns, see **Table 4.2**.)

In the 1984 Report (p.36), Ken Young questioned whether NATO was perceived broadly as a European alliance or as an American-dominated one. So this year we asked some new questions to measure attitudes towards Britain's 'special relationship' with the United States – as compared with Europe – and towards the US and Soviet roles in international peace-keeping. First we asked:

On the whole, do you think that Britain's interests are better served by . . .

		%
. . .	closer links with Western Europe,	53
or –	closer links with America?	21
	Both equally	16
	Neither	3
	Don't know	7

As we shall see, distrust of America's nuclear policy may be one explanation for these figures. Another may be the comparative influence that Britain is thought to wield in Europe. It is interesting that even among those who wished to withdraw from the EEC, support for closer links with Western Europe was 50%, suggesting that an anti-EEC stance is more closely tied to perceptions of economic ill-effects than to a distrust of European political alliances as such.

Although people in Social Classes I and II (professionals and managers) and those who left school aged 17 or over were more favourably disposed to stronger links with Europe, Conservative identifiers as a whole were rather less likely than Labour or Alliance identifiers to take a pro-European stance on this question. And the distinction between the partisans in each party was larger still, as the following table shows.

	Total	Conservative		Alliance		Labour	
		partisans	others	partisans	others	partisans	others
	%	%	%	%	%	%	%
Closer links with:							
Western Europe	53	51	52	63	55	57	53
America	21	21	24	13	16	19	30
Both equally	16	24	15	17	17	13	8

Scepticism about America's international role is not a new phenomenon. For instance, according to a Gallup survey carried out in October 1979, 39% of respondents had very little or no confidence in the ability of the United States to deal wisely with world problems (Webb and Wybrow, 1981, p. 101). So we also asked respondents:

Which of the phrases on this card is closest to your opinion about threats to world peace?

	%
America is a greater threat to world peace than Russia	11
Russia is a greater threat to world peace than America	26
Russia and America are equally great threats to world peace	54
Neither is a threat to world peace	5

Given that the United States is a close ally of Britain and shares a common language, common institutions and a similar culture, these attitudes are quite remarkable. Over one half of the sample regarded the United States as being as much a threat to world peace as the Soviet Union. There was a slight but noticeable difference in attitudes between the Social Classes, with people from Social Classes I and II being more likely than people from Social Classes IV and V to think that the USA and the Soviet Union were equally great threats to world peace (57% compared with 51%). Level of education and party identification were, however, more powerful discriminators. Alliance identifiers were much more likely than those in other parties to think that the two superpowers were equally great threats to world peace, while Conservatives, not surprisingly, were more likely to feel that the Soviet Union was a greater threat. Labour identifiers, by contrast, were more likely to nominate the United States as a greater threat, though this view was held by only a small minority of Labour identifiers.

	Conservative identifiers %	Alliance identifiers %	Labour identifiers %
America greater threat to world peace than Russia	8	9	17
Russia greater threat to world peace than America	34	20	20
Russia and America equally great threats	50	64	56
Neither a threat	6	3	4

The Alliance profile on the combination of these issues was an interesting one; Alliance identifiers were markedly more favourable towards the EEC than Labour identifiers, and less favourable towards closer ties with America. Their perceptions of threats to world peace suggest that this discrepancy may stem partly from their distrust of America's foreign and defence policies and partly from their generally more pro-European sympathies by comparison with those in other parties.

Attitudes to defence and nuclear weapons

Scepticism about cooperation with the United States is linked to people's attitudes towards nuclear missiles. As in 1983 we asked respondents about the siting of American missiles in Britain, as well as about Britain's own nuclear missiles. Again the intervening election campaign may have made some difference to opinions on this issue.

	1983	1984
American nuclear missiles make Britain:	%	%
safer	38	36
less safe	48	51
no difference	1	3
British independent nuclear missiles make Britain:		
safer	60	56
less safe	28	32
no difference	5	2

As can be seen, there was little change in the proportions answering 'safer' to both questions, though there is a suggestion of a decline in pro-nuclear attitudes. In both years, respondents made a sharp distinction between American nuclear missiles in Britain (under American control) and Britain's own missiles. Support for Britain's membership of NATO among respondents certainly did not guarantee support for the siting of American cruise missiles in Britain; on the contrary, even among supporters of NATO 48% felt that the presence of these missiles made Britain a less safe place in which to live. Attitudes to American nuclear missiles varied greatly according to perceptions of America and Russia as threats to world peace, as the following table shows.

	America is greater threat to world peace	Russia and America are equally great threats to world peace	Russia is greater threat to world peace
American nuclear missiles make Britain:	%	%	%
safer	22	31	51
less safe	71	56	35
no difference	1	4	2

What is important about the figures above is that even among people who regarded the two superpowers as equally threatening, a large majority was against an American nuclear presence in Britain. Younger people were particularly likely to feel that American nuclear missiles made Britain less safe, with 61% of 18-24 year olds holding this belief, compared with 48% of respondents over the age of 54. And, as expected, there was a marked difference according to party identification, with Labour identifiers much more likely to feel that American nuclear missiles made Britain less safe (71%), compared with both Conservatives (34%), and Alliance identifiers (51%). (For a full breakdown by strength of party identification see **Table 4.6**.)

Attitudes towards Britain's nuclear missiles followed similar patterns, with most variation in responses arising from party identity and age. But there was a clear majority (56% to 32%) who supported the notion that British missiles made Britain a safer place. Indeed the only subgroup we identified in the sample which contained more opponents of British nuclear missiles than supporters was Labour partisans. In all other groups, including the younger age groups, there were more people who thought Britain was safer with its own nuclear missiles.

Our measure of support for unilateral nuclear disarmament also showed a small increase since 1983, a period in which there was not only a General Election but continued demonstrations against nuclear missiles at Greenham and elsewhere.

	1983 %	1984 %
Britain should:		
rid itself of nuclear weapons while persuading others to do the same	19	23
keep its nuclear weapons until we persuade others to reduce theirs	77	73

Nonetheless, the unilateralist position was still held by a minority of respondents. While the 18-24 and the 25-34 age groups contained a slightly higher proportion who would get rid of nuclear weapons now (27%), this difference was not perhaps as great as might popularly be believed. Men and women overall shared similar views and even among social classes there were not marked differences. Nevertheless, party identification produced striking differences and showed that most unilateral disarmers (57%) identified politically with the Labour party. The following table shows the breakdown by party and partisanship.

	Total	Conservative partisans	others	Alliance partisans	others	Labour partisans	others
	%	%	%	%	%	%	%
Britain should:							
get rid of nuclear weapons	23	9	17	9	18	43	29
retain its nuclear weapons	73	88	81	83	77	54	68

At the time of the 1983 General Election the three parties differed clearly over the question of nuclear weapons and defence. The Conservatives favoured extra spending on defence in line with NATO's commitment to increase defence spending by three per cent per annum in real terms. They favoured the siting of US cruise missiles in Britain, and the replacement of Polaris by Trident missile submarines. The Alliance parties opposed unilateral disarmament by Britain, but did not support the Trident programme and were somewhat equivocal about American cruise missiles. Labour, by contrast, opposed Trident and cruise, and wanted to phase out Polaris within the lifetime of a parliament, although its leadership was split on this last issue. All parties favoured continued British membership of NATO.

Insofar as public opinion is associated with the policy commitment of the parties then we would expect to see Conservative identifiers most committed to nuclear weapons in Britain, Labour identifiers most opposed, and Alliance identifiers in between. As we have shown, this pattern was broadly what we found. Moreover, people's attitudes to nuclear missiles corresponded fairly closely to their perceptions of which party was closest to their views, as the following table shows.

	Party perceived as closest on defence views		
	Conservative %	Alliance %	Labour %
American nuclear missiles make Britain:			
safer	61	21	11
less safe	26	68	84
no difference	4	5	1
British nuclear missiles make Britain:			
safer	79	53	30
less safe	13	36	65
no difference	2	3	1
Britain should:			
rid itself of nuclear weapons while persuading others to do the same	4	20	55
keep its nuclear weapons until we persuade others to reduce theirs	94	73	43

We cannot of course infer a causal relationship between attitudes to defence and party support from this table; political support for a party might influence attitudes, or it might be that individuals choose parties which are in line with pre-existing views.

One of the important developments in contemporary British politics is the decline of partisan attachments amongst the electorate (Särlvik and Crewe, 1983). This has been taking place since the early 1970s and has obvious implications for public opinion. If party loyalties are declining in the electorate, then there will be a corresponding weakening of the influence of parties on public opinion. Which will mean, in turn, that public opinion will be increasingly open to other influences, principally the media.

Newspapers and defence policy

A full analysis of the relationship between media exposure and public opinion would require detailed evidence of respondent viewing and reading habits, together with information about the policy positions taken on various matters in the television programmes watched and the newspapers read. Nevertheless it is of interest to examine whether respondents' attitudes to defence varied according to the daily newspapers they read. It is possible to classify daily newspapers into two groups for this purpose.

The first group contains newspapers which supported the Conservatives in the 1983 election, and which are also generally in favour of Conservative policies on defence and nuclear disarmament. These are the Daily Mail, the Daily Star, the Sun, the Daily Telegraph, the Daily Express and The Times. The second group consists of newspapers which supported Labour in 1983, that is the Daily Mirror and the Daily Record in Scotland; we can also include in this group the Morning Star (which supported Labour only in preference to the other main parties) and The Guardian, which did not support Labour in 1983, but which has given prominent and sympathetic coverage to issues of nuclear disarmament. We have omitted a third category of mainly regionally based newspapers, since their impact does not extend to the whole of Great Britain.

Responses to our questions on nuclear defence varied significantly by newspaper readership.

Attitudes to nuclear issues

	Newspaper readership	
	Conservative inclined papers	Labour inclined papers
	%	%
US nuclear missiles make Britain:		
safer	44	22
less safe	41	69
UK nuclear missiles make Britain:		
safer	64	47
less safe	25	45
UK policy should be to:		
get rid of nuclear weapons	16	32
keep nuclear weapons	81	63

One possible interpretation of these results is that newspapers influenced people's opinions about nuclear disarmament; another is that individuals read newspapers which favoured their own views. In reality we might expect the relationship between newspaper readership and attitudes to be a mixture of these effects. And we can examine this further by taking respondents with the same party attachments and examining their attitudes and readership habits. We can then see whether newspaper readership has an independent association from that of party.

As the following table shows, readership and party identification combined to discriminate between four groups which illustrates the importance of political allegiance and the media as reinforcements, and possibly even creators, of opinions about nuclear weapons.

As we saw earlier Conservative identifiers generally felt safer than Labour identifiers did with British nuclear weapons on British soil. But in both groups there were clear differences between those who read Conservative inclined newspapers and those who read Labour inclined newspapers. The latter were more likely to oppose US and UK missiles, and were more likely to favour unilateralism, regardless of party attachments. So newspapers did have an independent association with attitudes.

Attitudes to defence issues

| | Conservative identifiers who read: | | Labour identifiers who read: | |
	Conservative inclined papers %	Labour inclined papers* %	Conservative inclined papers %	Labour inclined papers %
US nuclear missiles make Britain:				
safer	58	33	26	19
less safe	28	56	62	77
UK nuclear missiles make Britain:				
safer	74	67	49	43
less safe	15	26	42	52
UK policy should be:				
get rid of nuclear weapons	9	24	28	39
keep nuclear weapons	88	76	70	58

* There were only 49 respondents in this group.

In addition to asking about defence issues, we also asked respondents to assess the likelihood of such events as a future war in Europe, or a nuclear bomb being dropped somewhere in the world, within the next ten years. Only three per cent of our sample believed a war involving Britain and Europe was *very* likely in the next ten years, but another 18% thought it was quite likely. A rather higher proportion (nine per cent) thought it very likely that a nuclear bomb would be dropped somewhere in the world during the same period and 26% thought it quite likely; so around one in three people seemed to be pessimistic about the world's chances of avoiding a nuclear attack of some sort in the not too distant future.

As might be expected from the earlier findings, Labour identifiers were more pessimistic, and Conservatives less so, with Alliance identifiers in between. Among the groups who were more pessimistic about both events were those who felt that America was a greater threat to world peace than Russia, and those aged 18-24 years, particularly the latter group. As shown below, about

	All respondents %	Those aged 18-24 years %
War involving Britain and Europe:		
very likely	3	7
quite likely	18	27
Nuclear bomb will be dropped:		
very likely	9	19
quite likely	26	31

half these young people anticipated a nuclear bomb being dropped somewhere in the world during the next decade or so, and a third of them anticipated that Britain and Europe might once again be involved in a war during that period. We intend asking more about these issues in next year's questionnaire.

The influence of social background on attitudes

Before closing this chapter, it might be helpful to show briefly how the findings of this survey may be used by social and political scientists to explore theoretical debates, in this case the influence of social backgrounds on attitudes.

Inglehart (1977, 1981) has put forward a thesis that the underlying value systems of western societies have shifted significantly in the last two decades from an overwhelming emphasis on material well-being and physical security towards a greater emphasis on the quality of life and individual participation in politics. Individuals preoccupied with economic and physical security are described by Inglehart as 'materialists' and individuals preoccupied with the quality of life are described as 'post-materialists'.

Inglehart postulates that individuals acquire these basic values in adolescence and that they are a product of the socio-economic environment which they experience at that time. A further proposition in the theory is that once individuals have acquired these basic value orientations in their youth, they tend to carry them more or less unchanged into adulthood. Thus once individuals have acquired a materialist outlook they will tend to maintain it even if their adult life is later characterised by affluence and physical security.

Inglehart also argues that the shift towards post-materialist values brings with it increasing political skills and an increased desire for political participation. He believes that two classes of factors are influential in stimulating individuals to acquire post-materialist values. Firstly, generational changes combined with greater affluence engender support for these values. Thus young people are more likely to be post-materialist than older people, because they are more likely to have acquired their basic value orientation at a time of relative affluence and physical security, while the basic orientations of older people will have been acquired during the pre-war depression or the Second World War. Similarly, people with a high socio-economic status are more likely to be post-materialists than people with low status. Thus age and socio-economic status interact to produce patterns of values. Generational change produces new cohorts within the adult population who have been socialised in periods of relative affluence, while social structural change produces a higher proportion of people than there used to be who have relative economic and physical security.

A second correlate of the materialist/post-materialist distinction is education. Individuals who have experienced higher education are also more likely to hold post-materialist values. In survey data from a variety of advanced industrial countries Inglehart found significant relationships between age, social class, education and post-materialism.

Applying these hypotheses to our dataset is instructive. Looking first at responses to the nuclear defence questions by age, we would expect young people and those in the non-manual Social Classes to be more 'unilateralist' in their attitudes than their counterparts. As the table below shows, this relationship holds to some extent, though not as much, perhaps, as Inglehart's theory might lead one to expect. In particular, when we look at age within Social Class, we should expect to find a more pronounced post-materialist outlook in young, high status groups for whom affluence and generational replacement reinforce one another. In low status groups, by contrast, generational replacement is counteracted by experience of economic scarcity, unemployment and so on. Although there is some evidence of this in the table below, it must be remembered that party identification also influences attitudes within the manual and non-manual categories. So we cannot tell, in the absence of further multivariate analyses, whether post-materialist explanations or party identification is the more important predictor of responses.

Attitudes to nuclear weapons by age within occupational groups

	Age groups			
	18-24	25-34	35-54	55+
	%	%	%	%
NON-MANUAL WORKERS				
US nuclear missiles make Britain:				
safer	30	32	38	49
less safe	61	58	47	39
UK nuclear missiles make Britain:				
safer	54	51	55	65
less safe	38	37	32	22
UK policy should be:				
get rid of nuclear weapons	23	27	22	13
keep nuclear weapons	73	71	74	83
MANUAL WORKERS				
US nuclear missiles make Britain:				
safer	31	35	35	32
less safe	59	51	57	54
UK nuclear missiles make Britain:				
safer	46	56	58	56
less safe	46	34	32	33
UK policy should be:				
get rid of nuclear weapons	26	25	24	25
keep nuclear weapons	73	73	74	72

It can be seen that the differences between the age cohorts in the case of manual workers were quite small; by contrast the differences between the age cohorts of non-manual workers were fairly substantial. This confirms the expectation that socio-economic status and age interact to produce differences in attitudes. The fact that non-manual workers have higher incomes, greater job security and better conditions of service makes them more likely than manual workers to develop post-materialist values in the younger age cohorts.

Post-materialists are also more likely than materialists to be politically active, according to Inglehart. First, as they are more highly educated than the population as a whole, they will tend to have more skills to help them participate in politics; there is a good deal of evidence to suggest that political participation is higher in the more highly educated groups in society (Verba, Nie and Kim, 1978). Second, post-materialists are supposed to place positive value on political participation. This indeed is one of the defining characteristics of post-materialism (Inglehart, 1977). However, as Inglehart points out, their involvement is not necessarily in orthodox politics. He argues that post-materialists are more likely to be involved in 'elite-challenging' rather than 'elite-directing' political activity. That is, they are more concerned with challenging the *status quo* over certain clearly defined issues than with working within the system by getting new elites elected to positions of power. Third, post-materialists tend to be of a higher socio-economic status than the rest of society, which – along with education – makes for greater political involvement on their part.

In the light of this theory, it is interesting to observe whether or not attitudes to nuclear disarmament were associated with propensities for political action among our respondents. Respondents were asked if they would undertake various courses of action if 'an unjust law' was being considered by Parliament. (For detailed analysis of this question, see Chapters 1 and 6.) The courses of action were as follows:

> Contact my MP
> Speak to influential person
> Contact a government department
> Contact radio, TV or newspaper
> Sign a petition
> Raise the issue in an organisation I already belong to
> Go on a protest or demonstration
> Form a group of like-minded people

On the whole, these actions are fairly orthodox, with the possible exception of the protest or demonstration. At its simplest, the *number* of different courses of action each respondent said he or she was willing to take turns out to be significantly related to attitudes to US nuclear weapons. Those who would get involved in several courses of action were more likely to see US missiles as a threat (rather than a help) to Britain's security. They were, in the language of Inglehart, more post-materialist on this issue.

Respondents were also asked which of these actions would be the most effective in influencing outcomes. Interestingly, 68% of those who thought a protest or demonstration was the most effective form of action also thought that US missiles would make Britain less safe (compared with 51% of the total sample). Thus opponents of the US nuclear presence were more likely than supporters to favour 'elite-challenging' forms of political participation.

This last point leads to the question of the relationship between attitudes to nuclear weapons and a willingness to break the law in pursuit of political (or conscientious) objectives. We asked respondents whether *in general would you say that people should obey the law without exception, or are there exceptional occasions on which people should follow their consciences even if it means breaking the law?* As the table below shows, unilateralists and opponents of

American missiles in Britain were much more likely than their counterparts to support the claims of conscience against those of law.

Attitudes to nuclear weapons	Attitudes to the law	
	Always obey the law %	Follow conscience on occasions %
US nuclear missiles make Britain:		
safer	43	27
less safe	44	60
UK nuclear missiles make Britain:		
safer	62	49
less safe	27	40
UK policy should be:		
get rid of nuclear weapons	18	29
keep nuclear weapons	78	68

The various findings we have presented combine to pose an intriguing question about the likely direction of political protest in Britain. Our data suggest, first, that an anti-nuclear stance is becoming more prevalent, though slowly – see also Chapter 6. They suggest too, as Inglehart does, that this stance is part of the growth of post-materialist values. Post-materialists are, moreover, more sympathetic than others towards 'unorthodox' political activity and more likely, it appears, to prefer the claims of conscience to those of law. It would be foolish to predict from these findings that the future will thus be dominated by unlawful political protest actions on these or other issues. It would equally be foolish, however, to ignore the tendencies in that direction, particularly as it is among the young that pessimism about the prospect of war is most consistent and widespread.

References

BUTLER, D. and SLOMAN, A., *British Political Facts 1900-1979*, Macmillan, London (1980).

BUTLER, D. and STOKES, D.E., *Political Change in Britain*, Macmillan, London (1974).

HEATH, A., JOWELL, R. and CURTICE, J., *How Britain Votes*, Pergamon, Oxford (forthcoming, 1985).

INGLEHART, R., *The Silent Revolution: Changing Values and Political Styles among Western Publics*, Princeton University Press, Princeton N.J. (1977).

INGLEHART, R., 'Post-materialism in an Environment of Insecurity', *American Political Science Review 75*, (1981) pp. 880-900.

JOWELL, R. and AIREY, C. (eds.), *British Social Attitudes: The 1984 Report*, Gower, Aldershot (1984).

JOWELL, R. and HOINVILLE, G. (eds.), *Britain into Europe,* Croom Helm, London (1976).
SÄRLVIK, B., CREWE, I., *Decade of Dealignment,* Cambridge University Press, Cambridge (1983).
SÄRLVIK, B., CREWE, I., ALT, J. and FOX, A., 'Britain's Membership of the EEC: a Profile of Electoral Opinions in the Spring of 1974 – with a postscript on the Referendum', *European Journal of Political Research 4,* (1976) pp. 83-114.
VERBA, S., NIE, N.H. and KIM, J.O., *Participation and Political Equality,* Cambridge University Press, Cambridge (1978).
WEBB, N. and WYBROW, R., *The Gallup Report,* Sphere Books, London (1981).
WHITELEY, P., *The Electoral Future of the Labour Party,* University of Bristol (unpublished, 1984).
WORLD BANK, *World Development Report 1984,* Oxford University Press, Oxford (1984).

4.1 MEMBERSHIP OF EEC AND NATO (Q9 a, b) by sex, age and current/last social class

BASE: ALL RESPONDENTS	WEIGHTED BASE	SEX		18-24	25-34	35-54	55+	NO INF.	CURRENT / LAST SOCIAL CLASS				
		MALE	FEMALE						I,II	III NON MAN.	III MAN.	IV,V MAN.	NEVER WORKED /N.C.
UNWEIGHTED BASE	1675	780	895	217	309	525	610	14	352	380	383	388	172
WEIGHTED BASE	1645	775	871	214	311	517	590	14	341	378	369	380	177

Should Britain continue to be a member of the EEC or should it withdraw?

	WEIGHTED BASE	MALE	FEMALE	18-24	25-34	35-54	55+	NO INF.	I,II	III NON MAN.	III MAN.	IV,V MAN.	NEVER WORKED /N.C.
SHOULD CONTINUE	788 48%	381 49%	407 47%	92 43%	168 54%	260 50%	258 44%	10	234 69%	207 55%	142 38%	125 33%	80 45%
SHOULD WITHDRAW	746 45%	363 47%	383 44%	102 48%	125 40%	230 45%	286 48%	3	90 26%	141 37%	208 56%	226 59%	81 46%
DON'T KNOW	97 6%	24 3%	73 8%	17 8%	17 5%	20 4%	43 7%	1	16 5%	24 6%	16 4%	28 7%	13 7%
NOT ANSWERED	14 1%	7 1%	8 1%	3 1%	3 1%	7 1%	3 0%	0	1 0%	6 1%	4 1%	1 0%	3 2%

Should Britain continue to be a member of NATO or should it withdraw?

	WEIGHTED BASE	MALE	FEMALE	18-24	25-34	35-54	55+	NO INF.	I,II	III NON MAN.	III MAN.	IV,V MAN.	NEVER WORKED /N.C.
SHOULD CONTINUE	1304 79%	682 88%	622 71%	156 73%	249 80%	434 84%	455 77%	10	302 88%	315 83%	308 83%	250 66%	129 73%
SHOULD WITHDRAW	181 11%	74 10%	107 12%	29 14%	45 14%	48 9%	59 10%	0	26 8%	27 7%	36 10%	67 18%	26 14%
DON'T KNOW	147 9%	14 2%	133 15%	26 12%	16 5%	29 6%	72 12%	3	13 4%	30 8%	23 6%	60 16%	20 12%
NOT ANSWERED	14 1%	5 1%	9 1%	2 1%	2 1%	5 1%	5 1%	1	1 0%	6 .2%	3 1%	2 0%	3 1%

4.2 MEMBERSHIP OF EEC AND NATO (Q9 a, b) by detailed party identification

DETAILED PARTY IDENTIFICATION

Should Britain continue to be a member of the EEC or should it withdraw?

BASE: ALL RESPONDENTS	WEIGHTED BASE	CON: TOTAL	PART-ISAN	SYMP.	RESID. ID.	LAB: TOTAL	PART-ISAN	SYMP.	RESID. ID.	SDP/LIB/ALL: TOTAL	PART-ISAN	SYMP.	RESID. ID.	OTHER PARTY	NO POLIT. ALLEG.	OTHER D.K / N.A
UNWEIGHTED BASE	1675	640	388	172	80	595	326	168	101	220	68	83	69	24	105	91
WEIGHTED BASE	1645	635	384	167	85	575	317	160	98	219	72	80	67	28	102	86
SHOULD CONTINUE	788 48%	421 66%	269 70%	101 60%	51 61%	167 29%	80 25%	53 33%	35 36%	110 50%	39 54%	42 53%	28 42%	9	40 39%	41 47%
SHOULD WITHDRAW	746 45%	187 29%	99 26%	58 35%	30 35%	368 64%	220 69%	98 61%	50 51%	94 43%	30 41%	31 39%	33 49%	16	49 48%	31 36%
DON'T KNOW	97 6%	25 4%	14 4%	8 4%	3 4%	34 6%	15 5%	8 5%	11 11%	12 5%	2 2%	5 6%	6 8%	3	11 11%	13 15%
NOT ANSWERED	14 1%	2 0%	2 1%	0 0%	0 0%	6 1%	3 1%	2 1%	2 2%	3 1%	2 3%	1 1%	0 0%	0	2 2%	2 2%

Should Britain continue to be a member of NATO or should it withdraw?

BASE: ALL RESPONDENTS	WEIGHTED BASE	CON: TOTAL	PART-ISAN	SYMP.	RESID. ID.	LAB: TOTAL	PART-ISAN	SYMP.	RESID. ID.	SDP/LIB/ALL: TOTAL	PART-ISAN	SYMP.	RESID. ID.	OTHER PARTY	NO POLIT. ALLEG.	OTHER D.K / N.A
SHOULD CONTINUE	1304 79%	562 88%	350 91%	146 87%	66 78%	400 70%	224 71%	118 74%	57 59%	188 86%	65 91%	69 87%	53 80%	19	69 67%	65 76%
SHOULD WITHDRAW	181 11%	35 6%	11 3%	13 7%	12 14%	108 19%	56 18%	28 18%	23 24%	13 6%	1 1%	4 5%	8 12%	5	12 12%	8 9%
DON'T KNOW	147 9%	35 6%	20 5%	9 5%	7 8%	64 11%	36 11%	11 7%	17 17%	14 6%	4 5%	5 6%	6 8%	4	18 18%	11 13%
NOT ANSWERED	14 1%	3 0%	3 1%	0 0%	0 0%	4 1%	1 0%	3 2%	0 0%	3 1%	2 3%	1 1%	0 0%	0	3 3%	2 2%

4.3 BRITAIN'S LINKS WITH WESTERN EUROPE AND AMERICA (Q10)
by sex, age and current/last social class

BASE: ALL RESPONDENTS	WEIGHTED BASE	SEX MALE	SEX FEMALE	AGE 18-24	AGE 25-34	AGE 35-54	AGE 55+	NO INF.	I,II	III NON MAN.	III MAN.	IV,V	NEVER WORKED /N.C.
									(CURRENT / LAST SOCIAL CLASS)				
UNWEIGHTED BASE	1675	780	895	217	309	525	610	14	352	380	383	388	172
WEIGHTED BASE	1645	775	871	214	311	517	590	14	341	378	369	380	177
CLOSER LINKS WITH WESTERN EUROPE	870 53%	463 60%	408 47%	102 48%	180 58%	278 54%	304 51%	6	207 61%	197 52%	200 54%	183 48%	83 47%
CLOSER LINKS WITH AMERICA	346 21%	144 19%	202 23%	61 28%	63 20%	106 21%	113 19%	3	52 15%	83 22%	80 22%	96 25%	35 20%
or: BOTH EQUALLY	257 16%	124 16%	133 15%	27 13%	43 14%	95 18%	90 15%	2	67 20%	62 16%	54 15%	44 12%	31 17%
NEITHER	52 3%	23 3%	29 3%	6 3%	5 2%	11 2%	29 5%	1	10 3%	7 2%	14 4%	16 4%	6 3%
DONT KNOW	115 7%	20 3%	95 11%	16 7%	18 6%	24 5%	55 9%	2	5 1%	27 7%	21 6%	41 11%	21 12%
NOT ANSWERED	5 0%	2 0%	3 0%	2 1%	2 1%	1 0%	0 0%	0	0 0%	2 1%	1 0%	0 0%	2 1%

4.4 BRITAIN'S LINKS WITH WESTERN EUROPE AND AMERICA (Q10)
by detailed party identification

DETAILED PARTY IDENTIFICATION

BASE: ALL RESPONDENTS	WEIGHTED BASE	CON: TOTAL	CON PART-ISAN	CON SYMP.	CON RESID. ID.	LAB: TOTAL	LAB PART-ISAN	LAB SYMP.	LAB RESID. ID.	SDP/LIB/ALL: TOTAL	SDP PART-ISAN	SDP SYMP.	SDP RESID. ID.	OTHER PARTY	NO POLIT. ALLEG.	OTHER /D.K /N.A
UNWEIGHTED BASE	1675	640	388	172	80	595	317	181	87	220	125	45	50	24	105	91
WEIGHTED BASE	1645	635	384	167	85	575	317	160	98	219	72	80	67	28	102	86
CLOSER LINKS WITH WESTERN EUROPE	870 53%	327 51%	196 51%	86 52%	45 53%	317 55%	181 57%	87 54%	49 50%	125 57%	45 63%	50 63%	30 45%	14 50%	44 43%	43 50%
CLOSER LINKS WITH AMERICA	346 21%	143 23%	82 21%	43 26%	17 21%	136 24%	59 19%	43 27%	13 13%	33 15%	9 13%	13 15%	11 19%	4	19 19%	11 13%
or: BOTH EQUALLY	257 16%	129 20%	91 24%	21 12%	17 20%	59 10%	40 13%	13 8%	6 6%	37 17%	12 17%	12 15%	13 19%	3	12 12%	13 15%
NEITHER	52 3%	7 1%	4 1%	3 2%	0 0%	22 4%	16 5%	4 2%	2 2%	6 3%	3 4%	2 3%	1 1%	1	9 9%	4 5%
DONT KNOW	115 7%	28 4%	10 2%	13 8%	5 6%	41 7%	21 7%	12 8%	8 8%	15 7%	1 2%	4 5%	10 15%	0	16 15%	15 17%
NOT ANSWERED	5 0%	1 0%	1 0%	1 0%	0 0%	0 0%	0 0%	0 0%	0 0%	2 1%	1 1%	1 1%	1 1%	0	2 2%	0 0%

4.5 SITING OF NUCLEAR MISSILES IN BRITAIN (Q11 a, b)
by sex, age and current/last social class

	WEIGHTED BASE	SEX		AGE					CURRENT / LAST SOCIAL CLASS				
BASE: ALL RESPONDENTS		MALE	FEMALE	18-24	25-34	35-54	55+	NO INF.	I,II	III NON MAN.	III MAN.	IV,V	NEVER WORKED /N.C.
UNWEIGHTED BASE	1675	780	895	217	309	525	610	14	352	380	383	388	172
WEIGHTED BASE	1645	775	871	214	311	517	590	14	341	378	369	380	177

Do you think that the siting of American nuclear missiles in Britain makes Britain a safer or a less safe place to live?

	WEIGHTED BASE	MALE	FEMALE	18-24	25-34	35-54	55+	NO INF.	I,II	III NON MAN.	III MAN.	IV,V	NEVER WORKED /N.C.
MAKES BRITAIN SAFER	590 36%	301 39%	290 33%	61 28%	104 33%	190 37%	229 39%	6	140 41%	143 38%	134 36%	115 30%	58 33%
MAKES BRITAIN LESS SAFE	841 51%	377 49%	464 53%	131 61%	171 55%	255 49%	281 48%	3	155 46%	191 51%	190 51%	222 58%	83 47%
NO DIFFERENCE	49 3%	34 4%	15 2%	3 2%	12 4%	20 4%	14 2%	0	14 4%	10 3%	14 4%	7 2%	3 2%
DON'T KNOW	156 9%	58 7%	98 11%	16 7%	22 7%	50 10%	63 11%	4	31 9%	32 8%	30 8%	34 9%	29 16%
NOT ANSWERED	10 1%	5 1%	5 1%	3 1%	2 1%	1 0%	3 1%	1	1 0%	2 1%	2 1%	1 0%	4 2%

Do you think that having our own independent nuclear missiles makes Britain a safer or a less safe place to live?

	WEIGHTED BASE	MALE	FEMALE	18-24	25-34	35-54	55+	NO INF.	I,II	III NON MAN.	III MAN.	IV,V	NEVER WORKED /N.C.
MAKES BRITAIN SAFER	923 56%	455 59%	469 54%	106 50%	165 53%	295 57%	352 60%	6	197 58%	213 56%	210 57%	204 54%	100 56%
MAKES BRITAIN LESS SAFE	534 32%	248 32%	287 33%	91 43%	112 36%	159 31%	169 29%	4	108 32%	115 30%	125 34%	136 36%	51 29%
NO DIFFERENCE	31 2%	19 3%	12 1%	1 1%	9 3%	10 2%	11 2%	0	7 2%	9 2%	11 3%	2 1%	2 1%
DON'T KNOW	144 9%	45 6%	99 11%	12 6%	22 7%	52 10%	55 9%	3	26 8%	39 10%	22 6%	38 10%	20 11%
NOT ANSWERED	12 1%	8 1%	4 0%	3 1%	2 1%	2 0%	4 1%	1	3 1%	3 1%	2 1%	0 0%	4 2%

4.6 SITING OF NUCLEAR MISSILES IN BRITAIN (Q11 a, b) by detailed party identification

DETAILED PARTY IDENTIFICATION

Do you think the siting of American nuclear missiles in Britain makes Britain a safer or less safe place to live?

BASE: ALL RESPONDENTS	WEIGHTED BASE	CON: TOTAL	CON PART-ISAN	CON SYMP.	CON RESID. ID.	LAB: TOTAL	LAB PART-ISAN	LAB SYMP.	LAB RESID. ID.	SDP/LIB/ALL: TOTAL	SDP PART-ISAN	SDP SYMP.	SDP RESID. ID.	OTHER PARTY	NO POLIT. ALLEG.	OTHER D.K / N.A
UNWEIGHTED BASE	1675	640	388	172	80	595	326	168	101	220	68	83	69	24	105	91
WEIGHTED BASE	1645	635	384	167	85	575	317	160	98	219	72	80	67	28	102	86
MAKES BRITAIN SAFER	590 36%	329 52%	220 57%	72 43%	37 43%	123 21%	52 17%	47 30%	24 24%	73 33%	29 40%	23 29%	22 32%	4	33 33%	28 32%
MAKES BRITAIN LESS SAFE	841 51%	216 34%	110 29%	69 41%	38 45%	408 71%	245 77%	100 63%	63 64%	112 51%	32 44%	44 56%	36 53%	23	48 47%	34 39%
NO DIFFERENCE	49 3%	23 4%	13 3%	8 5%	2 3%	8 1%	4 1%	4 2%	1 1%	11 5%	6 8%	4 5%	1 1%	1	0 0%	6 7%
DON'T KNOW	156 9%	65 10%	38 10%	18 11%	8 9%	33 6%	16 5%	9 5%	9 9%	21 10%	5 7%	8 10%	9 13%	1	17 17%	18 21%
NOT ANSWERED	10 1%	3 0%	3 1%	0 0%	0 0%	0 0%	0 0%	0 0%	2 2%	2 1%	1 1%	1 1%	0 0%	0	3 3%	0 0%

Do you think that having our own independent nuclear missiles makes Britain a safer or less safe place to live?

BASE: ALL RESPONDENTS	WEIGHTED BASE	CON: TOTAL	CON PART-ISAN	CON SYMP.	CON RESID. ID.	LAB: TOTAL	LAB PART-ISAN	LAB SYMP.	LAB RESID. ID.	SDP/LIB/ALL: TOTAL	SDP PART-ISAN	SDP SYMP.	SDP RESID. ID.	OTHER PARTY	NO POLIT. ALLEG.	OTHER D.K / N.A
MAKES BRITAIN SAFER	923 56%	439 69%	278 72%	113 68%	48 57%	258 45%	128 40%	84 53%	46 47%	118 54%	47 65%	34 43%	37 55%	12	51 50%	44 51%
MAKES BRITAIN LESS SAFE	534 32%	118 19%	58 15%	35 21%	25 30%	277 48%	165 52%	69 43%	42 43%	67 31%	15 20%	24 43%	18 27%	14	34 34%	24 28%
NO DIFFERENCE	31 2%	17 3%	11 3%	3 3%	2 3%	5 1%	5 1%	0 0%	1 1%	7 3%	4 5%	2 3%	1 1%	0	0 0%	2 2%
DON'T KNOW	144 9%	56 9%	33 9%	14 9%	9 11%	32 6%	18 6%	6 4%	8 8%	24 11%	6 8%	8 10%	10 15%	3	13 13%	16 18%
NOT ANSWERED	12 1%	4 1%	4 1%	0 0%	0 0%	1 0%	1 0%	0 0%	1 1%	3 1%	1 1%	1 1%	1 1%	0	3 3%	0 0%

4.7 NUCLEAR DISARMAMENT (Q12)
by sex, age and current/last social class

BASE: ALL RESPONDENTS	WEIGHTED BASE	SEX		AGE					CURRENT / LAST SOCIAL CLASS				
		MALE	FEMALE	18-24	25-34	35-54	55+	NO INF.	I,II	III NON MAN.	III MAN.	IV,V	NEVER WORKED /N.C.
UNWEIGHTED BASE	1675	780	895	217	309	525	610	14	352	380	383	388	172
WEIGHTED BASE	1645	775	871	214	311	517	590	14	341	378	369	380	177
BRITAIN SHOULD RID ITSELF OF NUCLEAR WEAPONS UNILATERALLY	373 23%	174 22%	199 23%	59 27%	83 27%	112 22%	117 20%	2	72 21%	75 20%	83 22%	102 27%	41 23%
BRITAIN SHOULD KEEP ITS NUCLEAR WEAPONS UNTIL OTHERS REDUCE THEIRS	1207 73%	579 75%	628 72%	149 70%	223 72%	381 74%	446 76%	9	261 77%	288 76%	280 76%	265 70%	113 64%
NEITHER OF THESE	48 3%	18 2%	30 3%	2 1%	4 1%	21 4%	20 3%	1	8 2%	11 3%	4 1%	11 3%	14 8%
DON'T KNOW	10 1%	1 0%	9 1%	1 0%	0 0%	1 0%	7 1%	1	0 0%	3 1%	3 1%	2 0%	5 3%
NOT ANSWERED	7 0%	3 0%	4 0%	3 1%	2 1%	1 0%	0 0%	1	0 0%	2 1%	1 0%	0 0%	4 2%

4.8 NUCLEAR DISARMAMENT (Q12)
by detailed party identification

DETAILED PARTY IDENTIFICATION

BASE: ALL RESPONDENTS	WEIGHTED BASE	CON :				LAB :				SDP/LIB/ALL :				OTHER PARTY ALLEG.	NO POLIT. ALLEG.	OTHER / D.K / N.A
		TOTAL	PART-ISAN	SYMP.	RESID. ID.	TOTAL	PART-ISAN	SYMP.	RESID. ID.	TOTAL	PART-ISAN	SYMP.	RESID. ID.			
UNWEIGHTED BASE	1675	640	388	172	80	595	326	168	101	220	68	83	69	24	105	91
WEIGHTED BASE	1645	635	384	167	85	575	317	160	98	219	72	80	67	28	102	86
BRITAIN SHOULD RID ITSELF OF NUCLEAR WEAPONS UNILATERALLY	373 23%	77 12%	34 9%	22 13%	21 25%	212 37%	137 43%	48 30%	27 28%	33 15%	7 9%	17 22%	10 15%	11	22 22%	18 21%
BRITAIN SHOULD KEEP ITS NUCLEAR WEAPONS UNTIL OTHERS REDUCE THEIRS	1207 73%	541 85%	337 88%	142 85%	62 74%	347 60%	171 54%	109 68%	67 68%	174 79%	60 83%	58 73%	55 82%	15	69 67%	63 73%
NEITHER OF THESE	48 3%	13 2%	10 3%	3 2%	0 0%	13 2%	10 3%	1 1%	3 3%	7 3%	4 6%	2 3%	1 1%	3	8 8%	4 5%
DON'T KNOW	10 1%	3 0%	2 0%	0 0%	1 2%	3 0%	0 0%	3 2%	0 0%	3 1%	1 1%	1 1%	1 1%	0	1 1%	1 1%
NOT ANSWERED	7 0%	2 0%	2 0%	2 1%	0 0%	0 0%	0 0%	0 0%	1 1%	2 1%	1 1%	1 1%	0 0%	0	2 2%	0 0%

4.9 THREATS TO WORLD PEACE (Q14)
by sex, age and school leaving age

		SEX		AGE					SCHOOL LEAVING AGE				
BASE: ALL RESPONDENTS		MALE	FEMALE	18-24	25-34	35-54	55+	NO INF	16 OR UNDER	17-18	19+	STILL IN F.T. EDUC.	NO INF
UNWEIGHTED BASE	1675	780	895	217	309	525	610	14	1297	215	122	27	14
WEIGHTED BASE	1645	775	871	214	311	517	590	14	1265	222	119	27	12
AMERICA IS A GREATER THREAT THAN RUSSIA	183 (11%)	97 (12%)	87 (10%)	28 (13%)	34 (11%)	52 (10%)	67 (11%)	2	154 (12%)	19 (9%)	7 (6%)	1	2
RUSSIA IS A GREATER THREAT THAN AMERICA	426 (26%)	180 (23%)	246 (28%)	47 (22%)	53 (17%)	121 (23%)	201 (34%)	4	342 (27%)	46 (21%)	32 (26%)	6	1
RUSSIA AND AMERICA ARE EQUALLY GREAT THREATS	889 (54%)	440 (57%)	449 (52%)	119 (56%)	200 (64%)	299 (58%)	264 (45%)	7	650 (51%)	137 (62%)	76 (63%)	20	7
NEITHER IS A THREAT	84 (5%)	44 (6%)	40 (5%)	10 (5%)	15 (5%)	32 (6%)	27 (5%)	0	70 (6%)	11 (5%)	2 (2%)	0	1
DONT KNOW	54 (3%)	10 (1%)	44 (5%)	7 (3%)	7 (2%)	12 (2%)	27 (5%)	0	44 (4%)	6 (3%)	3 (3%)	0	1
NOT ANSWERED	10 (1%)	4 (1%)	6 (1%)	3 (1%)	2 (1%)	1 (0%)	3 (1%)	1	6 (0%)	2 (1%)	0 (0%)	0	1

4.10 THREATS TO WORLD PEACE (Q14)
by detailed party identification

DETAILED PARTY IDENTIFICATION

		CON :				LAB :				SDP/LIB/ALL :				OTHER PARTY ID.	NO POLIT. ALLEG.	OTHER / D.K / N.A
BASE: ALL RESPONDENTS		TOTAL	PART-ISAN	SYMP.	RESID. ID.	TOTAL	PART-ISAN	SYMP.	RESID. ID.	TOTAL	PART-ISAN	SYMP.	RESID. ID.			
UNWEIGHTED BASE	1675	640	388	172	80	595	326	168	101	220	68	83	69	24	105	91
WEIGHTED BASE	1645	635	384	167	85	575	317	160	98	219	72	80	67	28	102	86
AMERICA IS A GREATER THREAT THAN RUSSIA	183 (11%)	49 (8%)	26 (7%)	14 (8%)	9 (11%)	96 (17%)	66 (21%)	17 (11%)	13 (13%)	20 (9%)	5 (7%)	6 (8%)	10 (15%)	2	9 (9%)	7 (9%)
RUSSIA IS A GREATER THREAT THAN AMERICA	426 (26%)	218 (34%)	141 (37%)	50 (30%)	28 (33%)	113 (20%)	49 (15%)	36 (23%)	28 (28%)	45 (20%)	18 (25%)	17 (21%)	10 (15%)	8	19 (19%)	23 (27%)
RUSSIA AND AMERICA ARE EQUALLY GREAT THREATS	889 (54%)	315 (50%)	180 (47%)	98 (59%)	37 (44%)	322 (56%)	185 (58%)	96 (60%)	40 (41%)	140 (64%)	46 (64%)	51 (64%)	42 (63%)	17 (61%)	51 (50%)	46 (53%)
NEITHER IS A THREAT	84 (5%)	40 (6%)	27 (7%)	8 (5%)	4 (5%)	21 (4%)	8 (3%)	8 (5%)	6 (6%)	8 (4%)	2 (3%)	4 (5%)	2 (3%)	1 (4%)	9 (9%)	5 (6%)
DONT KNOW	54 (3%)	11 (2%)	7 (2%)	2 (1%)	2 (2%)	22 (4%)	8 (3%)	4 (3%)	10 (10%)	5 (2%)	1 (1%)	1 (1%)	3 (4%)	0 (0%)	11 (11%)	5 (6%)
NOT ANSWERED	10 (1%)	3 (0%)	1 (0%)	1 (1%)	1 (1%)	2 (0%)	1 (0%)	1 (1%)	0 (0%)	1 (1%)	1 (1%)	0 (0%)	0 (0%)	0 (0%)	3 (3%)	0 (0%)

5 Right and wrong in public and private life

*Michael Johnston and Douglas Wood**

Rules of social behaviour

When the deeds of John G. L. Poulson, T. Dan Smith, George Pottinger and company came to light in the early 1970s, the scandal, investigations and reports which followed raised fundamental questions about the rules defining acceptable and unacceptable conduct in Britain. The debates which were touched off have hardly settled the issue. They have rather shown us how many different conceptions of right and wrong co-exist in British society, and how those systems of rules can conflict. The law is different for the public and private sectors. There may be nothing legally wrong in a company manager behaving in a way which could lead to criminal charges against a public official. Also, officials may develop informal rules very different from those spelled out in the law, as Doig (1984) and Chibnall and Saunders (1977) have pointed out. And citizens will develop rules of their own out of everyday experiences within circles of co-workers (Mars, 1982) and acquaintances (Henry, 1978).

In this chapter, we examine the results from a section of our questionnaire intended to establish how people judged a series of situations involving members of the public, private sector employees and public officials. From people's answers on the rightness and wrongness of these situations, we can try to identify some of the considerations people take into account and some of the rules they employ in judging social behaviour.

These social rules are important in a number of ways. First, citizens' "intrinsic trust" (Marsh, 1977, p.117) in the honesty of political leaders and institutions, and their willingness to abide by the laws made by those

---

* Michael Johnston is Associate Professor of Political Science at the University of Pittsburgh.
Douglas Wood is a Research Director at Social and Community Planning Research, London.

institutions, depend in part upon their evaluation of official conduct. Political trust may influence aspects of political behaviour, from voting to protest (Marsh, 1977).

Secondly, popular conceptions of right and wrong are important because the law itself is often vague. The Prevention of Corruption Act of 1906, as Chibnall and Saunders (1977, pp.145-6) note, penalised "any agent [who] . . . corruptly accepts or obtains . . . from any person . . . any gift or consideration as an inducement or reward for doing or forebearing to do . . . any act in relation to his principal's affairs or business." But what is the meaning of "corruptly"? This problem was remedied somewhat by the 1916 Prevention of Corruption Act. But in the trial of Poulson and Pottinger, prosecutors still made repeated appeals to 'common sense' norms governing friendships, transactions and secrecy in arguing that what Poulson and Pottinger saw as friendly gifts were in fact bribes:

> "What friend gives a house to a friend? The nature of the gifts was to take every financial responsibility for the man's whole living. He was living in a Poulson house, driving a Poulson car, wearing Poulson suits, and travelling at Poulson's expense . . . The gifts point not to a friendship, but to buying a man, making him dependent." (Quoted in Chibnall and Saunders, 1977, p.147.)

Thus, popular conceptions of right and wrong were critical in filling in the gaps of the law (Chibnall and Saunders, 1977).

Thirdly, fiddling and the black economy have long been a fact of life (see, for example, Mars, 1982; and Henry, 1978). Whether or not people fiddle depends, in part, no doubt, upon whether or not they see it as wrong. An understanding of how people view the ethical aspects of everyday situations is a first step toward understanding the black economy from the inside out.

We are, in short, concerned with one of the basic problems in the relationship between state and society – the extent to which official rules agree with, or differ from, popular conceptions of right and wrong. "[It] is important that public and private morality share a degree of compatibility or similarity. Any divergence or predominance in relation to one may encourage a tendency to neglect or ignore the other . . ." (Doig, 1984, p.349). In contrast, Small (1976) reminds us that the law and morality are different things, and that to neglect this fact is to risk concluding not only that all laws are moral, but also that morality consists solely of not breaking the law.

Judging 'wrongness'

Because of severe limits on space, the section of the questionnaire dealing with these issues was able to identify only a few of the most prominent features of the area rather than mapping it in detail. The method we used was one developed to study public attitudes to political corruption in the USA (Johnston, 1985). It involves presenting people with a series of situations and asking them to judge the rightness or wrongness of each one. By varying the elements of the situations and therefore the focus of the judgements, we sought to establish the sorts of factor which lead to differing judgements.

We asked people to judge situations on a four-point scale:

> *It is not at all wrong*
> *It is a bit wrong*
> *It is wrong*
> *It is seriously wrong*

There was much discussion about the form of this scale while the questions were being devised. There were three main problems.

First, we debated whether to ask people to score situations ("How many out of ten . . .?") or to rate them on a verbal scale. We decided to use a verbal scale, partly because scoring made the questions sound trivial, partly because we could not put any meaning to the top end of a numerical scale of wrongness.

The second problem was the nature of the verbal scale. The American work on which our questions were based used a verbal scale of *corruption*. But our focus was less explicitly political than that of the American work and, in any case, 'corruption' seems to have a more restricted meaning in Britain than it does in the USA. Instead, we chose to use a scale of wrongness. We did not specify whether 'wrong' meant morally wrong, legally wrong or wrong by reference to some other standard. This may leave the nature of judgements ambiguous, but it seems to us that such ambiguity is inevitable. Situations often arise that involve a mixture of legal and moral considerations, or where loyalty or friendship conflict with other expectations. People's judgements of a situation will vary according to the weight they attach to its various elements. In using a simple scale of wrongness we were aiming at the final overall evaluation, whatever the considerations that led to it.

The third issue was how many positions to have on the scale. How many levels of right or wrong can people actually distinguish? An initial suggestion was for a scale of two points only. If something is wrong, it is wrong and there is not much more to say. But this did not seem to fit well to the judgements people actually make. In piloting, we used a three-point scale (nothing wrong, wrong, seriously wrong) and, because of the pilot results, we extended this to four points. In the conclusions to this chapter we suggest that we might have gone further.

Private transactions

Most of the situations we asked people to judge involved company managers, public officials or policemen. Since few people hold these sorts of jobs, answering the questions meant judging the behaviour of others. To put these judgements into some perspective and to bring things a little closer to home, we also asked for judgements of three fairly ordinary situations, probably within the experience of most of the sample.

The three situations we chose were:

> *A householder is having a repair job done by a local plumber. He is told that if he pays cash he will not be charged VAT. So he pays cash.*

> *A man offers the dustmen £5 to take away rubbish they are not supposed to pick up.*

A man gives a £5 note for goods he is buying in a big store. By mistake, he is given change for a £10 note. He notices but keeps the change.

Once people had judged each of these three transactions on the 'wrongness' scale, we followed up with a further question:

Might you do this if the situation came up?

The ways in which people judged these situations were:

	Evading VAT	Bribing dustmen	Pocketing wrong change
	%	%	%
Nothing wrong in it	31	32	6
A bit wrong	31	35	15
Wrong	32	29	61
Seriously wrong	3	3	16
Don't know	3	2	1

Views on VAT evasion and bribing dustmen were nearly identical. In both cases the sample divided more or less equally between the first three points on the scale. Pocketing wrong change was judged much more harshly. Almost all saw something wrong in it. Three in four saw it as wrong or seriously wrong.

The views people expressed about what they themselves might do in these situations should not be taken as reliably predicting their behaviour. It is a commonplace of survey research on delinquency and offending that admissions of actual deviant behaviour (shoplifting, drug use, etc.) tend to be improbably low. There is no reason why this should not also apply to statements about possible actions which might be subject to disapproval. But the comparison between answers on different situations remains interesting. The answers were:

	Evade VAT	Bribe dustmen	Pocket wrong change
	%	%	%
I might do it	66	58	18
Don't know/no answer	7	4	5
I would not do it	27	38	77

In each case, the number of people who thought they might do things was considerably greater than the number who saw nothing wrong in them. Two in three said they might connive at VAT evasion, even though two in three had said that they saw something wrong in it. Fewer, but still well over half, said that they might bribe the dustmen. About one in five said they might pocket the wrong change, although only one in twenty had said there was nothing wrong in doing so.

These answers follow the pattern of people's judgements on how wrong these things broadly are, but by no means exactly. To see more clearly what is happening, we can look at the proportions of those rating each action on each point of our scale of wrongness who *also* said that they might do it.

	Judgement of situation			
	Nothing wrong in it	A bit wrong	Wrong	Seriously wrong
Might do it				
Evade VAT	95%	78%	37%	19%
Bribe dustmen	87%	66%	23%	7%
Pocket change	86%	43%	10%	3%

A very high proportion (nearly four in five) of those who said it was a bit wrong to evade VAT also said that, faced with the situation, they might do so. But only just over two in five of those who said it was a bit wrong to pocket the wrong change thought they might do that themselves. Bribing dustmen came in between. There is a similar pattern in the answers of those who thought these things wrong or seriously wrong.

So people's statements about their own possible behaviour did not follow wholly from their judgements of how wrong that behaviour might be. A possible explanation lies in the provenance of each situation. In the case of VAT evasion, the plumber takes the initiative in suggesting to the householder that they cheat the government to their mutual advantage. With the dustmen, it is the householder who proposes the mutually beneficial breach of the rules. Perhaps people see themselves as more likely to be led into temptation than to lead others into it, or perhaps the possibility of being tempted is easier to admit. In the case of pocketing change, the shop assistant is neither a co-initiator nor a co-beneficiary. There is no 'informal agreement'. Responsibility for the action rests solely with the respondent.

People's judgements on these everyday situations varied sharply with age, older people tending to judge more harshly. But keeping the wrong change was generally taken much more seriously than VAT evasion or bribing dustmen by people of all ages. The variation by age in the numbers who thought they might actually do things followed the same pattern.

	18-24 %	25-34 %	35-54 %	55+ %
Might do it				
Evade VAT	80	80	73	50
Bribe dustmen	70	65	63	45
Pocket change	40	27	17	6

A further factor related to people's judgements of the three situations was religion. Those who professed religious beliefs tended to be more censorious than those who did not and, among the religious, those who attended services regularly judged the three situations more harshly than those who were less frequent in observance, as the following table shows.

	No religious beliefs	Religious – attend services:		
		Once a year or less	2-26 times a year	Weekly
	%	%	%	%
Might do it				
Evade VAT	75	65	65	50
Bribe dustmen	67	55	55	44
Pocket change	28	18	12	3

Age and religion are, of course, related to each other. Older people are more likely to say they have religious beliefs and more likely to be regular attenders at services. Only 19% of people aged 55 or over said they had no religion as compared with 61% of those under 25. Nonetheless, age and religion did appear to have independent effects and to reinforce each other. Taking attendance at services twice a year as a minimum definition of observance, the proportions who said they might keep the wrong change, analysed by religious observance within age group, were:

	Religious observers	Non-observers
Might pocket wrong change		
18-34	15%	37%
35-54	12%	20%
55+	3%	8%

We cannot show a full table in more detail, since some of the cells (particularly those for young observers) become too small to produce reliable data. The extremes, however, were that 45% of those under 25 who professed no religion said they might pocket the wrong change as compared with no-one aged 55 or over who attended services once a week.

Relative to the differences by age and by religious observance, differences in judgement of the three situations between other subgroups of the sample were small. There was no appreciable difference in judgements of the three situations between men and women, although men were a little more likely to say that they themselves might do each of the three things. There was no clear pattern of difference by Social Class, as conventionally measured through occupation. And there was no difference whatever by party identity.

Public servants and private sector managers

We wanted also to see whether people have different standards for the behaviour of public servants and the behaviour of managers in the private sector. As a test of this, we asked people to make two separate judgements of each of four situations. The situations can broadly be described as expensive entertainment, accepting gifts, fiddling expenses, and soliciting gifts. For one judgement, we put a private sector manager in the situation. For the second, we replaced the manager with a council official. We chose a council official rather than a civil servant on the assumption that the council official is a more familiar figure.

Entertaining actual or potential private customers is a commonplace of private sector business. The entertainment of public officials by businesses at least on a moderate scale, may be less common but is not infrequent. In fact, the question of appropriate practice in this area was a matter of much dispute as long ago as during the Poulson trials. We asked people to judge two situations:

A firm selling products to another company regularly takes a manager in that company to expensive lunches.

A firm supplying services to the council regularly takes a council official to expensive lunches.

People's judgements of these two situations were:

| | Expensive entertainment of: | |
	company manager %	council official %
Nothing wrong in it	39	22
A bit wrong	27	22
Wrong	26	41
Seriously wrong	6	13
Don't know	2	2

As far as the private sector is concerned, six out of ten people saw something wrong in regular expensive entertainment. But only three in ten saw it as more than just a bit wrong. So judgements on private sector entertainment came very close to the judgements made on VAT evasion and bribing dustmen. And, as we have seen, these were things most people thought they themselves might do if given the chance. We cannot tell, of course, whether the same pattern of answers would apply to this transaction. Unlike the other two private transactions, business entertainment is outside the common experience of many of our respondents.

There was a substantial difference between judgements on private sector entertaining and judgements on entertaining of the public sector. Three-quarters of the sample saw something wrong in entertainment for council officials. Half thought it more than just a bit wrong. It was judged more harshly than VAT evasion or bribing dustmen, although not quite as harshly as pocketing the wrong change.

The second practice we looked at was the business gift. Accepting such gifts would normally be a breach of the terms of service of public officials. It would be variably regarded by private sector employers. The situations we asked people to judge were:

A company manager accepts a Christmas present worth £50 from a firm from which he buys products.

A council official accepts a Christmas present worth £50 from a private firm that supplies services to the council.

Judgements on these situations were:

| | Presents for: | |
| | company manager | council official |
	%	%
Nothing wrong in it	39	13
A bit wrong	23	14
Wrong	29	43
Seriously wrong	7	28
Don't know	2	3

Views on gifts in the private sector were virtually identical to views on private sector entertainment. Views on gifts to public sector officials were much harsher, and considerably harsher than views on public sector entertainment. Perhaps the official's acceptance of a specific gift, even under the guise of a 'Christmas present', was perceived as more of an explicit *quid pro quo* than the same official regularly accepting lunches. As many as 85% saw something wrong in a council official accepting a gift worth £50. A quarter saw it as seriously wrong. This was significantly higher than the number who thought it seriously wrong to pocket £5 of wrong change.

The third practice we looked at was the fiddled expenses claim – something which would be seen as illegitimate by both public and private sector employers and that could, in theory, form a basis for prosecution. The situations we asked people to judge were:

A company employee exaggerates his claims for travel expenses over a period and makes £50.

A council official exaggerates his claims for travel expenses over a period and makes £50.

Judgements on these two situations were:

| | Expenses fiddled by: | |
| | company manager | council official |
	%	%
Nothing wrong in it	4	2
A bit wrong	17	12
Wrong	54	52
Seriously wrong	23	33
Don't know	2	2

We have seen earlier that entertainment and gifts for the private sector manager, things which could be regarded as perks, were generally seen as wrong, but not much more so than evading VAT. Here we move to the active fiddle and judgements become a good deal harsher. Almost everyone saw something wrong in a manager fiddling his expenses. More than three in four saw it as wrong or seriously wrong. But, to put it in perspective, judgements of a manager fiddling £50 in expenses were only a little more severe than judgements of a member of the public pocketing £5 of wrong change.

As with the two situations already discussed, a council official fiddling his expenses was judged more harshly than a private sector manager. But the difference was smaller than it was for entertainment and accepting gifts.

We also asked for people's views on the active soliciting of gifts from suppliers. The situations we put to them were:

A manager asks a firm from which he buys products for a £50 gift for himself.

A council official asks a firm that supplies services to the council for a £50 gift for himself.

Judgements on these two situations were:

	Gifts solicited by:	
	company manager	council official
	%	%
Nothing wrong in it	2	1
A bit wrong	6	4
Wrong	46	38
Seriously wrong	44	56
Don't know	2	1

Views on this sort of behaviour were, overall, much more severe than views on any of the situations so far discussed. Judgements were harsh for both managers and officials. The official was judged more severely but, as with fiddling expenses, the difference was much less than it was for entertainment or accepting gifts.

To summarise, there were, overall, clear differences between people's judgements of the situations we put before them. Soliciting gifts was judged more harshly than fiddling expenses, whether it was done by public or private sector workers. And, whoever was doing it, fiddling expenses was judged more harshly than accepting gifts or accepting entertainment. For council officials, accepting gifts was judged more harshly than entertainment. In all four situations, judgements were more severe if a public sector official rather than a private sector manager was involved. The distinctions drawn are best shown by a cross-analysis, for each situation, of the judgements on council officials as against private sector managers.

We used only four situations as examples and the pattern is not completely regular. But the suggestion in the figures is that the more the situation involves active 'taking' or soliciting, and the more severely a situation is judged overall, the less difference it makes whether it involves someone in the public or someone in the private sector. People had higher expectations of the standards of the public sector, but especially over smaller things.

Rating for official compared with manager:	Expensive entertainment %	Accepting gifts %	Fiddling expenses %	Soliciting gifts %
More censorious of council official	37	53	24	21
Same	56	40	66	70
Less censorious of council official	5	3	2	2
Unclear	3	3	2	2

We go on now to discuss differences in ratings between subgroups of the public. One general point about the results of subgroup analysis needs to be stressed first. The differences we will report are in *rating* rather than ranking. They are differences, sometimes quite large, in evaluations of the degree of 'wrongness' of situations. But in all the subgroup analyses we have carried out the relative ranking of situations remains virtually constant. Specifically, all subgroups rated all situations more seriously when they involved public officials than when they involved private sector managers. So the differences we are discussing are between subgroups in the general severity of their judgements, or between their evaluations of individual situations too small to affect their ranking relative to other situations.

As with the personal transactions discussed earlier, the most important factor was age. For three of the four pairs: entertainment, the acceptance of gifts and the fiddling of expenses; judgements tended to be progressively harsher with increasing age. This pattern is consistent with the results of the American research on judgements of "corruptness" (Johnston, 1985). This did not apply, however, to the fourth pair, the soliciting of gifts. Judgements of this pair of situations, which overall were harshest, showed no clear age pattern.

Proportion thinking it wrong or seriously wrong	18-24 %	25-34 %	35-54 %	55+ %
Expensive entertainment				
for a manager	22	26	34	37
for a council official	39	48	56	61
Gifts accepted				
by a manager	22	32	38	42
by a council official	45	62	77	81
Expenses fiddled				
by a manager	65	68	82	83
by a council official	73	77	90	89
Soliciting gifts				
by a manager	86	86	95	89
by a council official	91	93	97	93

When discussing personal situations, we noted the relationship between religious observance and age, but showed also that religious observance had an independent relationship to people's views. In the context of the behaviour of managers and officials there was also a relationship between frequent religious observance and harsher views on expensive entertainment, accepting gifts and fiddling expenses. But the relationship was not as strong as it was for the personal situations, and if standardised for age, it virtually disappeared. Not surprisingly, perhaps, religion appeared to have more influence on evaluations of everyday personal transactions than it did on judgements of more distant relationships in business and government.

But other factors, which were not relevant to the more personal situations, did appear to relate to views about the behaviour of managers and officials. One of these was party identification. Labour identifiers tended to take a more severe view than Conservatives of expensive entertainment and of managers accepting presents.

	Party identification	
Proportion thinking it	Conservative	Labour
wrong or seriously wrong	%	%
Expensive entertainment		
for a manager	27	40
for a council official	50	61
Gifts accepted		
by a manager	32	40

There was a smaller difference by party identification in views on council officials accepting gifts but there were no notable differences in views on fiddling expenses or soliciting gifts. Conservatives, in other words, were more tolerant than Labour identifiers of executive perks, but political opinions had no effect on judgements of executive fiddles or of more seriously regarded forms of executive wrong doing. Once again, respondents' personal characteristics seemed to affect judgements more strongly when the behaviour in question lay within an ethically "grey zone" (Noel-Baker, 1961). Where wrong doing was more clear-cut by formal standards, subgroup variations were smaller.

For those respondents with jobs, a further relevant factor was whether they themselves worked in the public or the private sector of the economy. Public sector workers tended to take a more censorious view of all four situations, whether they involved council officials or managers. They appeared to expect higher standards overall, but particularly from the private sector. So whereas the judgements of public sector workers were a bit harsher than those of private sector workers when a *council official* was involved they were a good deal harsher than those of private sector workers if the person involved was a company manager. For entertainment and the acceptance of gifts, the detailed comparison is shown in the following table. Answers on fiddling expenses and soliciting gifts followed a similar pattern. We saw earlier that Social Class had no very clear relationship to people's views on the three personal situations. It had no clear relationship either to three of the four pairs of situations involving managers and officials – entertainment, accepting gifts and fiddling.

| | Situation involves: | | | |
| | Official | | Manager | |
	Public sector workers %	Private sector workers %	Public sector workers %	Private sector workers %
Entertainment				
Nothing wrong	16	28	32	50
A bit wrong	25	20	29	23
Wrong/seriously wrong	58	52	39	26
Accepting gifts				
Nothing wrong	9	16	32	45
A bit wrong	14	15	22	22
Wrong/seriously wrong	76	68	47	32

With the fourth pair, involving the soliciting of gifts, a definite class pattern did emerge in people's answers. Those in Social Classes I and II judged the soliciting of gifts more severely than those in Social Class III, who in turn judged it more severely than those in Social Classes IV and V.

| | Social Class | | | |
Soliciting gifts seriously wrong	I or II %	III Non-manual %	III Manual %	IV or V %
in a council official	69	59	52	47
in a manager	62	42	43	37

Public servants compared

In all the situations discussed so far, we have compared a council official, representing someone in a position of public trust, with a private sector manager. But is is quite possible that people judge similar sorts of behaviour differently according to the type of official involved or the area of public life in which the official operates. To get an indication whether this was so, we asked people to judge some similar situations involving on the one hand a council official and on the other a policeman.

One pair of transactions involved soliciting money in return for a specific action. This differs from the soliciting of gifts already discussed in that here it is made explicit what will be provided in return. The two transactions we posited were:

A council tenant applies for a transfer to a better house. An official in the housing department asks for £50 to put the application near the front of the queue.

A policeman stops a driver for speeding. The policeman asks for £50 to forget the incident.

Judgements on these two situations were:

| | Bribe sought by: | |
	council official	policeman
	%	%
Nothing wrong in it	*	*
A bit wrong	1	1
Wrong	26	17
Seriously wrong	72	81
Don't know	1	1

The great majority judged both these situations to be seriously wrong. For an official to solicit money in return for a specific breach of duties was, overall, regarded as decidedly worse than soliciting gifts, particularly in the case of a policeman. It needs to be borne in mind, however, that because of the difference in their duties, we were not able to present exactly matching situations for council officials and policemen. The difference may thus come from the situation rather than the role. On the other hand, a policeman's job is almost certainly regarded as rather more critical than that of a housing officer. So a policeman may well be expected to uphold the law and the rules of his job more stringently.

There was no clear pattern in the answers by age, religious observance or party identity. Nor, interestingly, did it make any difference in judging the housing official's behaviour whether or not people were themselves council tenants. But, as with the soliciting of gifts, there was a difference by Social Class.

Soliciting bribe

| | Social Class | | | |
	I or II	III Non-manual	III Manual	IV or V
	%	%	%	%
Bribe seriously wrong:				
in a council official	80	74	72	66
in a policeman	86	84	81	77

Insofar as it measures anything, conventional Social Class is, we suppose, a measure of occupational status. One possibility is that the direct soliciting of gifts or bribes by officials was seen as more subversive of the established social system than any of the other situations we presented and, therefore, seen as more threatening by people who held jobs of higher status within that system. But this is conjecture.

As a contrast to public servants seeking bribes, we asked people to judge two parallel situations in which members of the public offered bribes. These were:

A council tenant applies for a transfer to a better house. He offers an official in the housing department £50 to put the application near the front of the queue.

A policeman stops a driver for speeding. The driver offers him £50 to forget the incident.

Judgements on these situations were:

	Bribe offered to:	
	council official	policeman
	%	%
Nothing wrong in it	1	1
A bit wrong	4	4
Wrong	41	36
Seriously wrong	53	59
Don't know	1	1

Hypothetical members of the public who offered bribes to public servants were generally judged harshly. It did not make much difference to the judgement whether the bribe was offered to a council official or a policeman. Twelve per cent regarded the offer to an official as worse. Eighteen per cent regarded it as worse if the offer was made to a policeman. The rest rated the two situations in the same way.

But in both cases, especially that of the policeman, offering a bribe was not, overall, judged as harshly as when a public servant *asked* for one. The comparison between the ratings for offering and asking was:

	for council official	for policeman
	%	%
Rating of request for bribe		
as compared with offer		
More censorious about soliciting bribe	23	40
Same	73	53
Less censorious about soliciting bribe	4	6
Unclear	1	1

As with judgements of officials asking for bribes, there was no obvious relationship between judgements of people who offered bribes and age, religion or party identity. And again council tenants did not judge the offer to the housing official much differently from anyone else. There was a slight relationship to Social Class, which was in the same direction as, but weaker than, the relationship between Social Class and judgements of officials who asked for bribes.

'Favoured treatment'

Finally, we looked at attitudes to favours by officials – illegitimate acts by officials done not for money but from motives of friendship or personal obligation. The situations we asked people to judge were:

A council tenant applies for a transfer to a better house. An official in the housing department notices that the application is from an old friend. He decides to put the application near the front of the queue.

A policeman stops a driver for speeding. The driver is an old friend. The policeman decides to forget the incident.

A council official uses his influence to get a relative a job with the council.

Judgements on these three situations were:

	Favour done by:		Nepotism by
	council official	policeman	council official
	%	%	%
Nothing wrong in it	2	3	11
A bit wrong	11	14	19
Wrong	52	51	45
Seriously wrong	33	31	23
Don't know	2	1	1

Most thought it wrong or seriously wrong for a council official or a policeman to take the sort of action described from motives of friendship. It made no notable difference to people's opinions whether a council official or a policeman was involved. But in either case only one in three saw it as seriously wrong. Doing something of this sort as a favour to a friend was judged very much less censoriously than asking for money to do it. And doing a special favour for a *relative* was generally viewed even more tolerantly. Less than a quarter saw it as seriously wrong for a council official to use his influence to get a relative a job.

The pattern by Social Class noted in the answers on bribery was not repeated in the answers on favours for friends or relatives. Indeed it was reversed in the case of the favour done by the housing official. Here the judgements of those in Social Classes I and II tended to be somewhat more tolerant than the judgements of those in Social Classes IV and V. Perhaps people in Social Classes IV and V were less likely to have friends among the officials? This result, too, is consistent with the findings of the American survey on "corruptness". There, lower-status respondents took a much more critical view of perceived favouritism than did their upper-status counterparts (Johnston, 1985). There was no strong pattern by Social Class in the answers on the favour done by the policeman or in the answers on nepotism.

Conclusions

The findings we have discussed suggest some broad conclusions about the sorts of judgements people make about the rightness or wrongness of various transactions in public and business life and about the content of these judgements.

A first important point is that people could answer the questions. The proportion of 'don't know' responses did not rise above 3% for any of the eighteen situations. Interviewers are often asked to seek definite answers where it is possible to do so, but in this survey they are specifically instructed to accept 'don't knows' as legitimate responses. So the results strongly suggest that people did not find the task they were asked to perform difficult or puzzling or the situations they were asked to judge too morally ambiguous. When public behaviour is put in terms of concrete situations, people do appear to have standards by which they can judge it.

A second important point is that people did, overall, distinguish between the situations we put to them. Their answers, in aggregate, produce a fairly clear ranking of the wrongness of the different situations. The proportions rating particular situations as *seriously* wrong varied from 3% to 81%, with considerable differences in the rating of individual situations in between. The figures are:

Thinking situation seriously wrong	general public	Main person involved company manager	council official	policeman
'bribing' dustmen	3%			
evading VAT	3%			
expensive entertainment		6%	13%	
nepotism			23%	
accepting gift		7%	28%	
keeping wrong change	16%			
fiddling expenses		23%	33%	
doing illegitimate favour			33%	31%
soliciting gift		44%	56%	
offering bribe to official	53%			
offering bribe to police	59%			
soliciting bribe			72%	81%

As noted earlier, men and women differed little in the overall severity of their judgements. But a look at specific situations in which judgements differed significantly between the sexes suggests that to some degree women and men may react differently to misconduct of different types. Men, for example, tended to disapprove more strongly of wrongdoing in official or business settings (managers and officials accepting or soliciting lunches or Christmas presents, or an employee fiddling expenses) than did women. Women, on the other hand, were stricter than men in their judgements of favouritism or wrongdoing in more private situations – such as an official deciding to give precedence to a friend's housing application, a policeman deciding to forget a friend's speeding or a householder bribing the dustmen. These contrasts may reflect differences in male and female roles and occupations, and thus in the types of situations frequently encountered. Or it could partly be a function of the different age profiles among men and women. It may also be, though, that men perceived themselves as being 'victimised' more frequently by the power of money and tangible resources, while women felt more threatened by favouritism (of which sex discrimination might be an example). But this too remains conjecture in the absence of supporting evidence.

At the beginning of this chapter we mentioned our preliminary discussions about how many points we should have on our scale of wrongness. We decided on four. But in rating the situation where a policeman solicits a £50 bribe, 81% of the people we interviewed used the fourth scale position, 'seriously wrong'. It is evident that, if we had wanted to cover anything more serious than a policeman soliciting a bribe, we would have needed a further, even more serious category on the scale to elicit distinctions.

Another important general point about the answers is that the ranking implied by the table of 'seriously wrong' ratings is robust. Groups within the sample differed in their rating of particular situations or sets of situations, but there were few differences between subgroups in the rank order of wrongness that their ratings imply. Broadly, standards were common between different groups; but groups differed in how seriously they applied them. Those situations rated less seriously by older people for example, tended to be rated much less seriously by younger people. But the rank order following from the ratings was almost identical.

Turning now to the content of people's judgements, it is clear that, overall people have rather higher standards for the behaviour of public officials than they do for the behaviour of people in the private sector. Over a series of transactions, the same behaviour was censured more strongly in a public official than in a private businessman. And it was judged decidedly worse for an official to ask for a bribe in return for a specific illegitimate act than it was for a member of the public to offer such a bribe.

Of the situations we looked at, the explicit and unambiguous seeking of bribes in return for illegitimate actions was judged more harshly than anything else. It was judged more severely than soliciting gifts without explicitly specifying something as reciprocation. This in its turn was judged more severely than accepting such gifts if they were given. In effect, the less an action could be construed as an explicit *quid pro quo*, the less harsh the judgements. Thus, where illegitimate action was taken in return for a bribe, the situation was judged more harshly than if the same action was taken as a favour to a friend. And the judgement tends to be even less harsh when illegitimate action is taken to help a relative.

Our judgements of right or wrong, in other words, involve a number of factors. Certainly our understandings of legality – even if vague and at times erroneous – are an important factor. But our judgements typically reflect a number of non-legal considerations too: if people break the law to help their children, we may judge matters more leniently. The taking of significant tangible assets – large sums of money or valuable goods – may be judged more harshly than situations in which the stakes are small or intangible. The identities and roles of the participants in an action may also affect our judgements (Smigel and Ross, 1970; Johnston, 1985). If prominent or socially-distant persons and organisations are perceived as breaking rules, judgements may be relatively strict. But if the wrongdoer is someone like themselves and the situation a familiar one, people tend to be less censorious. As we have seen, most people are willing to admit the possibility that they themselves might consider some forms of fiddling if the situation were to arise.

We did not expect, and did not produce, any clearcut boundary from our data between what is perceived as 'right' and what is perceived as 'wrong'. We covered a wide variety of actions and transactions – from the equivalent of illegitimate tipping, in the case of dustmen, to potentially serious corruption, in the case of policemen. In between we included a range of transactions which we expected would fall into Noel-Baker's "grey zone" – morally ambiguous situations such as illegitimately helping friends or relatives for no direct personal gain. On these we expected people's judgements to vary widely.

It is remarkable, therefore, that such variation among subgroups that exists is confined to the degree of seriousness with which they view a particular transaction, and does not apply to the derived ranking of 'wrongness' of the twelve different situations we presented. Unless we were to design a set of questions with that objective, we would be unlikely to produce so great a consensus on most other issues.

So, to the extent that a "grey zone" exists, it exists in respect of the relative tolerance or censoriousness of different subgroups towards particular actions, all of which were viewed as 'wrong' to some degree by most people. No more than one third of the sample said 'it is not wrong at all' in response to any of the twelve situations we offered.

In looking for explanations of censoriousness or tolerance, we do not find formal props, such as the legality or illegality of the action, very helpful. VAT evasion, for instance, which is unlawful, produced much less disapproval than, say, expensive entertainment which, within reason, is perfectly lawful. On the whole, variation between subgroups appeared greatest where the situations were complicated by questions of motive and where the circumstances were fairly distant from most people's everyday experiences. In those cases, people seemed to fall back on the norms of their social group, or generation, or personal philosophy. Which is where class, age and religion, for instance, came into play most powerfully. On the other hand, when laws or rules are known to be at odds with common practice, as in the case of tipping dustmen or evading VAT, people in all subgroups tended to come down in favour of practice; or at least they did not judge breaches of the rules very harshly.

It was to this tendency that Poulson, Smith and company tried to appeal when they argued that much of what they were accused of doing had become common business and political practice, and would no longer be regarded as wrong by the majority of people.

> "I will never believe I have done anything criminally wrong. I did what is business. If I bent any rules, who doesn't? If you are going to punish me, sweep away the system. If I am guilty, there are many others who should be by my side in the dock . . . What big company doesn't spend that much and more on entertaining and getting contracts?" (Poulson, quoted in Chibnall and Saunders, p.142.)

Although our data support the notion that many people will engage in various sorts of wrongdoing themselves, they do not support Poulson's view of his own actions. On the contrary, they suggest that he and his colleagues would have drawn little sympathy. He was right in pointing out that society operates under potentially conflicting conceptions of right and wrong, and that the law by no means automatically reflects society's prevailing mood. But he was wrong in suggesting, unless the mood has changed considerably since the early 1970s, that *his* actions would be viewed as morally ambiguous.

References

CHIBNALL, S. and SAUNDERS, P., 'Worlds Apart: Notes on the Social Reality of Corruption', *British Journal of Sociology 28*, (June 1977).
DOIG, A., *Corruption and Misconduct in Contemporary British Politics*, Penguin, Harmondsworth (1984).
HENRY, S., *The Hidden Economy: The Context and Control of Borderline Crime*, Martin Robertson, London (1978).
JOHNSTON, M., 'Right and Wrong in American Politics: Popular Conceptions of Corruption', *Polity* (forthcoming, 1985).
MARS, G., *Cheats at Work: An Anthropology of Workplace Crime*, George Allen and Unwin, London (1982).
MARSH, A., *Protest and Political Consciousness*, Sage, London (1977).
NOEL-BAKER, F., 'The Grey Zone', *Parliamentary Affairs 15*, London (1961).
SMALL, J. 'Political Ethics: A View of the Leadership', *American Behavioral Scientist 19*, (May-June 1976).
SMIGEL, E. O. and ROSS, H. L., *Crimes against Bureaucracy*, Van Nostrand Reinhold, New York (1970).

Acknowledgements

We are very grateful to the trustees of the Nuffield Foundation and to the University of Pittsburgh for their funding of this section of the study, and also to James Cornford and Pat Thomas for their advice and help.

5.1 JUDGEMENTS OF 'RIGHT' AND 'WRONG' (Q90 i, ii, iii, iv) by current/last social class, age and party identification

BASE: ALL RESPONDENTS	WEIGHTED BASE	CURRENT / LAST SOCIAL CLASS					AGE					PARTY I.D.				
		I.II	III NON MAN.	III MAN.	IV.V	NEVER WORKED /N.C.	18-24	25-34	35-54	55+	NO INF.	TORY	LAB.	ALLIANCE	OTHER	NON-ALIGN
UNWEIGHTED BASE	1675	352	380	383	388	172	217	309	525	610	14	640	595	220	24	196
WEIGHTED BASE	1645	341	378	369	380	177	214	311	517	590	14	635	575	219	28	188
A company employee exaggerates his claims for travel expenses over a period and makes £50.																
NOTHING WRONG (1)	63 4%	4 1%	6 2%	30 8%	21 6%	2 1%	17 8%	11 4%	15 3%	20 3%	0	11 2%	37 6%	5 2%	0	10 5%
BIT WRONG (2)	285 17%	52 15%	67 18%	62 17%	73 19%	32 18%	55 26%	86 27%	73 14%	68 12%	3	101 16%	109 19%	32 15%	3	40 21%
WRONG (3)	889 54%	196 57%	210 55%	192 52%	189 50%	103 58%	105 49%	155 50%	286 55%	337 57%	6	356 56%	290 50%	128 59%	21	93 50%
SERIOUSLY WRONG (4)	385 23%	90 26%	94 25%	86 23%	90 24%	26 15%	35 16%	57 18%	140 27%	150 25%	2	159 25%	132 23%	52 24%	5	37 20%
DONT KNOW	9 1%	0 0%	0 0%	0 0%	5 1%	3 1%	1 0%	1 0%	0 0%	1 0%	0	5 1%	1 0%	1 0%	0	3 1%
NOT ANSWERED	14 1%	0 0%	2 0%	0 0%	2 1%	10 5%	0 0%	2 1%	2 0%	7 1%	3	7 1%	2 1%	0 0%	0	5 3%
A company manager accepts a Christmas present worth £50 from a firm from which he buys products.																
NOTHING WRONG (1)	636 39%	105 31%	176 47%	141 38%	161 42%	54 30%	119 56%	129 41%	198 38%	187 32%	4	258 41%	221 39%	75 34%	14	68 36%
BIT WRONG (2)	372 23%	83 24%	88 23%	77 21%	70 18%	54 30%	44 21%	81 26%	114 22%	131 22%	2	162 26%	107 19%	60 28%	4	38 20%
WRONG (3)	483 29%	125 37%	87 23%	115 31%	113 30%	43 24%	40 19%	84 27%	157 30%	198 34%	4	166 26%	183 32%	70 32%	8	55 29%
SERIOUSLY WRONG (4)	117 7%	28 8%	22 6%	34 9%	23 6%	11 6%	8 4%	14 5%	42 8%	52 9%	1	40 6%	49 9%	10 5%	2	16 9%
DONT KNOW	23 1%	1 0%	3 1%	2 1%	10 3%	6 4%	3 1%	1 0%	5 1%	14 2%	0	3 1%	12 2%	2 1%	0	6 3%
NOT ANSWERED	15 1%	0 0%	2 1%	0 0%	3 1%	10 5%	0 0%	2 1%	2 0%	8 1%	3	7 1%	3 1%	1 0%	0	5 3%
A manager asks a firm from which he buys products for a £50 gift for himself.																
NOTHING WRONG (1)	37 2%	5 1%	7 2%	13 4%	11 3%	2 1%	5 2%	9 3%	7 1%	17 3%	0	10 2%	16 3%	4 2%	0	7 4%
BIT WRONG (2)	104 6%	11 3%	28 7%	22 6%	29 8%	13 7%	21 10%	33 11%	16 3%	33 6%	1	47 7%	32 6%	6 3%	3	15 8%
WRONG (3)	752 46%	115 34%	179 47%	173 47%	190 50%	95 54%	107 50%	121 39%	240 46%	279 47%	5	286 45%	270 47%	107 49%	10	79 42%
SERIOUSLY WRONG (4)	725 44%	210 62%	160 42%	158 43%	142 37%	54 31%	78 37%	146 47%	249 48%	246 42%	5	284 45%	247 43%	101 46%	16	78 41%
DONT KNOW	11 1%	0 0%	0 0%	0 0%	1 0%	4 2%	2 1%	0 0%	5 1%	8 1%	0	0 0%	7 1%	0 0%	0	3 2%
NOT ANSWERED	17 1%	0 0%	2 1%	1 0%	3 1%	10 5%	0 0%	2 1%	4 1%	8 1%	3	7 1%	4 1%	1 0%	0	6 3%
A firm selling products to another company regularly takes a manager in that company to expensive lunches.																
NOTHING WRONG (1)	645 39%	123 36%	159 42%	151 41%	149 39%	62 35%	114 53%	142 46%	202 39%	184 31%	3	274 43%	201 35%	77 35%	13	80 43%
BIT WRONG (2)	440 27%	113 33%	117 31%	83 23%	78 21%	49 27%	51 24%	85 28%	134 26%	167 28%	2	177 28%	129 22%	87 40%	10	38 20%
WRONG (3)	428 26%	85 25%	79 21%	105 28%	119 31%	40 23%	40 19%	62 20%	147 28%	175 30%	6	152 24%	186 32%	43 20%	4	42 22%
SERIOUSLY WRONG (4)	99 6%	19 6%	18 5%	27 7%	23 6%	11 6%	7 3%	19 6%	28 5%	44 8%	0	22 3%	46 8%	10 4%	2	20 11%
DONT KNOW	19 1%	1 0%	1 0%	3 1%	6 2%	6 3%	1 0%	1 0%	5 1%	12 2%	0	5 1%	10 2%	0 0%	0	3 2%
NOT ANSWERED	15 1%	0 0%	2 1%	0 0%	3 1%	10 5%	0 0%	2 1%	2 0%	7 1%	3	7 1%	3 1%	1 0%	0	5 3%

What do you think about the following situations:

5.2 JUDGEMENTS OF 'RIGHT' AND 'WRONG' (Q90 v, vi, vii) by current/last social class, age and party identification

BASE: ALL RESPONDENTS	ALL	CURRENT / LAST SOCIAL CLASS I,II	III NON MAN.	III MAN.	IV,V MAN.	NEVER WORKED /N.C.	AGE 18-24	25-34	35-54	55+	NO INF.	PARTY I.D. TORY	LAB.	ALLIANCE	OTHER	NON-ALIGN
UNWEIGHTED BASE	1675	352	380	383	388	172	217	309	525	610	14	640	595	220	24	196
WEIGHTED BASE	1645	341	378	369	380	177	214	311	517	590	14	635	575	219	28	188

A council official accepts a Christmas present worth £50 from a private firm that supplies services to the council.

	ALL	I,II	III NON MAN.	III MAN.	IV,V MAN.	NEVER WORKED /N.C.	18-24	25-34	35-54	55+	NO INF.	TORY	LAB.	ALLIANCE	OTHER	NON-ALIGN
NOTHING WRONG (1)	212 13%	30 9%	55 15%	45 12%	59 15%	23 13%	57 27%	64 21%	54 10%	37 6%	0	85 13%	65 11%	23 10%	9	30 16%
BIT WRONG (2)	224 14%	46 14%	61 16%	38 10%	51 13%	27 15%	57 27%	51 16%	60 12%	54 9%	1	91 14%	77 13%	27 12%	3	26 14%
WRONG (3)	707 43%	151 44%	160 42%	154 42%	166 44%	76 43%	66 31%	111 36%	238 46%	284 48%	8	278 44%	240 42%	117 53%	6	67 36%
SERIOUSLY WRONG (4)	463 28%	112 33%	94 25%	130 35%	93 25%	33 19%	31 15%	81 26%	158 31%	191 32%	2	171 27%	186 32%	49 23%	10	47 25%
DONT KNOW	25 2%	2 1%	5 1%	1 0%	8 2%	9 5%	2 1%	2 1%	5 1%	16 3%	0	4 1%	6 1%	2 1%	1	13 7%
NOT ANSWERED	14 1%	0 0%	2 0%	0 0%	2 1%	10 5%	0 0%	1 1%	2 0%	7 1%	3	7 1%	2 0%	1 0%	0	5 3%

A council official asks a firm that supplies services to the council for a £50 gift for himself.

	ALL	I,II	III NON MAN.	III MAN.	IV,V MAN.	NEVER WORKED /N.C.	18-24	25-34	35-54	55+	NO INF.	TORY	LAB.	ALLIANCE	OTHER	NON-ALIGN
NOTHING WRONG (1)	14 1%	1 0%	2 0%	5 1%	6 1%	1 0%	4 2%	4 1%	2 0%	5 1%	0	4 1%	4 1%	2 1%	0	5 3%
BIT WRONG (2)	62 4%	4 1%	15 4%	14 4%	23 6%	6 4%	15 7%	15 5%	10 2%	22 4%	1	20 3%	23 4%	6 3%	3	11 6%
WRONG (3)	622 38%	102 30%	137 36%	136 37%	170 45%	78 44%	87 41%	111 36%	191 37%	229 39%	5	226 36%	219 38%	94 43%	5	79 42%
SERIOUSLY WRONG (4)	924 56%	234 69%	222 59%	212 58%	177 47%	79 44%	108 50%	179 57%	311 60%	321 54%	5	377 59%	323 56%	116 53%	20	89 47%
DONT KNOW	8 0%	0 0%	0 0%	0 0%	3 1%	4 2%	1 0%	0 0%	1 0%	7 1%	0	2 0%	6 1%	0 0%	0	0 0%
NOT ANSWERED	15 1%	0 0%	2 1%	1 0%	2 1%	10 5%	0 0%	2 1%	2 0%	8 1%	3	7 1%	2 0%	2 1%	0	5 3%

A firm supplying services to the council regularly takes a council official to expensive lunches.

	ALL	I,II	III NON MAN.	III MAN.	IV,V MAN.	NEVER WORKED /N.C.	18-24	25-34	35-54	55+	NO INF.	TORY	LAB.	ALLIANCE	OTHER	NON-ALIGN
NOTHING WRONG (1)	361 22%	56 16%	92 24%	82 22%	91 24%	40 23%	75 35%	81 26%	117 23%	87 15%	1	155 24%	104 18%	37 17%	9	56 30%
BIT WRONG (2)	360 22%	87 25%	100 26%	59 16%	70 19%	44 25%	55 26%	77 25%	103 20%	123 21%	2	146 23%	108 19%	65 30%	6	35 18%
WRONG (3)	671 41%	141 41%	137 36%	168 45%	169 45%	57 32%	69 32%	107 34%	219 42%	269 46%	7	249 39%	258 45%	89 41%	10	65 34%
SERIOUSLY WRONG (4)	221 13%	56 16%	45 12%	57 16%	42 11%	20 12%	14 7%	43 14%	73 14%	90 15%	1	71 11%	94 16%	26 12%	4	26 14%
DONT KNOW	17 1%	2 1%	2 1%	2 1%	5 1%	6 3%	0 0%	1 0%	3 1%	13 2%	0	7 1%	9 2%	0 0%	0	2 1%
NOT ANSWERED	15 1%	0 0%	2 1%	1 0%	2 1%	10 5%	0 0%	2 1%	2 0%	8 1%	3	7 1%	2 0%	2 1%	0	5 3%

What do you think about the following situations:

5.3 JUDGEMENTS OF 'RIGHT' AND 'WRONG' (Q90 viii, ix) by current/last social class, age and party identification

	WEIGHTED BASE	CURRENT / LAST SOCIAL CLASS					AGE					PARTY I.D.				
		I.II	III NON MAN.	III MAN.	IV.V	NEVER WORKED /N.C.	18-24	25-34	35-54	55+	NO INF.	TORY	LAB.	ALLI-ANCE	OTHER	NON-ALIGN
BASE: ALL RESPONDENTS																
UNWEIGHTED BASE	1675	352	380	383	388	172	217	309	525	610	14	640	595	220	24	196
WEIGHTED BASE	1645	341	378	369	380	177	214	311	517	590	14	635	575	219	28	188
A council official uses his influence to get a relative a job with the council.																
NOTHING WRONG (1)	184 11%	35 10%	38 10%	38 10%	62 16%	12 7%	46 22%	29 9%	50 10%	56 10%	1	69 11%	69 12%	17 8%	6	23 12%
BIT WRONG (2)	319 19%	67 20%	94 25%	72 20%	63 17%	22 13%	37 17%	73 23%	107 21%	97 17%	4	145 23%	87 15%	47 22%	4	36 19%
WRONG (3)	742 45%	152 45%	157 41%	175 47%	163 43%	95 54%	77 36%	133 43%	241 47%	284 48%	6	277 44%	264 46%	108 49%	9	83 44%
SERIOUSLY WRONG (4)	375 23%	86 25%	87 23%	84 23%	83 22%	35 20%	52 24%	73 24%	115 22%	134 23%	0	135 21%	146 25%	46 21%	9	38 20%
DONT KNOW	12 1%	1 0%	1 0%	1 0%	7 2%	4 2%	1 0%	1 0%	1 0%	10 2%	0	2 0%	8 1%	0 0%	0	3 2%
NOT ANSWERED	14 1%	0 0%	0 0%	0 0%	2 1%	10 5%	0 0%	2 1%	2 0%	7 1%	3	7 1%	2 0%	0 0%	0	5 3%
A council official exaggerates his claims for travel expenses over a period and makes £50.																
NOTHING WRONG (1)	32 2%	1 0%	4 1%	16 4%	10 3%	2 1%	9 4%	5 2%	5 1%	13 2%	0	9 1%	17 3%	4 2%	0	3 1%
BIT WRONG (2)	191 12%	34 10%	44 12%	51 14%	40 11%	22 12%	46 22%	66 21%	41 8%	38 6%	0	65 10%	65 11%	25 11%	0	35 19%
WRONG (3)	856 52%	182 53%	191 51%	170 46%	208 55%	104 59%	105 49%	155 50%	282 55%	305 52%	9	335 53%	295 51%	119 55%	15	91 48%
SERIOUSLY WRONG (4)	540 33%	124 36%	133 35%	131 35%	116 30%	36 21%	51 24%	83 27%	184 36%	220 37%	2	218 34%	190 33%	70 32%	14	45 23%
DONT KNOW	12 1%	0 0%	3 1%	1 0%	4 1%	4 2%	3 1%	0 0%	3 1%	7 1%	0	2 0%	6 1%	0 0%	0	5 %
NOT ANSWERED	14 1%	0 0%	2 1%	0 0%	2 1%	10 5%	0 0%	2 1%	2 0%	7 1%	3	7 1%	2 0%	1 0%	0	5 %

5.4 JUDGEMENTS OF 'RIGHT' AND 'WRONG' (Q90 x, xi, xii) by current/last social class, age and party identification

What do you think about the following situations:

BASE: ALL RESPONDENTS

	WEIGHTED BASE	CURRENT / LAST SOCIAL CLASS					AGE					PARTY I.D.				
		I,II	III NON MAN.	III MAN.	IV,V	NEVER WORKED /N.C.	18-24	25-34	35-54	55+	NO INF.	TORY	LAB.	ALLIANCE	OTHER	NON-ALIGN
UNWEIGHTED BASE	1675	352	380	383	388	172	217	309	525	610	14	640	595	220	24	196
WEIGHTED BASE	1645	341	378	369	380	177	214	311	517	590	14	635	575	219	28	188

A council tenant applies for a transfer to a better house. An official in the housing department notices that the application is from an old friend. He decides to put the application near the front of the queue.

	WEIGHTED BASE	I,II	III NON MAN.	III MAN.	IV,V	NEVER WORKED /N.C.	18-24	25-34	35-54	55+	NO INF.	TORY	LAB.	ALLIANCE	OTHER	NON-ALIGN
NOTHING WRONG (1)	32 / 2%	8 / 2%	1 / 0%	15 / 4%	8 / 2%	1 / 1%	5 / 2%	3 / 1%	11 / 2%	14 / 2%	0	9 / 1%	11 / 2%	9 / 4%	1	3 / 2%
BIT WRONG (2)	186 / 11%	47 / 14%	47 / 13%	41 / 11%	31 / 8%	18 / 10%	32 / 15%	49 / 16%	54 / 10%	50 / 8%	1	81 / 13%	64 / 11%	22 / 10%	1	18 / 9%
WRONG (3)	862 / 52%	183 / 54%	211 / 56%	184 / 50%	194 / 51%	89 / 50%	95 / 44%	172 / 55%	258 / 50%	328 / 56%	9	338 / 53%	285 / 50%	121 / 56%	15	102 / 54%
SERIOUSLY WRONG (4)	542 / 33%	103 / 30%	116 / 31%	127 / 34%	141 / 37%	55 / 31%	79 / 37%	84 / 27%	190 / 37%	188 / 32%	1	197 / 31%	210 / 37%	65 / 30%	11	59 / 31%
DONT KNOW	9 / 1%	0 / 0%	1 / 0%	1 / 0%	2 / 1%	2 / 1%	2 / 1%	1 / 0%	2 / 0%	5 / 1%	0	3 / 0%	4 / 1%	1 / 0%	0	2 / 1%
NOT ANSWERED	14 / 1%	0 / 0%	2 / 1%	0 / 0%	2 / 1%	10 / 5%	0 / 0%	1 / 0%	2 / 0%	7 / 1%	3	7 / 1%	2 / 1%	1 / 0%	0	5 / 3%

A council tenant applies for a transfer to a better house. An official in the housing department asks for £50 to put the application near the front of the queue.

	WEIGHTED BASE	I,II	III NON MAN.	III MAN.	IV,V	NEVER WORKED /N.C.	18-24	25-34	35-54	55+	NO INF.	TORY	LAB.	ALLIANCE	OTHER	NON-ALIGN
NOTHING WRONG (1)	5 / 0%	0 / 0%	1 / 0%	2 / 1%	2 / 1%	0 / 0%	1 / 0%	0 / 0%	0 / 0%	3 / 0%	0	2 / 0%	2 / 0%	1 / 0%	0	0 / 0%
BIT WRONG (2)	21 / 1%	3 / 1%	3 / 1%	6 / 2%	9 / 2%	1 / 1%	4 / 2%	4 / 1%	5 / 1%	7 / 1%	0	3 / 1%	7 / 1%	5 / 0%	0	6 / 3%
WRONG (3)	423 / 26%	66 / 19%	95 / 25%	95 / 26%	116 / 31%	51 / 29%	55 / 26%	68 / 22%	106 / 21%	190 / 32%	4	157 / 25%	150 / 26%	52 / 24%	6	58 / 31%
SERIOUSLY WRONG (4)	1178 / 72%	272 / 80%	278 / 74%	266 / 72%	249 / 66%	113 / 64%	153 / 72%	237 / 76%	403 / 78%	380 / 64%	7	465 / 73%	411 / 71%	161 / 74%	22	119 / 63%
DONT KNOW	5 / 0%	0 / 0%	0 / 0%	0 / 0%	2 / 0%	3 / 1%	1 / 0%	0 / 0%	0 / 0%	5 / 1%	0	2 / 0%	4 / 1%	0 / 0%	0	0 / 0%
NOT ANSWERED	14 / 1%	0 / 0%	1 / 0%	0 / 0%	2 / 1%	10 / 5%	0 / 0%	1 / 0%	2 / 0%	7 / 1%	3	7 / 1%	2 / 1%	1 / 0%	0	5 / 3%

A council tenant applies for a transfer to a better house. He offers an official in the housing department £50 to put the application near the front of the queue.

	WEIGHTED BASE	I,II	III NON MAN.	III MAN.	IV,V	NEVER WORKED /N.C.	18-24	25-34	35-54	55+	NO INF.	TORY	LAB.	ALLIANCE	OTHER	NON-ALIGN
NOTHING WRONG (1)	15 / 1%	2 / 1%	3 / 1%	4 / 1%	6 / 2%	0 / 0%	7 / 3%	5 / 2%	2 / 0%	1 / 0%	0	8 / 1%	2 / 0%	1 / 1%	3	1 / 1%
BIT WRONG (2)	69 / 4%	12 / 4%	19 / 5%	16 / 4%	9 / 2%	12 / 7%	16 / 7%	20 / 6%	20 / 4%	12 / 2%	1	24 / 4%	21 / 4%	7 / 3%	4	12 / 7%
WRONG (3)	670 / 41%	127 / 37%	151 / 40%	152 / 41%	165 / 44%	75 / 43%	81 / 38%	128 / 41%	200 / 39%	257 / 44%	5	266 / 42%	220 / 38%	96 / 44%	8	80 / 43%
SERIOUSLY WRONG (4)	872 / 53%	200 / 59%	202 / 53%	196 / 53%	196 / 52%	78 / 44%	109 / 51%	156 / 50%	293 / 57%	309 / 52%	5	329 / 52%	327 / 57%	113 / 52%	14	90 / 48%
DONT KNOW	5 / 0%	0 / 0%	0 / 0%	1 / 0%	2 / 0%	3 / 1%	1 / 0%	0 / 0%	0 / 0%	5 / 1%	0	2 / 0%	4 / 1%	0 / 0%	0	0 / 0%
NOT ANSWERED	14 / 1%	0 / 0%	2 / 1%	0 / 0%	2 / 1%	10 / 5%	0 / 0%	1 / 0%	2 / 0%	7 / 1%	3	7 / 1%	2 / 1%	1 / 0%	0	5 / 3%

5.5 JUDGEMENTS OF 'RIGHT' AND 'WRONG' (Q90 xiii, xiv, xv) by current/last social class, age and party identification

BASE: ALL RESPONDENTS

	WEIGHTED BASE	CURRENT / LAST SOCIAL CLASS					AGE					PARTY I.D.				
		I.II	III NON MAN.	III MAN.	IV.V	NEVER WORKED /N.C.	18-24	25-34	35-54	55+	NO INF.	TORY	LAB.	ALLI-ANCE	OTHER	NON-ALIGN
UNWEIGHTED BASE	1675	352	380	383	388	172	217	309	525	610	14	640	595	220	24	196
WEIGHTED BASE	1645	341	378	369	380	177	214	311	517	590	14	635	575	219	28	188

A policeman stops a driver for speeding. The policeman asks for £50 to forget the incident.

	WEIGHTED BASE	I.II	III NON MAN.	III MAN.	IV.V	NEVER WORKED	18-24	25-34	35-54	55+	NO INF.	TORY	LAB.	ALLI-ANCE	OTHER	NON-ALIGN
NOTHING WRONG (1)	3 / 0%	0 / 0%	1 / 0%	1 / 0%	1 / 0%	0 / 0%	0 / 0%	0 / 0%	1 / 0%	2 / 0%	0	1 / 0%	1 / 0%	1 / 0%	0	0 / 0%
BIT WRONG (2)	12 / 1%	3 / 1%	0 / 0%	1 / 0%	5 / 1%	3 / 2%	2 / 1%	0 / 0%	1 / *	7 / 1%	0	2 / 0%	4 / 1%	3 / 1%	0	3 / 2%
WRONG (3)	283 / 17%	45 / 13%	56 / 15%	67 / 18%	79 / 21%	36 / 20%	47 / 22%	41 / 13%	70 / 14%	122 / 21%	3	98 / 15%	101 / 18%	32 / 15%	6	46 / 24%
SERIOUSLY WRONG (4)	1330 / 81%	293 / 86%	319 / 84%	299 / 81%	292 / 77%	127 / 72%	164 / 77%	267 / 86%	441 / 85%	451 / 76%	8	526 / 83%	466 / 81%	182 / 83%	23	134 / 71%
DONT KNOW	3 / 0%	0 / 0%	0 / 0%	1 / 0%	0 / 0%	0 / 0%	0 / 0%	3 / 1%	0 / 0%	0 / 0%	0	2 / 0%	2 / 0%	0 / 0%	0	0 / 0%
NOT ANSWERED	15 / 1%	0 / 0%	2 / 1%	0 / 0%	3 / 1%	10 / 5%	0 / 0%	0 / 0%	2 / 1%	7 / 1%	3	7 / 1%	2 / 0%	1 / 0%	0	6 / 3%

A policeman stops a driver for speeding. The driver offers £50 to forget the incident.

	WEIGHTED BASE	I.II	III NON MAN.	III MAN.	IV.V	NEVER WORKED	18-24	25-34	35-54	55+	NO INF.	TORY	LAB.	ALLI-ANCE	OTHER	NON-ALIGN
NOTHING WRONG (1)	10 / 1%	0 / 0%	3 / 1%	5 / 1%	2 / 1%	0 / 0%	3 / 1%	3 / 1%	1 / 0%	3 / 0%	0	4 / 1%	4 / 1%	1 / 0%	1	1 / 1%
BIT WRONG (2)	61 / 4%	14 / 4%	15 / 4%	15 / 4%	13 / 3%	4 / 2%	16 / 8%	15 / 5%	17 / 3%	13 / 2%	0	21 / 3%	20 / 3%	7 / 3%	0	13 / 7%
WRONG (3)	594 / 36%	122 / 36%	115 / 30%	135 / 37%	155 / 41%	67 / 38%	89 / 42%	96 / 31%	188 / 36%	215 / 36%	7	223 / 35%	217 / 38%	75 / 35%	10	69 / 37%
SERIOUSLY WRONG (4)	964 / 59%	206 / 60%	243 / 64%	213 / 58%	206 / 54%	95 / 54%	106 / 49%	195 / 63%	310 / 60%	349 / 59%	4	380 / 60%	331 / 58%	134 / 61%	18	100 / 53%
DONT KNOW	4 / 0%	0 / 0%	0 / 0%	0 / 0%	1 / 0%	1 / 1%	0 / 0%	0 / 0%	0 / 0%	4 / 1%	0	2 / 0%	2 / 0%	0 / 0%	0	0 / 0%
NOT ANSWERED	14 / 1%	0 / 0%	2 / 1%	0 / 0%	3 / 1%	10 / 5%	0 / 0%	2 / 1%	2 / 0%	7 / 1%	3	7 / 1%	2 / 0%	1 / 0%	0	5 / 3%

A policeman stops a driver for speeding. The driver is an old friend. The policeman decides simply to forget the incident.

	WEIGHTED BASE	I.II	III NON MAN.	III MAN.	IV.V	NEVER WORKED	18-24	25-34	35-54	55+	NO INF.	TORY	LAB.	ALLI-ANCE	OTHER	NON-ALIGN
NOTHING WRONG (1)	48 / 3%	10 / 3%	6 / 2%	13 / 4%	12 / 3%	7 / 4%	7 / 3%	13 / 4%	13 / 3%	15 / 3%	0	17 / 3%	19 / 3%	5 / 2%	0	8 / 4%
BIT WRONG (2)	223 / 14%	63 / 18%	56 / 15%	49 / 13%	42 / 11%	12 / 7%	37 / 17%	44 / 14%	74 / 14%	67 / 11%	1	88 / 14%	76 / 13%	31 / 14%	2	26 / 14%
WRONG (3)	836 / 51%	173 / 51%	202 / 53%	179 / 48%	199 / 53%	84 / 47%	96 / 45%	163 / 52%	257 / 50%	316 / 53%	5	335 / 53%	276 / 48%	125 / 57%	16	84 / 44%
SERIOUSLY WRONG (4)	517 / 31%	96 / 28%	112 / 30%	127 / 34%	120 / 32%	62 / 35%	73 / 34%	89 / 29%	171 / 33%	180 / 30%	5	186 / 29%	200 / 35%	57 / 26%	10	64 / 34%
DONT KNOW	7 / 0%	0 / 0%	0 / 0%	0 / 0%	3 / 1%	3 / 1%	1 / 0%	0 / 0%	0 / 0%	6 / 1%	0	3 / 0%	3 / 0%	0 / 0%	0	2 / 1%
NOT ANSWERED	14 / 1%	0 / 0%	2 / 1%	0 / 0%	2 / 1%	10 / 5%	0 / 0%	2 / 1%	2 / 0%	7 / 1%	3	7 / 1%	2 / 0%	1 / 0%	0	5 / 3%

What do you think about the following situations:

5.6 JUDGEMENTS OF 'RIGHT' AND 'WRONG' (Q91, a, b) by age and frequency of religious attendance

What do you think about the following situation:

A man offers the dustmen £5 to take away rubbish they are not supposed to pick up.

BASE: ALL RESPONDENTS

	WEIGHTED BASE	AGE					FREQUENCY OF RELIGIOUS ATTENDANCE				
		18-24	25-34	35-54	55+	NO INFORMATION	ONCE A WEEK OR MORE	BETWEEN ONCE IN TWO WEEKS AND TWICE A YEAR	ONCE A YEAR OR LESS	NO RELIGION	NO INFORMATION
UNWEIGHTED BASE	1675	217	309	525	610	14	213	342	583	529	8
WEIGHTED BASE	1645	214	311	517	590	14	201	326	581	530	7
NOTHING WRONG (1)	520 32%	81 38%	124 40%	173 34%	137 23%	4	42 21%	98 30%	178 31%	201 38%	1
BIT WRONG (2)	576 35%	74 35%	112 36%	192 37%	194 33%	4	68 34%	118 36%	199 34%	191 36%	1
WRONG (3)	482 29%	52 24%	70 23%	138 27%	220 37%	2	76 38%	102 31%	179 31%	125 24%	0
SERIOUSLY WRONG (4)	42 3%	7 3%	3 1%	10 2%	23 4%	0	13 6%	7 2%	14 2%	9 2%	0
DONT KNOW	12 1%	0 0%	0 0%	0 0%	11 2%	0	2 1%	1 0%	6 1%	3 1%	0
NOT ANSWERED	13 1%	0 0%	0 0%	3 1%	7 1%	4	1 0%	2 1%	4 1%	1 0%	5

Might you do this if the situation came up?

	WEIGHTED BASE	18-24	25-34	35-54	55+	NO INFORMATION	ONCE A WEEK OR MORE	BETWEEN ONCE IN TWO WEEKS AND TWICE A YEAR	ONCE A YEAR OR LESS	NO RELIGION	NO INFORMATION
YES	948 58%	150 70%	201 65%	324 63%	265 45%	8	89 44%	181 55%	318 55%	358 68%	2
NO	626 38%	58 27%	103 33%	174 34%	288 49%	2	103 51%	133 41%	235 41%	155 29%	0
DONT KNOW	48 3%	5 3%	6 2%	14 3%	22 4%	0	4 2%	11 3%	19 3%	14 3%	0
NOT ANSWERED	23 1%	0 0%	1 0%	4 1%	15 3%	4	6 3%	2 1%	8 1%	2 0%	5

5.7 JUDGEMENTS OF 'RIGHT' AND 'WRONG' (Q92 a, b) by age and frequency of religious attendance

BASE: ALL RESPONDENTS	WEIGHTED BASE	AGE					FREQUENCY OF RELIGIOUS ATTENDANCE				
		18-24	25-34	35-54	55+	NO INFORMATION	ONCE A WEEK OR MORE	BETWEEN ONCE IN TWO WEEKS AND TWICE A YEAR	ONCE A YEAR OR LESS	NO RELIGION	NO INFORMATION
UNWEIGHTED BASE	1675	217	309	525	610	14	213	342	583	529	8
WEIGHTED BASE	1645	214	311	517	590	14	201	326	581	530	7

What do you think about the following situation:

A householder is having a repair job done by a local plumber. He is told that if he pays cash he will not be charged VAT. So he pays cash.

	WEIGHTED BASE	18-24	25-34	35-54	55+	NO INFORMATION	ONCE A WEEK OR MORE	BETWEEN ONCE IN TWO WEEKS AND TWICE A YEAR	ONCE A YEAR OR LESS	NO RELIGION	NO INFORMATION
NOTHING WRONG (1)	509 31%	99 46%	123 40%	152 29%	134 23%	1	47 23%	81 25%	185 32%	195 37%	1
BIT WRONG (2)	514 31%	68 32%	110 35%	173 34%	159 27%	4	53 27%	96 29%	186 32%	179 34%	0
WRONG (3)	524 32%	41 19%	71 23%	171 33%	236 40%	4	84 42%	132 40%	170 29%	137 26%	1
SERIOUSLY WRONG (4)	57 3%	3 1%	7 2%	14 3%	33 6%	1	12 6%	14 4%	20 3%	12 2%	0
DONT KNOW	26 2%	2 1%	0 0%	3 1%	20 3%	0	4 2%	2 1%	15 3%	5 1%	0
NOT ANSWERED	15 1%	0 0%	0 0%	3 1%	9 1%	4	1 0%	2 1%	5 1%	2 0%	5

Might you do this if the situation came up?

	WEIGHTED BASE	18-24	25-34	35-54	55+	NO INFORMATION	ONCE A WEEK OR MORE	BETWEEN ONCE IN TWO WEEKS AND TWICE A YEAR	ONCE A YEAR OR LESS	NO RELIGION	NO INFORMATION
YES	1093 66%	170 80%	248 80%	377 73%	292 50%	5	100 50%	214 66%	376 65%	401 76%	2
NO	443 27%	38 18%	53 17%	119 23%	230 39%	3	84 42%	96 29%	155 27%	108 20%	0
DONT KNOW	87 5%	6 3%	9 3%	17 3%	53 9%	2	11 5%	15 5%	43 7%	18 3%	0
NOT ANSWERED	22 1%	0 0%	0 0%	4 1%	15 3%	4	6 3%	2 1%	7 1%	2 0%	5

5.8 JUDGEMENTS OF 'RIGHT' AND 'WRONG' (Q93 a, b) by age and frequency of religious attendance

What do you think about the following situation:

A man gives a £5 note for goods he is buying in a big store. By mistake, he is given change for a £10 note. He notices but keeps the change.

BASE: ALL RESPONDENTS

	WEIGHTED BASE	AGE					FREQUENCY OF RELIGIOUS ATTENDANCE				
		18-24	25-34	35-54	55+	NO INFORMATION	ONCE A WEEK OR MORE	BETWEEN ONCE A WEEK OR TWO WEEKS AND ONCE IN A YEAR	ONCE A YEAR OR LESS	NO RELIGION	NO INFORMATION
UNWEIGHTED BASE	1675	217	309	525	610	14	213	342	583	529	8
WEIGHTED BASE	1645	214	311	517	590	14	201	326	581	530	7
NOTHING WRONG (1)	99 6%	35 16%	23 7%	28 5%	14 2%	0	2 1%	15 5%	34 6%	49 9%	0
BIT WRONG (2)	249 15%	53 25%	77 25%	68 13%	51 9%	0	13 7%	28 9%	96 16%	110 21%	1
WRONG (3)	1011 61%	112 52%	179 58%	348 67%	366 62%	6	132 65%	213 65%	366 63%	300 57%	1
SERIOUSLY WRONG (4)	269 16%	13 6%	33 11%	70 13%	150 25%	4	53 26%	67 21%	82 14%	67 13%	0
DONT KNOW	5 0%	0 0%	0 0%	1 0%	4 1%	0	1 0%	1 0%	1 0%	2 0%	0
NOT ANSWERED	13 1%	0 0%	0 0%	3 1%	7 1%	4	1 0%	2 1%	3 1%	2 0%	5

Might you do this if the situation came up?

YES	295 18%	84 40%	85 27%	89 17%	37 6%	0	5 3%	38 12%	104 18%	147 28%	1
NO	1268 77%	121 57%	204 66%	407 79%	526 89%	10	186 92%	278 85%	451 78%	352 67%	1
DONT KNOW	60 4%	8 4%	22 7%	18 4%	13 2%	0	4 2%	9 3%	19 3%	28 5%	0
NOT ANSWERED	21 1%	0 0%	0 0%	3 1%	15 3%	4	6 3%	2 1%	6 1%	2 0%	5

6 Local government and the environment

Ken Young[*]

In this chapter we deal with two broad issues that have become highly politicised in recent years. The first is the question of where control over local government and its finances should reside. Two government policies in particular – the proposed abolition of the Greater London and Metropolitan County Councils, and the setting of a maximum rate level for selected local authorities – have received wide publicity. In consequence, a new debate on the nature and future of local democracy has been started (Jones and Stewart, 1983).

Our findings on this broad issue are unequivocal. Few people of any political persuasion (even committed Conservatives) supported further inroads by central government into local government affairs, whether in general or in respect of rate controls. The only exception was the public's endorsement of central control over school curricula. But this issue is not as controversial or active at present as the other issues of central control we investigated.

As will be seen, such consistent support for local government autonomy may derive in part from the public's general feeling that local authorities are rather more accessible than central government is, and that councillors are considered easier to locate and persuade about matters of importance than MPs are. We shall deal with this issue in some detail.

The second question we address in this chapter is the possible emergence of environmental or 'green' issues as an important factor in British politics. We ask whether such issues are likely to be as influential here as they have been, for instance, in the Federal Republic of Germany; or whether, for the moment, the people who are concerned about them do not cohere sufficiently to form a significant political force. We conclude that although environmental issues such as noise, fumes, industrial pollution and traffic pollution are ones of very wide

[*] Senior Fellow, Policy Studies Institute.

public concern; as are issues to do with nuclear energy and nuclear arms, the two sets of issues seem to attract concern from rather different subgroups of the population. So it seems unlikely for the time being that a wider 'green' movement can be built as successfully in this country as it has been elsewhere. We shall carefully monitor attitudes to these issues over the years to detect changes.

The responsive local authority

In our 1984 Report we referred to the concept of *political efficacy,* that is people's expectations of being able to wield effective political influence. Chapter 1 has already explained this concept and explored the extent to which the individual's willingness to assert himself or herself against 'unjust or harmful' government actions is associated with Social Class, gender, generation and other factors. The discussion here confines itself to the extent to which our respondents distinguished between *central* and *local* government in their expressions of political assertiveness.

In the 1984 Report we noted an apparent increase in national assertiveness over a twenty-year period and suggested that it might be attributable to today's greater opportunities for participation at the local level. This year we have included measures of local assertiveness as well so as to contrast them with measures of national assertiveness. And, within the broad constraint of questions which are not strictly comparable, we have been able to make comparisons in local assertiveness over time, using the 1960 study, *The Civic Culture* (Almond and Verba, 1963), and the survey carried out for the Maud Committee on local government in the early months of 1965 (Maud, 1967).

We first asked respondents what action, if any, they would take if Parliament was considering a law which they regarded as *really unjust or harmful.* We then asked a further question: *Now suppose your local council was proposing a scheme which you thought was really unjust or harmful. Which, if any, of the things on this card do you think you would do? Any others?* The differences in national and local responses were quite marked and were sustained throughout the sample.*

As explained in Chapter 1, these responses may conveniently be conflated into two indices of political assertiveness – a Personal Action Index (PAI) and a Collective Action Index (CAI).

Taking the sample as a whole, the scores on these two indices were:

	National	Local
PAI	0.88	1.13
CAI	0.74	0.69

The maximum (activist) score for either index was four and the minimum minus

---

* Comparisons with our 1983 survey results should however take into account that the 1983 questionnaire included a preliminary question as to whether or not the respondent had ever regarded a proposed law as unjust or harmful. Dropping this preliminary question has had the effect of considerably inflating the proportions who say (hypothetically) that they would take some action.

one. So local government was seen as considerably more accessible to the complaining citizen than was central government. Alternative interpretations of the lower score on *collective* action for local government may be that local authorities were seen as less responsive to expressions of mass opinion, or that the direct and personal approach was more appropriate at this level of government. And it may indeed be the case, *contra* Almond and Verba, that recourse to collective action in our culture speaks more of a sense of personal futility than it does of a 'civic' spirit.

Responses to the prospect of unjust or harmful actions

	Parliament	Local council
Personal action:	%	%
Contact MP/councillor	55	61
Speak to influential person	15	14
Contact government department/council official	9	26
Contact radio, TV or newspaper	18	18
Take any personal action	69	79
Collective action:		
Sign petition	57	50
Raise issue in an organisation I belong to	8	6
Go on a protest or demonstration	9	8
Form a group of like-minded people	8	10
Take any collective action	66	61
None of these	8	5

How was the far higher score for local than national *personal* action achieved? First, the proportion of respondents willing to contact their councillor was higher than that proposing to contact their MP in the same circumstances, and these differences may relate to the considerable distinction drawn between the role of MP and councillor which emerged from last year's survey. But the most striking finding in this comparison is surely the one relating to the relative accessibility of the administrative officials of town hall and Whitehall. As many as 26% would approach the town or county hall offices direct, in marked contrast to the nine per cent who would contact a government department. There is a possible wording effect here, but it is unlikely to have distorted what are probably realistic assessments of the options for action at national and local levels.

In the light of these findings, the question of which form of political protest people believe to be the *most effective* assumes a particular importance. As in the 1983 survey, the proportions claiming any action to be effective fell below those citing it as something they would be likely to do, largely because they were offered up to eight distinct (and sometimes 'costless') courses of action. As the table shows, the differences between national and local perceptions of effectiveness were small. They are, however, quite instructive, for they hint at the somewhat greater perceived accessibility of local government officials as compared with civil servants.

The striking feature of these figures is the importance attached to elected representatives at both the central and local level. As we have seen, however,

Responses to the prospect of an unjust or harmful action by Parliament or local council: actions considered 'most effective'

	most effective nationally	most effective locally
Personal action:	%	%
Contact MP/councillor	43	38
Speak to influential person	4	5
Contact government department/council official	4	8
Contact radio, TV or newspaper	16	16
Collective action:		
Sign petition	12	14
Raise issue in an organisation I belong to	1	2
Go on a protest or demonstration	6	4
Form a group of like-minded people	3	5
None of these	7	5

there was generally a greater sense of citizen efficacy with respect to local than central government, which confirms the findings of the *Civic Culture* survey carried out in five countries some 25 years ago. Almond and Verba (1963, p.185) wrote that their finding of a consistently higher propensity to act in protest against the local authority confirmed "widely held views of the closer relatedness of citizens to their local governments because of their greater immediacy, accessibility, and familiarity". Direct numerical comparisons are fraught with difficulty owing to the differences in question form and reporting method between the *Civic Culture* survey and our own. But differences in response *within* each survey do bear comparison. A calculation of an approximate equivalent to PAI (local) for the 1960 survey would give a value considerably higher than the national score for that survey, and higher *by about the same margin* as we found in our own sample.

Local activism does, however, seem to have increased during the last twenty five years. In 1959-60 Almond and Verba asked: "Suppose a regulation were being considered by [your local council] that you considered very unjust or harmful. What do you think you would do? Anything else?". Five years later the Maud survey asked: "If there was something you felt strongly that the [borough or district] council ought or ought not to be doing – would you do anything to try to get them to change to your point of view?". The wording of the 1965 question is less likely to produce a positive reply and, while it is therefore possibly more appropriate, a direct comparison would be misleading. Nevertheless, all three surveys provide evidence of the greater willingness of individuals to act on their own account when roused by some proposed local

Local political action in 1960 and 1984

	1960*	1984
Percentage who would:	%	%
act alone	41	79
act with others	36	61
not act at all	22	5

* Source: Almond and Verba (1963).

action. We may repeat the Maud question at some stage to throw light on the fascinating issue of whether local government re-organisation, in which the smaller authorities were swept away, has had any impact upon citizen assertiveness.

For the most part, the subgroup differences in national political assertiveness discussed in our 1984 Report and in Chapter 1 of this report applied also to local assertiveness, with the middle-aged and better educated exhibiting higher scores, particularly for personal action, than the young, the old, and the less highly educated.

Personal action scores by age and school-leaving age

	PAI (national)	PAI (local)
Age:		
18-24	0.81	1.03
25-34	0.91	1.26
35-54	1.01	1.29
55 and over	0.77	0.97
School-leaving age:		
16 or under	0.81	1.04
17-18	1.05	1.47
19 or over	1.26	1.49
still in full-time education	1.22	1.41

Where we might have expected differences in local assertiveness – for instance between owner-occupiers and tenants – they were small, although the low scores of public sector tenants are noteworthy. Income differences as such exerted a less marked effect than education. (See **Tables 6.1** and **6.2** for further details.)

Personal action scores by tenure and income group

	PAI (national)	PAI (local)
Tenure:		
owner-occupier	0.90	1.18
rented (public)	0.79	1.02
rented (other)	0.92	1.14
Household income:		
under £5,000	0.76	1.03
£5,000-£7,999	1.01	1.24
£8,000-£11,999	0.93	1.24
£12,000 and over	1.07	1.34

We also explored the possibility that the perceived accessibility of local authorities might itself vary between different parts of the country and between say, the metropolitan and non-metropolitan areas, or the densely populated and mobile South East as opposed to the remoter rural regions. Clearly, the raw regional scores will be very responsive to occupational and income differences. However, examining the difference between national and local PAI scores within each region effectively holds these other factors constant and measures the relative accessibility of local government there. As the table below shows, we found no differences in the margin by which people were more inclined to intervene in local than in national issues between metropolitan and non-metropolitan areas. Even in Greater London, where a saturation poster campaign has compared the alleged responsiveness of government under the GLC and Whitehall rule, the margin does not deviate from the national average of 0.23. Nor is there a 'remoteness from Whitehall' pattern in either the national or local scores.

Personal action scores by region

	PAI (national)	PAI (local)
Scotland	0.64	0.90
North	0.84	1.18
North West	0.97	1.17
Yorkshire	0.94	1.32
West Midlands	0.94	1.17
East Midlands	1.03	1.18
Wales	0.66	0.98
South West	1.09	1.22
South East	0.83	1.12
Greater London	0.89	1.14
Metropolitan areas	0.91	1.18
Non-metropolitan areas	0.86	1.11
Total	0.88	1.11

As the table shows, however, there were some striking differences between individual regions in the margin by which local assertiveness exceeded national assertiveness. These were to some extent attributable to differences in the composition of the score which surely reflected local circumstances. For example, 25% of the Greater London respondents would contact their local newspaper or radio, while only 12% of the Scots would do so. In the Northern region, 34% of the respondents would contact a council official while only 22% of those in the West Midlands would. Interesting differences also emerge from inspection of the response to the question about the most effective forms of protest. Eleven per cent of the Welsh thought that none of the courses of action offered by the interviewers was likely to prove effective, while only one per cent of the Scots thought so. The perceived accessibility and effectiveness of councillors also varied widely between the regions. In Scotland, contact with councillors was thought the most effective avenue by 47% of the respondents, compared with only 29% of North Western respondents. This may partly be a function of the smaller scale of Scottish local authorities by comparison with England.

Of course, many of these inter-regional differences were small and should be interpreted cautiously, especially in view of the small number of sampling points in each area and the small numbers of respondents in some.

Nonetheless the results do suggest that regional and local factors – institutional, locational, cultural – influenced the relationship between the citizen and his or her local government. Further exploration over the years might shed more light upon these factors and begin to suggest what the consequences of the 1974 local government re-organisation have been for political representation in Britain. In any case, the time is surely ripe for a repeat of the 1965 Maud Committee survey.

Central *versus* local control

The greater apparent accessibility of local than national government to citizen involvement naturally raised the question of relations between the two levels of government. Here we asked a number of questions, including one asked last year, on whether central control of local government should be greater, less, or about the same. Since the responses to such a general question may well have reflected relative indifference, we also asked specific questions about where the responsibility for determining local rate and rent levels should lie. We anticipated that central measures to restrict rate levels would enjoy popular support. We then added a further issue on which central control might be seen as 'progressive' (in the sense of raising standards) and asked whether central or local government should determine the content of what is taught in the school curriculum. These questions are of considerable topical importance in the year of the Rates Act and of other significant incursions by the centre into what has been thought hitherto to be the proper sphere of local government.

Year-on-year differences are not expected to be large in a survey such as this, and at first sight very little has changed in the pattern of opinion on the general question of central control of local government. This year, as last, we asked:

Do you think that local councils ought to be controlled by central government more, less, or about the same amount as now?

	1983	1984
	%	%
More	13	14
About the same	45	42
Less	34	36
Don't know	8	8

The very small percentage changes away from 'about the same' are not significant in themselves. They suggest, however, that some polarisation of opinion may have occurred as a result of the intense political debates of the last year. If this is so, we would expect to see these differences amplified among people who identify with the two major parties for whom the issue of central control has proved so divisive. And indeed among both Conservative and Labour identifiers there has been a large shift from 'about the same' towards their respective party positions on the issue, so that there is now a substantial difference between party identifiers. But the differences were far from symmetrical: it remains the case that only 14% of our respondents would like to see greater central control over local government, including less than a fifth of those who aligned themselves with the Conservative party. (See **Table 6.3**.)

The partisan polarisation of issues, where it existed, tended to be amplified when we distinguished between each party's more committed identifiers – the *partisans* – and its less intense 'sympathisers' and 'residual identifiers'. The actual picture, as the following table shows, is that Labour partisans favoured a reduction of central control by a greater margin than any other group. Labour's other followers shared this view, but to a less marked degree. The figures for the Alliance suggested no clear pattern, while Conservative partisans confounded our expectation by being scarcely warmer towards increased central control than the other followers of that party and rather less supportive than

Alliance partisans. This is an important finding, because it appears to reinforce the proposition that *localism* is an important and often overlooked component of Conservative ideology (Young, 1975), one which a Conservative administration engaged in making inroads into local government autonomy ignores at its peril.

Attitudes to central control of local government by political identification

	Conservative		Alliance		Labour		Non-
	partisans	others	partisans	others	partisans	others	aligned
	%	%	%	%	%	%	%
More	19	17	24	5	11	11	10
About the same	49	46	34	39	32	43	43
Less	27	28	39	46	52	38	27
Don't know	3	7	3	7	4	7	16

There were also interesting relationships between attitudes to central government control and to the perceived responsiveness of local government. Broadly, those least in favour of central control had a correspondingly greater faith in the processes of local democracy, or at any rate in the effectiveness of approaching councillors as a means of achieving change. Sixty-nine per cent of those who wanted less central control would approach a local councillor by comparison with only 58% of those who wanted more central control.

These differing beliefs about the efficacy of various modes of protest were paralleled by differences in the expressed willingness to use them. As the next table shows, those who wished to see a reduction in central control of local government declared themselves more ready to take action in the face of an unjust or harmful local decision: they had a stronger sense of their own efficacy as citizens. Nor was this greater assertiveness confined to local political action; it was reflected too at the national level. The differences, however, were not large.

Attitudes to central control of local government by personal action scores

Central government control of local councils should be:	PAI (national)	PAI (local)
More	0.92	1.21
About the same	0.89	1.10
Less	0.97	1.27

So far we have referred only to an abstract notion of 'central control', and we would expect the pattern of opinion to differ when we consider specific issues which are closer to the everyday concerns of the respondent. The current controversy over central control revolves around just such a tangible issue: the central determination of local rate levels through the Rates Act 1984 and the subsequent rate-capping orders. Rates and charges – including housing rents – are the principal sources of local revenues available to local authorities. As the level of government grant is decided by the government itself, the determination of rates and charges could be regarded as the *sine qua non* of local self-government. We asked: *Do you think the level of rates should be up to the local council to decide, or should central government have the final say?* And we followed this question with: *How about the level of council rents? Should that be up to the local council to decide or should central government have the final say?* The answers in both cases revealed very considerable support for local determination of these local sources of revenue.

Who should finally decide the level of rates and rents?

	Rates	Rents
	%	%
Local council	74	76
Central government	19	17
Don't know	7	7

On both rates and rents this broad pattern of opinion was reflected throughout the sample, irrespective of Social Class, region or income. It was, however, an issue on which party influences were clearly apparent. Among Labour identifiers 84% favoured local determination and only 11% central determination of rates and rents. Conservatives were somewhat less emphatic with respect to rates, with 29% of them in favour of central government having the final say. When we distinguished between the partisans and the less committed adherents of the major parties, the differences became sharper still, but only in respect of the currently controversial issue of rates – shown in the table below – not rents. (See **Tables 6.3** and **6.4** for further details.)

Who should decide local rate levels?

	Conservative		Alliance		Labour	
	partisans	others	partisans	others	partisans	others
	%	%	%	%	%	%
Local council	62	69	88	76	86	82
Central government	33	22	9	17	9	13
Don't know	5	8	3	7	4	5

Owner-occupiers, generally thought to be the most rate-sensitive group in the population, were not notably more in favour of giving central government the final say over rates: 71% of them (compared with 74% of the sample as a whole) regarded rates as a matter for the local council. So there is scant evidence here of the 'ratepayer revolt' so often cited in justification of the Rates Act. Only party identification seemed to distinguish respondents and, even so, the government had not yet persuaded the majority of its most committed supporters of the necessity of the Rates Act powers. We should of course beware of over-interpreting this finding. The large number of Conservatives who were not prepared to accept central determination of rate levels may possibly have distinguished between such general propositions about local financial autonomy and the specific issue of rate-capping a small number of (Labour-controlled) councils. They might therefore have been more supportive of the government's actions than of the principles behind them. Nonetheless, even the strongest Conservative identifiers seemed to have a degree of ambivalence, at least, towards the provisions contained in the Rates Act.

The third and final specific instance of central control that we explored was the determination of the content of *the school curriculum*. Here we found a more evenly balanced pattern of opinion within the sample as a whole; 53% thought the curriculum ought to be the prerogative of the LEA, and 39% favoured central determination. Here, however, there were sharp divisions along class and income lines, reflected also in the length of time respondents had themselves spent in full-time education. We asked: *Do you think that what is taught in schools should be up to the local education authority to decide, or should central government have the final say?*

Control of the curriculum by Social Class, income and school-leaving age

	Social Class		Income		School-leaving age	
	Non-manual	Manual	£12,000 pa or over	Under £12,000 pa	17 or over	16 or under
	%	%	%	%	%	%
Decided by LEA	45	59	39	57	40	56
Final say by central government	47	34	54	36	53	35
Don't know	7	7	6	7	6	8

If we assume that dissatisfaction with schools and with what is taught in them would produce support for *central* control of standards, then we would expect to find that parents of children – of both pre-school and school age – would show a greater preference for central influence than those in adult only households. This proved to be the case, as can be seen from the following table. And it was not simply caused by an association with age: indeed, support for central intervention was relatively low in the 25-34 age group as a whole where a relatively high proportion of households with children are to be found. Yet assumed 'parental concern', while it had an effect on support for central control of the curriculum, was less important than the age at which the respondent himself or herself had left school. The figures suggest, then, that it was 'educational experience', rather than parental concern, that underpinned support for 'standards'.

Control of the school curriculum by household type

	Households with children 0-17	Adult only households
	%.	%
Should be decided by LEA	50	55
Final say should be by central government	45	35
Don't know	4	9

Given the associations between class, education and party support, we found the expected divisions on party lines also. But in this instance the basic party divisions (with 64% of Labour identifiers compared with only 42% of Conservatives favouring local determination) were *not* sharpened by partisanship. This suggests that it is the social basis of party alignment, rather than genuine partisan differences, that is being reflected here. Both Labour and

Conservative governments have sought greater influence over the school curriculum and the current Secretary of State's efforts in this direction have not been a matter of deep partisan contention. Moreover, divisions of class, income and educational experience serve to divorce the issue of central control of the curriculum from that of central control of rates and rents. What happens in schools is apparently not seen as a matter of constitutional significance but is approached more pragmatically. So there was no evident relationship between respondents' attitudes to central determination of the curriculum and their attitudes to other aspects of central control.

Concern for the environment

The relationship between the governors and the governed is coloured by the range of activities in which government engages. Since the war the citizen's experience of government has in many places been transformed by the carrying out of major public works with environmental impacts comparable in their magnitude with those of the railway upon the Victorian city. The construction of the post-war new towns presaged many of the issues that now attach to the building of motorways, airports or power stations and established the now familiar procedure of proposal, objection, public inquiry and ultimate decision.

Then, as now, little redress was available to the aggrieved person whose property or amenities stood to suffer from such development. His or her rights in the face of a public policy commitment were procedural rather than substantive. But three new tendencies are commonly said to have changed the atmosphere in which major developments now have to take place. First, arguments about new roads, airports or power stations have become overlaid with a more general concern for the conservation of amenity. Second, the spillovers – noise, pollution, fumes – which so often attend the higher levels of energy consumption associated with economic development of these kinds are regarded as more pervasive and more perturbing than they used to be. Third – and most crucially perhaps – the broad secular trend towards a more active and less deferential society is thought by some to raise the prospect of such major developments leading to protest or civil disobedience in place of the sullen acquiesence with which they have often been greeted hitherto.

This last fear has not materialised and the results we report in Chapter 1 do little to support the prediction of a 'revolt of the middle classes' in response to environmental (or indeed to other) issues. Nonetheless we did find an acute public sense of loss of amenity through urban and industrial pollution. Indeed, levels of concern about noise, fumes, and other forms of pollution were so high and the skew of opinion so great as to suggest a potential political force of some strength in these issues. We came to this conclusion by analysing the answers to a series of questions covering respondents' ratings of the seriousness of particular sources of pollution; their willingness to accept the costs of controlling industrial pollution in particular, and their attitudes towards nuclear energy and its associated risks. Several of these questions had already been asked in the 1983 survey, so we have the confidence of two readings to rely upon. They also cover much of the ground already reviewed by the Royal

Commission on Environmental Pollution in its 'overview' report of 1984 (Royal Commission on Environmental Pollution, 1984). We asked first:

How serious an effect on our environment do you think each of these things has?

		Very serious	Quite serious	Not very serious	Not at all serious	Don't know/ not answered
Noise from aircraft	%	7	24	50	17	2
Lead from petrol	%	45	39	11	2	2
Industrial waste in the rivers and sea	%	67	25	6	1	1
Waste from nuclear electricity stations	%	69	18	9	2	3
Industrial fumes in the air	%	46	40	11	2	2
Noise and dirt from traffic	%	20	45	29	4	2

The general level of concern about pollution can be gauged from the number of distinct sources of pollution which our respondents rated as 'very' or 'quite' serious. (See **Tables 6.5** and **6.6**.) *Most* respondents proved to be concerned about *most* sources of pollution: in all, 80% of those who filled in our self-completion questionnaire thought at least four of these sources had very or quite serious effects on the environment. We also found, much as expected, some association with population density; with slightly higher levels of concern being registered in metropolitan than in non-metropolitan areas, and much higher levels in respect of the distinctively urban sources of pollution. There was also a marked regional effect on levels of concern, again probably arising from the characteristics of different regions. Fewer people registered concern about all six sources of pollution in Scotland (16%), Wales and the North (18%) than in the industrial heartlands of the Midlands (21%) or London and the South East (27%). The most serious level of concern about *each* source, in relation to the population density of where people live is shown below:

Concern about pollution by place of residence

	Total	Greater London	Metropolitan areas	Non-metropolitan areas
'Very serious' source of pollution	%	%	%	%
Noise from aircraft	7	10	7	6
Lead from petrol	45	54	50	42
Industrial waste in the rivers and sea	67	75	72	64
Waste from nuclear electricity stations	69	66	72	68
Industrial fumes in the air	46	53	52	42
Noise and dirt from traffic	20	32	25	17

We will refer later to the fact that only 'nuclear waste', among all the sources, attracted less concern from Londoners. The other regional differences are probably accounted for to some extent by differences in occupation and income between regions. Those in Social Classes IV and V registered slightly lower levels of concern than those in Social Classes I to III, and there were marked differences by income group. Those with higher household incomes were much more likely than those with low incomes to describe these sources of pollution as 'serious'.

There were also still more striking associations of concern with household type. Adult households registered below average levels of concern, while households with children registered considerably higher levels. Indeed the people most worried about pollution were those in households with children under five (83%) and women in the 18-44 age group (82%). Women in the youngest (18-24) age group were also notably more concerned than men of the same age. (See **Table 6.5** for details.)

Each of the sources of pollution about which we asked merits separate attention. We begin with the least widespread (or most localised) concern – aircraft noise – and move through the other items in ascending order of concern, taking the proportion registering 'very serious' concern as our guide.

Aircraft noise was thought to be 'very serious' by only seven per cent of our respondents. More Londoners can however expect to experience the nuisance of aircraft noise, given the very high levels of air traffic there; as many as 46% of them found it to be 'very' or 'quite' serious, a proportion fully 11 points higher than that registered by any other region. There were also quite strong associations with housing tenure, with 34% of owner-occupiers expressing 'very' or 'quite' serious concern compared with 24% of public sector tenants. A similar size difference was found between non-manual and manual workers.

Age and sex differences also show interesting patterns. Men were slightly less concerned as a group than were women about aircraft noise, and middle-aged people (35-54) were rather more concerned than the younger and older groups. However, these broad categories conceal quite large age-within-sex differences. Thus, the higher levels of concern felt by women were accentuated in the younger age groups: as many as 36% of women aged 18-24 were concerned about aircraft noise, compared with only 19% of men of the same age. This margin became less marked with age so that the attitudes of men and women over the age of 60 were not dissimilar. (See **Table 6.5**.)

As we have shown, concern about *traffic noise and dirt* produced strong metropolitan/non-metropolitan distinctions, with residents of Greater London again registering the highest levels. Place proved to be the most important discriminator on this issue, although once again women registered more concern than men in most age groups, principally in this case in the 45-54 age group.

The pollution of the atmosphere by *lead in petrol* was regarded as far more serious than the noise and dirt nuisances of road traffic. Again, the metropolitan/non-metropolitan distinction was noticeable, as was the very high level of concern expressed by Londoners. Household *type* however proved to be of prime importance. We had expected that the publicity given to the effects of atmospheric lead upon the cognitive abilities of children in recent years (Wilson, 1983) would have shaped the attitudes of parents to some degree, but the extent to which this was so was surprising. As many as 54% of those households with under-fives registered 'very serious' concern, and a further 35% 'quite serious' concern; in other words only a negligible proportion of parents with young children expressed no real anxiety. The numbers were considerably lower for working age adult households (40% 'very serious' concern) and lowest for single persons over 60 years of age (30%). As before, women displayed a more intense concern than men of the same age on this issue, but, as before, this margin disappeared among those over 55 years of age.

The campaign for lead-free petrol (CLEAR) may well have had some effect in polarising political opinion on this issue. Although Social Class and income differences in levels of concern were not particularly marked, Conservative identifiers expressed less concern than Labour and Alliance identifiers about lead in petrol. These differences were also considerably amplified by partisanship, with the more committed Conservatives registering notably lower levels of concern than Conservative identifiers as a group.

Turning from traffic-generated fumes to *industrial fumes*, we encountered problems of discriminating between groups, since all of them expressed such very high levels of concern. The same feature characterises attitudes to the impact of *industrial waste* upon the rivers and the sea; there were few respondents who did not consider these sources of pollution to be serious. Only one per cent thought industrial waste in the rivers and sea to be a 'not at all serious' matter, and only two per cent gave that verdict on industrial fumes in the air. As this near unanimity circumscribes the possibilities for analysis, it is useful at this point to introduce the related issue we examined of how far respondents thought industry should be *prevented* from causing damage to the countryside and, more important perhaps, whether people were prepared to pay the price of such restraint. We posed just such a choice in the self-completion questionnaire, where we asked respondents to choose between two statements: *Industry should be prevented from causing damage to the countryside, even if this sometimes leads to higher prices OR Industry should keep prices down, even if this sometimes causes damage to the countryside.*

Control of industrial pollution versus prices

		Industry should be stopped from damaging the countryside, even if prices must rise	Industry should keep prices down, even if damage to the countryside results
Working, non-manual	%	85	14
Working, manual	%	73	26
Retired	%	71	27
Conservative identifiers	%	82	17
Alliance identifiers	%	83	17
Labour identifiers	%	73	25
Owner-occupiers	%	80	19
Public sector tenants	%	68	30
Household income: under £5,000	%	68	30
Household income: £12,000 and over	%	87	12
Men under 35	%	81	17
Men 35 and over	%	80	19
Women under 35	%	72	28
Women 35 and over	%	75	24

As many as 77% of respondents agreed with the first statement. Nevertheless, the question proved a more effective discriminator than those items which implied a generalised (and cost-free) concern for the environment. We would of course expect income to be associated with attitudes to a policy that raised prices. But, as the table above shows, there were also other factors which differentiated respondents.

The relationship of income, occupational status and housing tenure to attitudes on this issue was clear. It is reflected also in the fact that 'environmentalist' policies for industry are likely to have a greater appeal to supporters of the Conservative and Alliance parties than to Labour supporters among whom resistance to price increases is more acute. Of particular interest was the finding that this was the *sole* environmental issue where women proved not to take a 'greener' position than men. On the contrary, women under 35 – generally the most environmentally conscious group – showed little willingness, compared with most other groups, to trade off prices against environmental protection. Indeed, among the 18-24 age group, as many as 37% of women preferred lower prices, the strongest expression of preference from any group within the sample. This suggested a high degree of sensitivity to price amongst women in this age group, some of whom would have been managing a household budget. Otherwise we found somewhat higher levels of concern about industrial pollution among those subgroups who were perhaps most able to pay for control than among those who were not. (See **Tables 6.11** and **6.12** for further details.)

The 'nuclear' issue

We turn finally to what was seen to be the most serious of all the environmental issues we covered – the disposal of *nuclear waste*, and we relate this concern to other nuclear fears.

While concern about most sources of pollution was place-specific, this was *not* the case for nuclear waste disposal: only four percentage points separated the metropolitan and non-metropolitan areas. In addition, as we have noted, this was the only issue on which Londoners were less concerned than the sample as a whole. Such findings might at first suggest that the locations of the existing and proposed power stations and the very large areas which would be at risk from a nuclear accident simply serve to diffuse concern more widely across the country.

In fact, attitudes to nuclear waste disposal were strongly polarised, as indeed they were on the related issues of nuclear energy policy, nuclear risk, and the probability of a serious nuclear accident occurring at a British power station during the next decade. The polarisation arises from the highly symbolic nature of the nuclear issue. Nuclear power (and nuclear weaponry) seem to evoke wider social and moral questions, and therefore divide the population in a quite specific way. So we found some fairly strong associations with party identification. Nearly 80% of Labour identifiers thought nuclear waste disposal a 'very serious' problem, as against around 60% of Conservative identifiers.

Most of the more 'material' characteristics such as income, tenure or occupation failed to distinguish responses to the nuclear waste question to any great degree. At first sight men and women hardly differed on this issue; nor did young people from old. On further analysis, however, as we noted in the

1984 Report, these broad age and sex categories actually concealed very sharp divergences which cancelled each other out at higher levels of aggregation. In particular, women under 45 registered very high levels of concern in comparison with their male or their older counterparts, with 92% considering nuclear waste to be 'very' or 'quite' serious. These are rather different patterns of subgroup variation from those we found on the other environmental issues we covered. And they persisted when we turned from nuclear waste disposal to the wider set of questions relating to *nuclear energy and weapons*. They appeared, therefore, to mark out nuclear from non-nuclear issues. The most striking of these differences was the extent to which the age/sex differentiation and the partisan alignments ran through, and gave coherence to, nuclear issues *per se*.

For example, we asked respondents to choose between three options for future electricity generation: making do with existing power stations, building more coal-fuelled power stations, or building more nuclear power stations:

Which one of these three possible solutions to Britain's electricity needs would you favour most?

		Make do with the power stations we have already	Build more coal-fuelled power stations	Build more nuclear power stations
Conservative identifiers	%	40	33	24
Alliance identifiers	%	36	48	14
Labour identifiers	%	33	56	8
Men under 45	%	32	38	25
Men 45 and over	%	28	51	19
Women under 45	%	47	42	9
Women 45 and over	%	42	43	9

As can be seen, women were more opposed to further nuclear power stations than men were, but the differences between them were much greater in the younger age groups. Indeed, as the detailed figures in **Table 6.7** at the end of this chapter show, support for nuclear power was *strongest* among men (32%) in the very age group – the under 25s – where it was *weakest* (7%) among women. (See **Tables 6.7** and **6.8** for further details.)

Given the coincidence of our fieldwork with the onset of the national miners' strike, we might have expected to find such partisan divisions on energy policy issues. Yet, as we shall see, the partisan divisions also featured strongly in the assessment of the risks involved in nuclear energy. It seems that attitudes to energy generation are shaped largely by the perception of risk and the symbolic loading placed upon the prospect of a nuclear accident.

That the responses to the earlier question on energy policy were tapping an environmental rather than an industrial factor is suggested by the close association between attitudes on that question and the perception of risk. Only one per cent of that large number who thought that nuclear energy entailed 'very serious' risks favoured the construction of more nuclear power stations, compared with 39% of those who thought the risks to be 'slight' and as many as 56% of that small minority who thought there were 'hardly any' risks involved.

As far as nuclear power stations are concerned, which of these statements comes closest to your own feelings?

	Total %	Conservative %	Alliance %	Labour %
They create *very serious* risks for the future	37	24	33	52
They create *quite serious* risks for the future	30	32	37	27
	67	56	70	79
They create only *slight* risks for the future	23	32	22	14
They create *hardly any* risks for the future	8	10	7	5
	31	42	29	20
Don't know/not answered	2	2	1	1

The distinctiveness of the attitudes of younger women was also apparent in their perception of nuclear risk. Men under 45 were hardly more concerned than older men, but women of most age groups were distinctly more concerned than men. As many as 74% of women under 45 saw nuclear power stations as presenting 'very serious' or 'quite serious' risks for the future, and 70% of older women agreed.

We also asked (as we did last year) about the expectations of a number of specified 'catastrophes', including *a serious accident at a British nuclear power station*, within the next ten years. The overall figures showed a striking lack of confidence in the safety of nuclear power, with more than half of the whole sample (in both years) thinking such an eventuality was 'very' or 'quite' likely to occur. Again, the association with party identification showed up.

Expectations of a serious accident at a British nuclear power station

	Total %	Conservative identifiers %	Alliance identifiers %	Labour identifiers %
Very likely	13	8	8	20
Quite likely	40	33	41	47
Not very likely	36	45	41	23
Not at all likely	8	11	7	6
Don't know	2	1	1	2

What, if any, relationship obtains between attitudes to nuclear *energy* issues and attitudes to nuclear *weapons*? The table below relates perceptions of the risks involved in nuclear power generation to attitudes to nuclear weapons. The rows represent the respective responses to three sets of questions. The first couplet posed a choice between whether *Britain should rid itself of nuclear weapons while persuading others to do the same* and *Britain should keep its nuclear weapons until we persuade others to reduce theirs*. The second couplet shows responses to the question about whether *the siting of American nuclear missiles in Britain makes Britain a safer or a less safe place to live.* The third couplet shows responses to a similar question about *British* nuclear missiles.

Attitudes to nuclear weapons

	Perception of nuclear power risks:	
	'Very' or 'quite' serious risks	'Slight' or 'hardly any' risks
	%	%
British nuclear arms:		
retain	69	83
renounce	27	14
US missiles:		
make Britain safer	27	52
make Britain less safe	62	32
British missiles:		
make Britain safer	50	69
make Britain less safe	39	21

The pattern was remarkably consistent and symmetrical. A definite relationship existed between people's fear of nuclear energy and their views on disarmament (despite the skews of opinion against unilateralism *and* against nuclear power stations). Those who were the most worried about nuclear power were more likely to favour unilateralism, and to be nervous both of American and British nuclear missiles in Britain. This broad patterning of attitudes is almost replicated when we examine the relationship with the expectations of the probability of a British nuclear power station *accident* in the next ten years.

This leads us to ask whether there is already an important element of 'nuclear politics' in Britain. Our findings suggest that there is indeed a degree of coherence in people's attitudes towards nuclear issues, but perhaps less than expected, even among 'unilateralists', and still less among 'multilateralists'. Four-fifths of the 'unilateralists' saw nuclear energy as a risky business: but so did two-thirds of the total sample. About two-thirds of the unilateralists considered a nuclear power station accident a likely event; but so did around half of the total sample. Moreover, less than a quarter of our sample supported a unilateralist position. If there is a syndrome of nuclear concern, it centres on the linked issues of nuclear power and the perceived dangers of the *American* nuclear presence, indicating perhaps that a sense of *uncontrollability* lies at the heart of 'the nuclear threat'.

Where does this leave 'green' politics in Britain? If this term is seen as linking environmental concerns with the anti-nuclear movement on the West German pattern, it appears that green politics have yet to arrive as a coherent force. True, there was a substantial bedrock of concern about domestic nuclear issues, particularly among younger women and among Labour identifiers. But these associations, if anything, serve to distinguish the nuclear from the non-nuclear threats to the environment; for the latter concerns are more closely linked to household circumstances. So Britain does not appear to be on the threshold of the sort of politicisation of 'green' issues in which the anti-nuclear movement can provide the leading role. While it seems likely that opposition to the use of nuclear energy may become increasingly linked to opposition to nuclear weapons, a 'green' political movement, if it develops, will still be rather distinct from the anti-nuclear position, particularly in respect of the social base of its support.

Nor was there much indication that concern over pollution and opposition to developments that threaten the environment are likely to lead to widespread disaffection and middle-class civil disobedience. While there was widespread concern about pollution *and* widespread distrust of nuclear power on safety grounds, particularly among younger women, there were as we saw in Chapter 1, only shreds of support for political lawbreaking, and rather less among women than among men. Environmental issues therefore seem unlikely, for the time being, to radicalise hitherto quiescent social groups. But on our evidence they could turn out to be a potent factor in future electoral contests. For the time being, any of the three major party groupings could benefit from such a development.

References

ALMOND, G. A. and VERBA, S., *The Civic Culture*, Princeton University Press, Princeton N.J. (1963).
JONES, G. W. and STEWART, J. D., *The Case for Local Government*, Allen and Unwin, London (1983).
MAUD, J., *Committee on the Management of Local Government: Vol. 3: The Local Government Elector*, HMSO, London (1967).
ROYAL COMMISSION ON ENVIRONMENTAL POLLUTION *Tenth Report*, Cmnd. 9149, HMSO, London (1984).
WILSON, D., *The Lead Scandal*, Heinemann, London (1983).
YOUNG, K., *Local Politics and the Rise of Party*, Leicester University Press, Leicester (1975).

Acknowledgements

I am grateful to George Jones and John Stewart for their comments on an earlier version of this chapter.

6.1 PARLIAMENTARY PROTEST – ACTIONS RESPONDENTS WOULD TAKE (Q96 a) by accommodation of household, household income and school leaving age

Actions respondents would take in the event of a really unjust and harmful law being considered by Parliament:

BASE: ALL RESPONDENTS	UNWEIGHTED BASE	WEIGHTED BASE	ACCOMMODATION OF HOUSEHOLD					HOUSEHOLD INCOME					SCHOOL LEAVING AGE				
			OWNED/BEING BOUGHT	RENTED (LA/NEW TOWN)	RENTED (HOUS. ASS.)	RENTED (OTHER)	NO INF.	UNDER £5000	£5000-£7999	£8000-£11999	£12000+	NO INFORMATION	16 OR UNDER	17-18	19+	STILL IN F.T. EDUCATION	NO INF.
UNWEIGHTED BASE	1675	1107	428	14	118	8	510	374	302	285	204	1297	215	122	27	14	
WEIGHTED BASE	1645	1081	420	15	122	7	493	377	292	281	201	1285	222	119	27	12	
WOULD TAKE NO LISTED ACTIONS	136 8%	81 7%	42 10%	1	11 9%	1	62 13%	14 4%	16 5%	7 2%	38 19%	122 9%	11 5%	2 1%	0	2	
1 OR 2 LISTED ACTIONS TAKEN	1165 71%	766 71%	298 71%	12	86 70%	3	356 72%	269 71%	212 73%	193 69%	135 67%	918 73%	153 69%	67 57%	18	8	
3 OR 4 LISTED ACTIONS TAKEN	308 19%	207 19%	73 18%	2	22 18%	3	66 13%	89 24%	59 20%	67 24%	27 13%	207 16%	49 22%	42 35%	9	1	
5 OR MORE LISTED ACTIONS TAKEN	26 2%	19 2%	4 1%	0	3 2%	0	7 1%	6 2%	5 2%	8 3%	0 0%	12 1%	4 2%	9 7%	1	0	
ACTIONS: CONTACT MY MP	908 55%	618 57%	214 51%	6	65 53%	5	237 48%	225 60%	175 60%	186 66%	85 42%	667 53%	134 61%	84 70%	19	4	
SPEAK TO INFLUENTIAL PERSON	240 15%	152 14%	58 14%	1	25 20%	4	91 18%	49 13%	36 12%	38 14%	26 13%	169 13%	41 18%	24 20%	4	3	
CONTACT A GOVERNMENT DEPARTMENT	141 9%	99 9%	29 7%	2	11 9%	0	29 6%	39 10%	27 9%	29 10%	15 8%	98 8%	21 9%	18 15%	4	0	
CONTACT RADIO, TV OR NEWSPAPER	290 18%	190 18%	71 17%	3	25 20%	1	80 16%	82 22%	50 17%	56 20%	22 11%	208 16%	48 22%	26 22%	6	2	
SIGN A PETITION	942 57%	630 58%	230 55%	9	70 58%	3	256 52%	244 65%	185 63%	166 59%	90 45%	713 56%	130 59%	76 63%	18	5	
RAISE THE ISSUE IN AN ORGANISATION I ALREADY BELONG TO	130 8%	94 9%	30 7%	1	5 4%	0	27 6%	32 9%	33 11%	28 10%	10 5%	79 6%	24 11%	24 20%	3	0	
GO ON A PROTEST OR DEMONSTRATION	147 9%	92 9%	35 8%	3	15 13%	1	26 5%	42 11%	29 10%	34 12%	16 8%	93 7%	23 10%	19 16%	11	1	
FORM A GROUP OF LIKE MINDED PEOPLE	129 8%	81 7%	35 8%	2	11 9%	0	37 7%	29 8%	23 8%	28 10%	12 6%	95 8%	17 7%	16 13%	1	0	
DONT KNOW	2 0%	1 0%	0 0%	0	1 0%	0	2 0%	0 0%	0 0%	0 0%	0 0%	1 0%	0 0%	0 0%	0	0	
NOT ANSWERED	10 1%	8 1%	2 0%	0	0 0%	0	1 0%	0 0%	1 0%	6 2%	2 1%	6 0%	4 2%	0 0%	0	0	

6.2 COUNCIL PROTEST – ACTIONS RESPONDENTS WOULD TAKE (Q7 a) by accommodation of household, household income and school leaving age

Actions respondents would take in the event of a really unjust and harmful scheme being proposed by local council:

Column groups: columns 2–6 = ACCOMMODATION OF HOUSEHOLD; columns 7–11 = HOUSEHOLD INCOME; columns 12–16 = SCHOOL LEAVING AGE.

BASE: ALL RESPONDENTS	OWNED/ BEING BOUGHT	RENTED (LA/ NEW TOWN)	RENTED (HOUS. ASS.)	RENTED (OTHER)	NO INF.	UNDER £5000	£5000- £7999	£8000- £11999	£12000 +	NO INFORM- ATION	16 OR UNDER	17- 18	19 +	STILL IN F.T. EDUCAT- ION	NO INF.
UNWEIGHTED BASE 1675	1107	428	32	118	8	510	374	302	285	204	1297	215	122	27	14
WEIGHTED BASE 1645	1081	420	15	122	7	493	377	292	281	201	1265	222	119	27	12
WOULD TAKE NO LISTED ACTIONS 89 5%	48 4%	32 8%	1	6 5%	1	48 10%	5 1%	6 2%	3 1%	27 14%	84 7%	3 1%	1 1%	0	2
1 OR 2 LISTED ACTIONS TAKEN 1105 67%	722 67%	292 70%	12	77 63%	3	331 67%	252 67%	204 70%	173 62%	146 72%	883 70%	130 59%	69 58%	16	7
3 OR 4 LISTED ACTIONS TAKEN 407 25%	279 26%	85 20%	2	38 31%	3	106 21%	110 29%	74 25%	90 32%	27 14%	278 22%	76 34%	41 35%	9	2
5 OR MORE LISTED ACTIONS TAKEN 30 2%	24 2%	5 1%	0	1 1%	0	6 1%	8 2%	6 2%	6 2%	1 0%	12 1%	8 4%	8 7%	2	0
ACTIONS: CONTACT MY COUNCILLOR 1003 61%	686 63%	227 54%	4	82 67%	4	286 58%	231 61%	197 68%	194 69%	95 47%	749 59%	143 65%	87 73%	17	7
SPEAK TO INFLUENTIAL PERSON 233 14%	150 14%	60 14%	2	20 16%	2	74 15%	64 17%	31 11%	44 16%	20 10%	150 12%	56 25%	23 19%	4	1
CONTACT A COUNCIL OFFICIAL 427 26%	280 26%	113 27%	6	26 21%	3	124 25%	108 29%	81 28%	75 27%	39 20%	312 20%	74 33%	32 27%	9	1
CONTACT LOCAL NEWSPAPER OR RADIO 292 18%	209 19%	59 14%	2	21 18%	1	74 15%	70 19%	60 20%	66 24%	22 11%	191 15%	56 25%	36 30%	8	2
SIGN A PETITION 817 50%	549 51%	195 46%	10	60 49%	3	207 42%	205 54%	170 58%	151 54%	82 41%	627 50%	101 46%	68 57%	18	2
RAISE THE ISSUE IN AN ORGANISATION I ALREADY BELONG TO 105 6%	74 7%	25 6%	0	7 5%	0	32 7%	19 5%	21 7%	28 10%	5 2%	64 5%	18 8%	18 15%	3	1
GO ON A PROTEST OR DEMONSTRATION 133 8%	87 8%	28 7%	2	15 12%	0	28 6%	39 10%	21 7%	30 11%	16 8%	85 7%	19 9%	19 16%	9	1
FORM A GROUP OF LIKE-MINDED PEOPLE 166 10%	113 10%	43 10%	1	9 7%	0	43 9%	41 11%	28 10%	42 15%	12 6%	129 10%	19 9%	15 13%	3	0
DONT KNOW 6 0%	1 0%	4 1%	0	1 1%	0	3 1%	3 1%	0 0%	0 0%	1 0%	5 0%	0 0%	0 0%	0	1
NOT ANSWERED 9 1%	8 1%	1 0%	0	0 0%	1	0 0%	2 1%	1 0%	6 2%	1 0%	4 0%	5 2%	0 0%	0	1

6.3 CONTROL BY CENTRAL GOVERNMENT OR LOCAL GOVERNMENT (Q5 a, b) by detailed party identification

DETAILED PARTY IDENTIFICATION

BASE: ALL RESPONDENTS	WEIGHTED BASE	CON: TOTAL	PART-ISAN	SYMP.	RESID. ID.	LAB: TOTAL	PART-ISAN	SYMP.	RESID. ID.	SDP/LIB/ALL: TOTAL	PART-ISAN	SYMP.	RESID. ID.	OTHER PARTY	NO POLIT. ALLEG.	OTHER D.K / N.A
UNWEIGHTED BASE	1675	640	388	172	80	595	326	168	101	220	68	83	69	24	105	91
WEIGHTED BASE	1645	635	384	167	85	575	317	160	98	219	72	80	67	28	102	86
Control of local councils by central government ... SHOULD BE:																
MORE	225 14%	119 19%	75 19%	28 17%	16 19%	64 11%	36 11%	14 9%	14 14%	25 11%	17 24%	4 5%	4 5%	5	11 10%	2 2%
LESS	598 36%	173 27%	104 27%	46 27%	24 28%	261 45%	164 52%	66 41%	31 32%	96 44%	28 39%	39 49%	29 44%	12	28 27%	28 32%
SAME	692 42%	306 48%	188 49%	79 47%	38 45%	212 37%	101 32%	70 44%	41 42%	82 37%	24 34%	30 36%	27 41%	9	44 43%	39 45%
DON'T KNOW	107 7%	29 5%	12 3%	12 7%	6 7%	30 5%	12 4%	8 5%	10 10%	13 6%	2 3%	6 8%	5 7%	2	16 16%	17 20%
NOT ANSWERED	23 1%	8 1%	5 1%	2 1%	1 2%	8 1%	4 1%	2 1%	2 2%	3 1%	1 1%	0 0%	2 3%	0	3 3%	1 1%
Who should decide level of rates?																
DECIDED BY LOCAL COUNCIL	1219 74%	411 65%	237 62%	116 67%	57 67%	483 84%	272 86%	134 84%	77 78%	174 80%	64 88%	57 71%	54 81%	24	72 71%	56 65%
FINAL SAY BY CENTRAL GOVERNMENT	308 19%	183 29%	126 33%	36 21%	20 24%	64 11%	30 9%	19 12%	15 16%	32 14%	6 9%	17 21%	8 13%	3	13 12%	15 17%
DONT KNOW	111 7%	40 6%	18 5%	14 7%	7 9%	27 5%	14 4%	7 5%	6 6%	13 6%	2 3%	6 8%	5 7%	2	15 14%	15 17%
NOT ANSWERED	8 0%	2 0%	2 1%	0 0%	0 0%	2 0%	1 1%	0 0%	0 0%	0 0%	0 0%	0 0%	0 0%	0	3 3%	1 1%

6.4 CONTROL BY CENTRAL GOVERNMENT OR LOCAL GOVERNMENT (Q5 c)
by current/last social class, household income and school leaving age

Who should decide level of council rents?

BASE: ALL RESPONDENTS

		CURRENT / LAST SOCIAL CLASS					HOUSEHOLD INCOME					SCHOOL LEAVING AGE				
	WEIGHTED BASE	I,II	III NON MAN.	III MAN.	IV,V	NEVER WORKED /N.C.	UNDER £5000	£5000-£7999	£8000-£11999	£12000+	NO INF.	16 OR UNDER	17-18	19+	STILL IN F.T. EDUC.	NO INF.
UNWEIGHTED BASE	1675	352	380	383	388	172	510	374	302	285	204	1297	215	122	27	14
WEIGHTED BASE	1645	341	378	369	380	177	493	377	292	281	201	1265	222	119	27	12
DECIDED BY LOCAL COUNCIL	1255 76%	257 75%	299 79%	291 79%	286 75%	123 69%	398 81%	297 79%	212 72%	218 78%	130 65%	979 77%	164 74%	83 70%	19 70%	9
FINAL SAY BY CENTRAL GOVERNMENT	274 17%	64 19%	54 14%	63 17%	64 17%	29 16%	60 12%	66 18%	61 21%	52 18%	36 18%	206 16%	38 17%	26 21%	4 21%	1
DONT KNOW	107 6%	17 5%	23 6%	15 4%	29 8%	23 13%	32 6%	11 3%	20 7%	10 4%	33 17%	73 6%	19 8%	9 7%	5 7%	2
NOT ANSWERED	10 1%	3 1%	2 1%	1 0%	1 0%	3 2%	4 1%	3 1%	0 0%	1 0%	2 1%	7 1%	1 0%	2 1%	0	0

6.5 ENVIRONMENTAL NUISANCE (Q208) by age within sex

TABLE INCLUDES ONLY THOSE WHO THINK THE ENVIRONMENT IS SERIOUSLY AFFECTED BY:

BASE: THOSE RETURNING SELF-COMPLETION

AGE WITHIN SEX

	TOTAL	MALE									FEMALE								
		TOTAL	18-24	25-34	35-44	45-54	55-59	60-64	65+	NA	TOTAL	18-24	25-34	35-44	45-54	55-59	60-64	65+	NA
UNWEIGHTED BASE	1562	727	105	141	123	101	60	62	132	1	835	99	158	153	123	72	79	143	8
WEIGHTED BASE	1522	714	101	142	126	99	57	62	127	1	809	101	153	148	113	64	78	144	8
Noise from aircraft																			
VERY SERIOUS	99 7%	43 6%	2 2%	6 4%	8 6%	8 8%	4 6%	8 12%	9 7%	0	56 7%	9 9%	3 2%	7 5%	11 9%	6 10%	8 10%	13 9%	0
QUITE SERIOUS	369 24%	162 23%	17 17%	27 19%	32 26%	25 25%	11 20%	15 24%	34 27%	0	207 26%	27 27%	42 27%	45 31%	30 26%	10 16%	21 27%	29 20%	3
Lead from petrol																			
VERY SERIOUS	687 45%	323 45%	36 36%	77 54%	61 48%	41 41%	25 44%	31 50%	52 41%	0	364 45%	49 49%	74 48%	76 52%	62 55%	22 34%	25 32%	53 37%	3
QUITE SERIOUS	597 39%	270 38%	43 42%	49 35%	45 35%	44 44%	23 40%	22 36%	45 35%	0	327 40%	43 43%	67 44%	58 38%	35 31%	27 42%	41 52%	53 36%	5
Industrial waste in the rivers and sea																			
VERY SERIOUS	1015 67%	483 68%	66 65%	106 75%	90 72%	71 72%	39 69%	34 55%	77 61%	0	532 66%	73 72%	111 72%	99 67%	77 68%	36 56%	47 61%	86 59%	3
QUITE SERIOUS	381 25%	173 24%	23 23%	31 22%	32 25%	22 22%	13 23%	21 34%	30 24%	0	208 26%	25 25%	40 22%	34 27%	18 26%	18 29%	21 27%	36 25%	4
Waste from nuclear electricity stations																			
VERY SERIOUS	1051 69%	482 67%	65 64%	92 65%	92 73%	73 74%	36 65%	41 66%	82 65%	0	569 70%	81 80%	118 77%	110 74%	74 65%	45 71%	48 61%	91 63%	3
QUITE SERIOUS	267 18%	127 18%	18 18%	30 21%	20 16%	18 18%	13 23%	6 10%	22 17%	0	141 17%	17 17%	21 14%	24 16%	25 22%	11 16%	17 22%	22 15%	4
Industrial fumes in the air																			
VERY SERIOUS	695 46%	318 45%	39 39%	74 52%	70 56%	40 41%	24 43%	19 30%	52 41%	0	377 47%	56 56%	79 51%	60 41%	61 54%	26 40%	25 31%	68 47%	3
QUITE SERIOUS	606 40%	292 41%	45 44%	55 39%	43 34%	43 44%	23 40%	34 55%	49 39%	0	314 39%	38 37%	58 38%	72 49%	38 34%	24 38%	40 52%	40 27%	5
Noise and dirt from traffic																			
VERY SERIOUS	307 20%	127 18%	9 9%	28 20%	25 20%	13 13%	10 18%	10 16%	31 25%	0	179 22%	19 19%	26 17%	30 20%	31 27%	11 17%	18 23%	43 30%	2
QUITE SERIOUS	686 45%	325 46%	48 48%	64 45%	57 45%	47 47%	27 48%	34 55%	48 38%	0	361 45%	46 45%	75 49%	66 45%	51 45%	27 42%	42 54%	50 34%	5

6.6 ENVIRONMENTAL NUISANCE (208)
by party identification, household income and type of area

TABLE INCLUDES ONLY THOSE WHO THINK THE ENVIRONMENT IS SERIOUSLY AFFECTED BY:

BASE: THOSE RETURNING SELF-COMPLETION	WEIGHTED BASE	PARTY I.D.					HOUSEHOLD INCOME					TYPE OF AREA		
		TORY	LAB.	ALLIANCE	OTHER	NON-ALIGN	UNDER £5000	£5000-£7999	£8000-£11999	£12000+	NO INF.	GLC	METRO POLITAN	NON-METROP
UNWEIGHTED BASE	1562	602	551	208	23	178	471	359	290	277	165	149	534	1028
WEIGHTED BASE	1522	593	534	198	27	171	451	354	281	273	164	145	527	996
Noise from aircraft														
VERY SERIOUS	99 7%	26 4%	46 9%	13 6%	4	10 6%	40 9%	23 6%	11 4%	20 7%	6 3%	14 10%	39 7%	61 6%
QUITE SERIOUS	369 24%	152 26%	109 20%	60 31%	14	33 19%	101 22%	71 20%	81 29%	77 28%	38 23%	52 35%	132 25%	237 24%
Lead from petrol														
VERY SERIOUS	687 45%	224 38%	289 54%	91 46%	19	65 38%	203 45%	179 51%	139 49%	117 43%	49 30%	78 54%	265 50%	422 42%
QUITE SERIOUS	597 39%	252 43%	180 34%	83 42%	6	77 45%	162 36%	133 38%	113 40%	114 42%	76 46%	53 36%	192 37%	405 41%
Industrial waste in the rivers and sea														
VERY SERIOUS	1015 67%	364 61%	390 73%	137 69%	19	106 62%	286 63%	246 69%	202 72%	187 69%	95 58%	109 75%	381 72%	634 64%
QUITE SERIOUS	381 25%	162 27%	111 21%	53 27%	7	47 28%	113 25%	83 24%	67 24%	73 27%	45 27%	27 18%	114 22%	266 27%
Waste from nuclear electri-city stations														
VERY SERIOUS	1051 69%	354 60%	424 79%	141 71%	22	110 64%	315 70%	258 73%	202 72%	186 68%	91 56%	96 66%	377 72%	674 68%
QUITE SERIOUS	267 18%	123 21%	69 13%	40 20%	3	32 19%	70 15%	57 16%	56 20%	48 18%	37 23%	32 22%	94 18%	174 17%
Industrial fumes in the air														
VERY SERIOUS	695 46%	231 39%	275 52%	93 47%	16	80 47%	199 44%	170 48%	136 49%	121 44%	68 41%	77 53%	273 52%	422 42%
QUITE SERIOUS	606 40%	257 43%	189 35%	84 42%	9	67 39%	160 36%	142 40%	116 41%	122 45%	66 40%	48 33%	191 36%	415 42%
Noise and dirt from traffic														
VERY SERIOUS	307 20%	111 19%	130 24%	32 16%	6	28 17%	116 26%	65 18%	53 19%	48 18%	24 14%	47 32%	134 25%	172 17%
QUITE SERIOUS	686 45%	254 43%	225 42%	108 54%	15	85 50%	178 40%	159 45%	131 47%	138 50%	81 50%	64 44%	230 44%	457 46%

6.7 POSSIBLE SOLUTIONS TO BRITAIN'S ELECTRICITY NEEDS (Q209 a) by age within sex

BASE: THOSE RETURNING SELF-COMPLETION

AGE WITHIN SEX

	WEIGHTED BASE / TOTAL	MALE TOTAL	18-24	25-34	35-44	45-54	55-59	60-64	65+	NA	FEMALE TOTAL	18-24	25-34	35-44	45-54	55-59	60-64	65+	NA
UNWEIGHTED BASE	1562	727	105	141	123	101	60	64	132	8	835	99	158	153	123	72	79	143	8
WEIGHTED BASE	1522	714	101	142	126	99	57	62	127	8	809	101	153	148	113	64	78	144	8
MAKE DO WITH EXISTING POWER	574 / 38%	214 / 30%	36 / 36%	44 / 31%	38 / 31%	28 / 28%	13 / 23%	16 / 26%	38 / 30%	0	360 / 44%	59 / 58%	79 / 51%	50 / 34%	48 / 42%	24 / 37%	31 / 39%	66 / 45%	5
MORE COAL-FUELLED POWER STATIONS	663 / 44%	321 / 45%	28 / 28%	56 / 40%	58 / 46%	59 / 59%	27 / 49%	31 / 50%	58 / 46%	2	342 / 42%	33 / 33%	56 / 37%	78 / 53%	46 / 41%	32 / 50%	37 / 47%	58 / 40%	2
MORE NUCLEAR POWER STATIONS	236 / 15%	157 / 22%	32 / 32%	36 / 26%	25 / 19%	15 / 15%	15 / 27%	13 / 22%	24 / 19%	0	78 / 10%	7 / 7%	14 / 9%	16 / 11%	15 / 13%	7 / 11%	7 / 7%	15 / 10%	0
DONT KNOW	17 / 1%	2 / 0%	1 / 0%	0 / 0%	0 / 1%	1 / 1%	0 / 0%	0 / 0%	4 / 3%	1	15 / 2%	0 / 0%	1 / 1%	2 / 1%	3 / 3%	1 / 2%	3 / 4%	4 / 3%	0
NOT ANSWERED	33 / 2%	19 / 3%	4 / 4%	5 / 3%	4 / 3%	3 / 3%	1 / 1%	1 / 2%	4 / 3%	0	14 / 2%	2 / 2%	4 / 3%	2 / 1%	1 / 1%	3 / 2%	3 / 3%	2 / 2%	0

6.8 POSSIBLE SOLUTIONS TO BRITAIN'S ELECTRICITY NEEDS (Q209 a) by party identification, household income, combined working status and current social class

BASE: THOSE RETURNING SELF-COMPLETION

	WEIGHTED BASE / TOTAL	PARTY I.D. TORY	LAB.	ALLI-ANCE	OTHER	NON-ALIGN	HOUSEHOLD INCOME UNDER £5000	£5000-£7999	£8000-£11999	£12000+	NO INF.	WORKING MAN.	NON-MAN.	NOT WORKING RET-IRED	UNEMP	HOME
UNWEIGHTED BASE	1562	602	551	208	23	178	471	359	290	277	165	402	417	262	99	292
WEIGHTED BASE	1522	593	534	198	27	171	451	354	281	273	164	388	409	251	96	290
MAKE DO WITH EXISTING POWER	574 / 38%	239 / 40%	178 / 33%	70 / 36%	20 / 39%	67 / 39%	177 / 39%	134 / 38%	97 / 35%	90 / 33%	75 / 45%	120 / 31%	164 / 40%	91 / 36%	37 / 38%	128 / 44%
MORE COAL-FUELLED POWER STATIONS	663 / 44%	198 / 33%	296 / 56%	96 / 48%	7 / 26%	67 / 39%	213 / 47%	163 / 46%	128 / 45%	109 / 40%	51 / 31%	186 / 48%	162 / 40%	116 / 46%	38 / 40%	125 / 43%
MORE NUCLEAR POWER STATIONS	236 / 15%	140 / 24%	42 / 8%	28 / 14%	0 / 0%	25 / 15%	38 / 8%	53 / 15%	48 / 17%	66 / 24%	30 / 19%	73 / 19%	73 / 18%	34 / 13%	14 / 14%	28 / 10%
DONT KNOW	17 / 1%	5 / 1%	5 / 1%	2 / 1%	0 / 0%	6 / 3%	10 / 2%	2 / 0%	3 / 1%	3 / 1%	3 / 0%	1 / 0%	5 / 1%	5 / 2%	1 / 1%	4 / 1%
NOT ANSWERED	33 / 2%	11 / 2%	13 / 2%	2 / 1%	1 / 2%	6 / 4%	14 / 3%	5 / 0%	5 / 2%	5 / 2%	8 / 5%	9 / 2%	5 / 1%	6 / 2%	6 / 7%	5 / 2%

6.9 PERCEPTION OF RISKS FROM NUCLEAR POWER STATIONS (Q209 b) by age within sex

BASE: THOSE RETURNING SELF-COMPLETION

AGE WITHIN SEX

	TOTAL	MALE TOTAL	18-24	25-34	35-44	45-54	55-59	60-64	65+	NA	FEMALE TOTAL	18-24	25-34	35-44	45-54	55-59	60-64	65+	NA
UNWEIGHTED BASE	1562	727	105	141	123	101	60	64	132	1	835	99	158	153	123	72	79	143	8
WEIGHTED BASE	1522	714	101	142	126	99	57	62	127	1	809	101	153	148	113	64	78	144	8
VERY SERIOUS RISKS	569 37%	240 34%	29 29%	53 37%	43 34%	44 45%	16 28%	17 27%	38 30%	0	330 41%	53 53%	64 42%	59 40%	39 34%	28 44%	30 38%	56 39%	1
QUITE SERIOUS RISKS	457 30%	205 29%	28 28%	38 27%	41 33%	23 23%	18 32%	19 31%	37 29%	0	252 31%	28 28%	48 32%	47 32%	36 32%	19 29%	26 34%	43 30%	4
ONLY SLIGHT RISKS	348 23%	191 27%	29 29%	43 30%	30 24%	23 23%	13 23%	18 31%	34 27%	0	157 19%	15 15%	31 20%	31 21%	27 24%	14 21%	13 16%	28 19%	3
HARDLY ANY RISKS	118 8%	67 9%	12 12%	6 4%	13 10%	6 6%	9 16%	6 10%	15 12%	0	51 6%	3 3%	8 5%	9 8%	7 7%	2 3%	4 5%	13 9%	0
DONT KNOW	14 1%	1 0%	0	0 0%	0 0%	0 0%	0 0%	0 0%	0 0%	0	13 2%	0 0%	1 1%	1 1%	2 2%	1 1%	5 6%	4 2%	0
NOT ANSWERED	15 1%	9 1%	2 2%	2 1%	0 0%	2 2%	0 0%	2 2%	2 2%	0	6 1%	1 1%	1 1%	1 1%	2 2%	1 1%	1 1%	1 1%	0

6.10 PERCEPTION OF RISKS FROM NUCLEAR POWER STATIONS (Q209 b) by party identification, household income, combined working status and current social class

BASE: THOSE RETURNING SELF-COMPLETION

	WEIGHTED BASE	PARTY I.D. TORY	LAB.	ALLIANCE	OTHER	NON-ALIGN	HOUSEHOLD INCOME UNDER £5000	£5000-£7999	£8000-£11999	£12000+	NO INF.	COMBINED WORKING STATUS AND CURRENT SOCIAL CLASS — WORKING MAN.	NON-MAN.	NOT WORKING RETIRED	UNEMP	HOME
UNWEIGHTED BASE	1562	602	551	208	23	178	471	359	290	277	165	402	417	262	99	292
WEIGHTED BASE	1522	593	534	198	27	171	451	354	281	273	164	388	409	251	96	290
VERY SERIOUS RISKS (4)	569 37%	143 24%	279 52%	65 33%	22	60 35%	198 44%	149 42%	92 33%	82 30%	49 30%	155 40%	124 30%	83 33%	52 55%	122 42%
QUITE SERIOUS RISKS (3)	457 30%	189 32%	142 27%	73 37%	2	51 30%	131 29%	108 30%	94 33%	77 28%	48 29%	105 27%	130 32%	85 34%	23 24%	83 29%
ONLY SLIGHT RISKS (2)	348 23%	192 32%	77 14%	43 22%	1	35 21%	74 16%	69 19%	75 27%	89 33%	42 26%	91 23%	122 30%	51 20%	13 13%	54 19%
HARDLY ANY RISKS (1)	118 8%	57 10%	28 5%	14 7%	3	16 9%	36 8%	27 8%	18 6%	23 8%	18 10%	32 8%	24 6%	27 11%	6 6%	23 8%
DONT KNOW	14 1%	5 1%	5 1%	1 1%	0	4 2%	7 2%	1 0%	2 1%	2 1%	2 1%	2 1%	1 0%	4 1%	0 0%	6 2%
NOT ANSWERED	15 1%	7 1%	3 1%	1 1%	0	5 3%	6 1%	1 0%	1 0%	0 0%	7 4%	4 1%	5 1%	1 0%	1 1%	2 1%

6.11 PRIMARY SOCIAL RESPONSIBILITY OF INDUSTRY (Q210)
by age within sex

BASE: THOSE RETURNING SELF-COMPLETION

AGE WITHIN SEX

	WEIGHTED BASE TOTAL	MALE TOTAL	M 18-24	M 25-34	M 35-44	M 45-54	M 55-59	M 60-64	M 65+	M NA	FEMALE TOTAL	F 18-24	F 25-34	F 35-44	F 45-54	F 55-59	F 60-64	F 65+	F NA
UNWEIGHTED BASE	1562	727	105	141	123	101	60	64	132	1	835	99	158	153	123	72	79	143	8
WEIGHTED BASE	1522	714	101	142	126	99	57	62	127	1	809	101	153	148	113	64	78	144	8
INDUSTRY SHOULD BE PREVENTED FROM CAUSING DAMAGE TO THE COUNTRYSIDE	1169 77%	572 80%	73 73%	123 87%	104 83%	77 77%	48 85%	51 83%	95 75%	0	596 74%	63 62%	119 77%	117 79%	88 77%	49 75%	53 68%	105 73%	5
INDUSTRY SHOULD KEEP PRICES DOWN, EVEN IF CAUSES DAMAGE	335 22%	134 19%	24 24%	18 13%	22 17%	21 22%	7 13%	10 17%	30 23%	1	201 25%	37 37%	33 21%	31 21%	26 23%	15 23%	21 27%	37 25%	2
DONT KNOW	8 1%	2 0%	1 1%	0 0%	0 0%	0 0%	0 0%	0 0%	1 1%	0	6 1%	0 0%	0 0%	0 0%	0 0%	1 1%	3 4%	2 1%	1
NOT ANSWERED	11 1%	5 1%	2 2%	0 0%	0 0%	1 1%	0 0%	1 2%	1 1%	0	5 1%	1 1%	2 1%	0 0%	0 0%	0 0%	1 1%	2 1%	0

6.12 PRIMARY SOCIAL RESPONSIBILITY OF INDUSTRY (Q210)
by party identification, household income, combined working status and current social class

BASE: THOSE RETURNING SELF-COMPLETION

	WEIGHTED BASE	PARTY I.D. TORY	LAB.	ALLI-ANCE	OTHER	NON-ALIGN	HOUSEHOLD INCOME UNDER £5000	£5000-£7999	£8000-£11999	£12000+	NO INF.	COMBINED WORKING STATUS AND CURRENT SOCIAL CLASS — WORKING MAN.	NON-MAN.	NOT WORKING RET-IRED	UNEMP	HOME
UNWEIGHTED BASE	1562	602	551	208	23	178	471	359	290	277	165	402	417	262	99	292
WEIGHTED BASE	1522	593	534	198	27	171	451	354	281	273	164	388	409	251	96	290
INDUSTRY SHOULD BE PREVENTED FROM CAUSING DAMAGE TO THE COUNTRYSIDE	1169 77%	484 82%	391 73%	165 83%	20	109 63%	308 68%	261 74%	243 87%	238 87%	119 73%	284 73%	348 85%	179 71%	73 77%	213 73%
INDUSTRY SHOULD KEEP PRICES DOWN, EVEN IF CAUSES DAMAGE	335 22%	99 17%	136 25%	33 17%	8	60 35%	134 30%	92 26%	36 13%	33 12%	40 24%	101 26%	58 14%	68 27%	19 20%	74 26%
DONT KNOW	8 1%	5 1%	2 0%	0 0%	0 0%	2 1%	4 1%	0 0%	0 0%	1 0%	2 1%	1 0%	1 0%	4 2%	0 0%	2 1%
NOT ANSWERED	11 1%	5 1%	5 1%	0 0%	0 0%	1 1%	6 1%	1 0%	1 0%	0 0%	3 2%	2 1%	3 1%	0 0%	3 3%	1 0%

7 Measuring individual attitude change

Denise Lievesley and Jennifer Waterton *

All respondents to the first Social Attitudes Survey in 1983 were asked at the end of the interview whether or not we could approach them again the following year. Ninety-two per cent said we could.

We had in mind the possibility of introducing a panel element into the survey as a means of enhancing its measurement potential. With the support of the Economic and Social Research Council, a panel was selected and interviewed a year later in 1984. It is to be re-visited in 1985 and, if funding permits, in future years too.

The annual cross-sectional survey reported in the rest of this book is, of course, valuable as a means of measuring aggregate changes and trends in public attitudes and expectations over the years. What it cannot do, however, is to measure individual change – the way in which particular people alter their views or values over time in response, perhaps, to changes in circumstances or other stimuli. To construct this sort of dynamic model, a panel element is essential.

The presence of a panel alongside the cross-sectional surveys also increases the precision of the measurement of aggregate change. The panel data are more precise (that is they have lower sampling errors) than the cross-sectional data, and the higher the correlation between individuals' answers in successive years, the greater these gains in precision will be. Thus the panel data will also assist the interpretation of cross-sectional changes, helping to identify which changes ought to be treated with more caution than others. In this respect a panel is an invaluable diagnostic tool both at the design and at the analysis stages.

A panel approach does, however, have two principal potential drawbacks.

* Denise Lievesley is a Research Director and Jennifer Waterton a Researcher in SCPR's Survey Methods Centre.

The first is 'attrition' – the inevitable depletion of a panel in successive rounds through non-response, death, migration, and so on. Attrition need not be very large if appropriate measures are taken to minimise it, but it cannot be eliminated. It need not be a serious problem either, provided that its effects are uniformly distributed; but that is unlikely. The danger is that selective depletion may cause the panel to become increasingly unrepresentative of the population it seeks to represent. We therefore need to be alert to the possible effects of attrition on a panel and to assess them at successive rounds.

The second potential drawback of a panel is 'conditioning' – the process by which repeated contact with respondents may lead them to change their attitudes or behaviour, or more simply, their answers – and which, may cause the panel to become unrepresentative (see Bochel and Denver, 1971; Traugott and Katosh, 1979). Conditioning is not necessarily a bad thing – its effect may be to improve data quality and to provide estimates which are closer to the truth. However, we need to assess whether conditioning has been taking place before we can use panel results as a reliable measure of attitudinal or behavioural change.

With this in mind, the first part of this chapter assesses and discusses the possible effects of attrition and conditioning in the panel before going on to illustrate some of its measurement benefits.

A **Technical Note** at the end of this chapter gives details of the panel's response rates, and includes examples of its comparative precision. It should be noted here, however, that the panel element comprised 553 successful re-interviews carried out in a random 57 of the 114 polling districts used for the main survey, selected systematically from a stratified list.

Comparing the cross-section with the panel

The cross-sectional samples are subject to possible non-response biases arising from the fact that only about 70% of the original selection participated in the survey. The response rates for the 1983 and 1984 cross-sectional surveys were similar and there were no striking differences between the demographic structures of the two samples; the few differences which did emerge can be accounted for by definitional or wording changes. The panel sample is subject to the same initial non-response effects but also to attrition and, perhaps, to conditioning.

There are various sources of attrition. Some people will, at the first interview, refuse permission for recall: others will subsequently withdraw or refuse. Some people will have moved and be untraceable or too expensive to follow. Others will be unable (through illness, etc.) to participate. Some will have died; some will simply not be contacted by the interviewer. The numbers in each of these categories are too small for their separate effects to be assessed, so we have concentrated upon examining their composite effect. In any case, analysis of non-response frequently shows that people lost for different reasons differ in an off-setting manner (Sobol, 1959). Thus when we conclude that attrition has had little effect on the composition of the panel it may be because the various biases are compensatory.

To disentangle the effects of attrition and conditioning, we must look at the sample's characteristics in both years on the same measures. From the 769 people who were randomly selected for the panel from the 1983 cross-section, 216 did not participate for one reason or another. So the first question we ought to ask is whether or not the 553 who did participate (the 'maintained' panel) were a random subset of the 'selected' panel.

Attrition and demographic characteristics

There were no significant differences between those we managed to interview and those we did not with respect to sex, marital status, employment status, social class, income or household size. It was also particularly reassuring to find that there were no significant differences between the two groups in their geographical distribution. Thus, despite the fact that there had been a demonstrable difference in response by region at the first round of interviewing, the subsequent attrition seems to be very stable across the regions. Similarly, if we group the sampled areas into metropolitan and non-metropolitan, we find that the attrition rates are similar in both categories.

There is a considerable body of literature demonstrating a relationship between age and response rates. Kemsley (1975), for instance, describes a fairly constant reduction in response rate with age: a fitted regression line gave the result that response fell by two per cent for each increase of five years. So we expected attrition levels to go up with age. But we also expected that the young, being more mobile and hence more difficult to re-contact might be under-represented. And this is what happened. The panel appears to under-represent both the young and the elderly, and thus to contain proportionately too many people aged 25-64, although these differences are not statistically significant at the five per cent level.

		Age of respondent					
		18-24	25-34	35-54	55-64	65+	Weighted base
Selected for panel	%	13.1	17.5	34.4	14.5	19.9	746
Dropped out	%	13.4	14.4	30.6	13.9	26.4	216
Maintained panel	%	12.8	18.7	36.0	14.8	17.1	530

The effect of attrition on attitudes and behaviour

Having found no major effects of attrition on the demographic composition of the panel, we then examined its effects on attitudinal and behavioural variables. We concentrated on those questions that had been asked in the same form of the 1983 cross-section, the 1984 cross-section and the 1984 panel.

We began by identifying all the significant differences between the maintained panel and the 1984 cross-section. Whenever a significant difference occurred we compared the maintained panel with those who dropped out, using the answers given in 1983, to see if the difference could be accounted for by attrition. In fact only a small number of variables were found to have significant attrition (well within the number we would expect by chance). So our conclusion is that the attitudinal and behavioural profile of the maintained panel is broadly similar to that of the selected panel. The main differences we found, discussed below, related to interest levels and the propensity to answer 'don't know'.

Attrition and interest levels

There is a common finding in longitudinal research that people who are uninterested in, or uninformed about, the subject matter of a study are more likely to drop out than others (see, for example, Sobol, 1959). Our study bears this out. The small number of behavioural variables which *did* show significant attrition were mainly ones associated with the respondents' level of interest.

Consider, for instance, newspaper readership: we might expect more interested and informed respondents to have higher levels of readership. In 1984, 72% of the cross-section claimed to read a daily morning newspaper at least three times a week compared with 79% of the panel. The cross-sectional result is close to readership levels found in the National Readership Survey. Further, those people who dropped out of the panel between 1983 and 1984 had lower levels of readership (by ten percentage points) than those who stayed in the panel.

We also found that panel respondents were less likely than the cross-section to be political 'passivists', according to one of the measures in the survey. We asked people (see Chapters 1, 4 and 6) to say what action they would take if they believed a law being considered by Parliament was 'really unjust and harmful'. Panel members were less likely to say that they would take no action and more likely to say they would sign a petition. A similar question asked about 'local' actions elicited similar differences.

These differences between the panel and the cross-section are attributable to differential attrition. In the 1984 Report (p.23) Ken Young calculated indices of political efficacy – a *personal action index* and a *collective action index* – which ranged between minus one and four – with higher values indicating greater propensity for action. The table below shows the results for the cross-section and the panel in both years, and also for the selected panel and those who dropped out in 1983.

	Personal action index	Collective action index
Parliamentary question, 1983		
Cross-section	0.63	0.64
Selected panel	0.69	0.68
Maintained panel	0.75	0.77
Dropped out	0.68	0.46
Parliamentary question, 1984		
Cross-section	0.88	0.74
Panel	0.95	0.87
Local council question, 1984		
Cross-section	1.13	0.69
Panel	1.16	0.79

We can see the maintained panel were indeed more potentially politically active than those who dropped out, and this finding is reinforced in 1984 in the comparisons between the cross-section and the panel. The differences are small, except for the collective action index of those who dropped out, which is much lower than that of those in the maintained panel. This is consistent with the hypothesis that people who remain in the panel appear to have a somewhat keener sense of social and political awareness than those who drop out.

Answering 'don't know'

Another way in which we can assess a respondent's interest in, or knowledge about, the survey topics is by the number of times he or she fails to answer a question or replies 'don't know'. A count of the 'don't know' and 'not answered' categories (hereafter abbreviated to DKs) across 118 questions asked in 1984 showed that panel respondents were much less likely to answer DK:

	Higher % of DKs in the panel	Same % of DKs in panel and cross-section	Higher % of DKs in the cross-section
Number of questions	5	30	83
Percentage of questions	4	26	70

If indeed there is a lower level of interest in the survey subject matter among those who drop out, we might expect the fall in the incidence of DKs to be caused by attrition. Many years ago Lazarsfeld (1941) demonstrated a greater tendency for people who have responded DK to a number of questions on earlier interviews to drop out at some later date. However, it is clear from an analysis of several questions that differential attrition accounts for only *part* of the fall in DKs. The rest of the fall is attributable to conditioning.

For instance, at a question about the extent to which local councils should be controlled by central government, the proportion answering DK amongst the panel members fell from seven per cent in 1983 to two per cent in 1984. As expected, those who dropped out of the panel were more likely to reply DK but even if we remove them from the analysis (so that we are looking at the *same* people in 1983 and 1984) we find that the percentage of DKs falls from five per cent to two per cent. This fall is not mirrored in the cross-section in which DKs remained stable at eight per cent each year. This finding was repeated many times throughout the questionnaire.

The lower incidence of DKs in 1984 among the continuing panel members is an example of conditioning. Interestingly this tendency seems to have affected not only questions asked in both 1983 and 1984, but also questions asked for the *first* time in 1984. For example, a new set of questions was introduced in 1984 on attitudes towards public and private 'rule-breaking' (see Chapter 5). Respondents were presented with 15 situations and asked for their views on the impropriety of each. In every case the panel had lower DK rates than the cross-section.

It may be that the 1983 interview had aroused greater interest among the panel members, but it is very unlikely that this greater interest encompassed the enormous range of survey topics including some not touched on in the initial interview. A more plausible hypothesis is that respondents have acquired the skills of being interviewed in an attitude survey; they have learned that interviewers accept all answers even when it is clear that respondents are unsure of their opinions. This is of course a feature of attitude surveys, in which a respondent's orientation, rather than his or her precise position, is being sought.

Other conditioning effects

Three further questions on rule-breaking introduced the following situations:

> *A householder is having a repair job done by a local plumber. He is told that if he pays cash he will not be charged VAT. So he pays cash.*

> *A man offers the dustman £5 to take away rubbish he is not supposed to pick up.*

> *A man gives a £5 note for goods he is buying in a big store. By mistake he is given change for a £10 note. He notices but keeps the change.*

In each case we asked respondents first whether, and to what extent, they thought the action was wrong, and then whether or not they would do it 'if the situation came up'.

We found that panel members were more prepared than the cross-section to say that they *would* do it. In the case of keeping the incorrect change the difference was only marginal, but it rose to a five per cent difference in respect of 'tipping' the dustman and to eight per cent for VAT evasion. These differences occurred even though the panel members were no less likely than the cross-section to rate the actions as wrong. We should not discount the possibility that the differences may be due to attrition, that is we may have lost from the panel a disproportionate number who would have replied that they would *not* take the specified actions; since the 1983 survey did not include this series of questions we cannot measure attrition directly.

As a proxy, however, we can examine other questions relating to 'deviant' behaviour and attitudes, which were asked in both years. We found, for example, that a lower proportion of the panel than the cross-section (53% v. 57%) thought people should obey the law without exception; a higher proportion (32% v. 29%) said they might break a law to which they were opposed; and a higher proportion (43% v. 36%) admitted to being very or a little prejudiced against people of other races. We then divided the selected panel into those continuing into 1984 and the rest, to determine whether attrition explained these differences. As in the case of DKs, attrition did indeed account for some but by no means all of the difference.

There seems to be persuasive evidence, therefore, that the reporting of the panel members has changed. They were more likely to admit to deviant behaviour – perhaps because they were more used to, and therefore more relaxed in, the interview setting. In view of the fact that people are unlikely to over-report deviant behaviour, we would argue that the panel estimates may therefore be closer to the 'truth'.

These conditioning effects did not seem to apply uniformly to all subgroups. As **Figure 1** shows, young and old panel members were more likely than their cross-section counterparts to say that they might 'tip' the dustman or evade VAT, whereas differences between the middle-aged panel and cross-section respondents were within sampling error. The analysis of these questions in Chapter 5 suggests that religious observance is an important discriminator. But, as **Figure 2** shows, the panel members' answers were less likely than the cross-section's answers to be influenced by religion. So in this example the panel and cross-sectional datasets would actually have led to different conclusions.

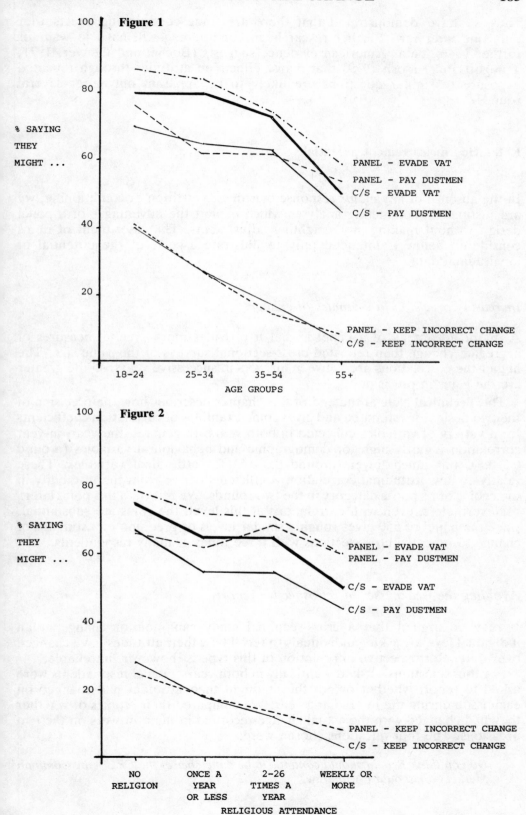

Figure 1

% SAYING
THEY
MIGHT ...

PANEL – EVADE VAT
PANEL – PAY DUSTMEN
C/S – EVADE VAT
C/S – PAY DUSTMEN

PANEL – KEEP INCORRECT CHANGE
C/S – KEEP INCORRECT CHANGE

18–24   25–34   35–54   55+

AGE GROUPS

Figure 2

% SAYING
THEY
MIGHT ...

PANEL – EVADE VAT
PANEL – PAY DUSTMEN

C/S – EVADE VAT

C/S – PAY DUSTMEN

PANEL – KEEP INCORRECT CHANGE
C/S – KEEP INCORRECT CHANGE

NO   ONCE A   2–26   WEEKLY OR
RELIGION   YEAR   TIMES A   MORE
            OR LESS   YEAR

RELIGIOUS ATTENDANCE

Thus we have demonstrated that there are some conditioning effects after only one interview. Further research on conditioning will have to wait for further years' data. American evidence suggests (Bochel and Denver, 1971; Traugott and Katosh 1979) that major effects on attitudes through repeated exposure to similar questions are likely to be apparent only after several rounds.

Enhancing measurement potential

In the absence of any *major* response bias due to attrition or conditioning, we are justified in conducting analyses which exploit the advantages of a panel design without making any weighting adjustments. The assortment of items considered below is intended only to illustrate aspects of the potential of longitudinal data.

Increasing precision in estimates of change

A major advantage of a panel is that it provides more precise measures of aggregate change than repeated cross-sectional surveys of the same size. The higher the correlations are between answers in successive years, so the greater are the gains in precision.

The **Technical Note** at the end of this chapter describes how the precision of the two designs is estimated and gives some examples of correlation coefficients for a variety of variables collected in both years. In general, the year-on-year correlation is fairly high for demographic and behavioural variables (around 0.7-0.8), but much lower (around 0.3-0.5) for attitudinal variables. These relatively low attitudinal correlation coefficients derive from the instability in the choice of response category in the two rounds. We return to this point later.

Nevertheless, even with correlations at this level, the gains are substantial, since the panel of 550 gives roughly similar levels of precision on estimates of change to repeated cross-sections with three times as many respondents.

Avoiding the weaknesses of retrospective reports

It may be argued that a cross-sectional study can monitor change at an individual level by asking individuals to recall how their attitudes have changed over time. Retrospective information of this type is, however, unreliable.

For four questions – asked identically in both years – panel respondents were asked to report whether or not they thought their attitudes had changed on each issue during the intervening year. We compared their reports of whether they had changed with the actual change recorded in their answers on the two occasions. The four questions chosen were:

> *Do you think Britain should continue to be a member of the EEC – the Common Market – or should it withdraw?*

If the government had *to choose between keeping down inflation or keeping down unemployment, to which do you think it should give highest priority?*

There is a law in Britain against racial discrimination, that is against giving unfair preference to a particular race in housing, jobs and so on. Do you generally support or oppose the idea of a law for this purpose?

Generally speaking, what is your opinion about private schools in Britain? Should there be more private schools, about the same number as now, fewer private schools, or no private schools at all?

The table shows the extent of agreement between the change as measured directly ('actual' change) and that perceived by the respondent ('reported' change). Any respondent who replied 'don't know' in either year has been omitted.

	Common Market	Unemployment/ inflation	Racial discrimination	Private education
Reported changes	10%	7%	2%	2%
Actual changes	16%	22%	29%	26%
Reported no change but actually changed	13%	19%	28%	26%
Correlation between reported and actual change	0.14	0.02	−0.05	0.02
Base	509	499	525	511

At all four questions, the proportion who reported a change was substantially lower than the proportion who had actually given a different response. The first three of these questions were dichotomies (continue/withdraw, unemployment/inflation, support/oppose) where change involved moving from one view to its opposite. The fourth question had four answer categories (more/same/fewer/none), and most respondents (two-thirds) who reported 'no change' on this issue – but who had actually changed – moved only one category in either direction on the scale.

Correlation between reported and actual change for these four questions is very low indeed (averaging only about 0.03), partly because some people who reported changing their views did not actually change their response; this could mean that their views had changed but not enough to make them alter 'sides'. So it was not necessarily an error. But the number falling into this group was very small. Of more concern was the large number who had changed their response but reported no change in their view. More than 60% of the panel were 'wrong' in this respect for one or two of the four questions. About five per cent of them were wrong for three or four of the questions. This latter group may have misunderstood or paid little attention to the questions. In any event, their answers were, in effect, haphazard. One might hypothesise that this behaviour would be more common amongst the elderly or the non-aligned politically, but this did not prove to be the case.

The findings here provided convincing evidence that respondents' retrospective reports of changes in attitude are not a reliable proxy for actual changes. Our conclusions support those of Smith (1984) who attributes faulty recall of attitudes to two biases: a 'social desirability bias' which leads to over-reporting of positive attitudes and behaviours in order to be consistent with positive self-images, and 'a conservative bias' which increases support of the establishment. He argues that there is also a tendency to draw the past to the present, and demonstrates that recall can interact with other variables making the reconstructing of associations between variables difficult.

The panel as a diagnostic tool

Longitudinal data collected in a panel survey may be of use in identifying malfunctioning questions and hence in improving questionnaire design. For example, the very marked change in answers to the question on racial discrimination to which we referred earlier, may well be attributable to unsatisfactory question wording. We would have expected little change at an individual level over a 12-month period on this variable – and indeed the marginal distribution is reassuringly stable. The magnitude of change in individuals' answers leads us to suppose that respondents may have misinterpreted the question on one of the two occasions. Looking again at the question, we find that it incorporates a double negative in the phrase 'against giving unfair preference', which may well have caused problems of interpretation and, therefore, invalid answers.

Another aspect of this diagnostic function is that the panel provides us with the opportunity to assess the extent of recording errors (either in the field or in the office) and hence to improve the accuracy of the 'clean' data tape which is used at the analysis stage. For example, some variables (such as the respondent's sex or ethnic group) are stable; the answers ought to be consistent between the two interviews! If they are not, something has gone wrong either in the interview or the coding stage or in transfer to tape. We found, for example, that two people were coded as 'black' on one occasion and as 'white' on the other, and that six people were coded as 'other non-white' in 1983 but as 'white/European' in 1984. Ethnic group classifications are notoriously unreliable, but on this occasion some of the discrepancies were probably explained by the introduction of an amended coding frame in which the categories were re-ordered and given slightly different labels precisely with a view to improving their reliability.

We did not exploit this diagnostic aspect to the full, preferring in 1984 to err on the side of reducing interview length and avoiding the intrusive potential of repeating questions on variables which could not have changed. In subsequent rounds however, with a core of respondents who are committed to continuing as members of the panel, we will build in a number of validity checks. Thus the panel should be a valuable means of increasing the reliability of questions and of improving the survey instrument.

Gross change versus net change

Using panel data it is possible to distinguish between '*net*' change – that is the change in the aggregate results between the two years, and '*gross*' change – that is the change in individual attitudes. In the absence of panel data, no net change is often taken as indicating stable attitudes, but such an interpretation may well be erroneous (see Duncan, 1984). The following question on educational standards was asked identically in both years:

In general, how would you compare the overall standards of education in schools today with the standards when you were at school? Would you say that standards today are higher, lower or about the same? [If higher or lower] *A lot or a little?*

The answers yielded the following cross-tabulation (omitting 'don't knows' and 'not answereds').

	Numbers answering in 1984:					
	A lot higher	A little higher	About the same	A little lower	A lot lower	Total
Numbers answering in 1983:						
A lot higher	**78**	22	3	9	8	120
A little higher	32	**24**	13	14	12	95
About the same	4	16	**39**	13	3	75
A little lower	8	14	21	**33**	26	102
A lot lower	8	10	4	30	**77**	129
Total	130	86	80	99	126	521

Since this is a question which asks, for the most part, about an event quite far in the past, and compares it with what one imagines would be a fairly stable yardstick (i.e., an impression of present overall educational standards in schools), we would have expected a fairly stable overall distribution between the years, and this was the case. Nonetheless, only 48% of respondents actually put themselves in the *same* category on both occasions (although 81% were within one point in either direction). The correlation between the answers given in the two years is 0.60 on the 5-point scale. Collapsing to a 3-point scale (higher/same/lower) does not significantly alter the correlation.

This pattern of small net change accompanied by large gross change suggests response variability. Even though a respondent's underlying attitudes may remain relatively constant, he or she may choose a different response category on different occasions simply because, unlike with some factual questions, there is no uniquely correct answer category that represents his or her views. Interpretation of the answer categories may also vary between occasions. But if this is the case, it affects our ability to compare *different* people who are even more likely to define the question categories differently. And this problem is likely to be more acute for questions of low saliency or for those which have several answer categories from which to choose. Large gross change can therefore serve as a useful indicator of an abstruse or otherwise difficult question.

A combination of no net change with some gross change should not, however, automatically be attributed to difficulties of question wording or content. It may also be an indication of genuine volatility that just happens to balance out. This may, for example, have applied in the case of party identification. Between 1983 and 1984 there was little net change (a few more Labour supporters in 1984). Yet there does seem to have been considerable volatility at the individual level.

Numbers identifying with each party in 1984:

	Conservative	Labour	Liberal	SDP	Alliance	Other/ Non-aligned	Total
Numbers identifying with each party in 1983:							
Conservative	**193**	11	7	4	4	8	227
Labour	4	**161**	4	2	2	6	180
Liberal	3	4	**28**	4	1	4	44
SDP	4	6	3	**16**	1	2	32
Alliance	2	1	2	3	**1**	0	9
Other/non aligned	12	19	5	3	0	**22**	61
Total	216	202	49	32	10	42	553

Thus, 131 people (about a quarter of the panel) changed their answers in the intervening year. Shifts between Labour and Conservative parties were rare, but, even if we discount the shifts *among* the Alliance parties, there was quite a lot of movement in and out of the Liberal, SDP and Alliance groupings. The smaller number of non-aligned in 1984 than in 1983 might be attributable to the effect of the intervening General Election which may have helped to focus the ideas of those who were previously undecided. Even though party identification is now thought to be more volatile than it used to be, political scientists have nonetheless treated it (as distinct from voting behaviour which can swing more quickly) as an enduring attachment to a party which is relatively unaffected by intervening events such as elections and which is *not*, therefore, time-specific. Our panel results cast doubt upon such an interpretation. It is interesting that the correlation coefficient, even when we omit the 'others' and the 'non-aligned' and treat the Liberal/SDP/Alliance grouping as the middle point on an ordered scale with Labour and Conservative at opposite ends, is only 0.87.

The availability of measures of gross change also offers a greater opportunity to assess directly the impact of world events, changes in legislation or government decisions, by providing 'before' and 'after' measures. Such assessments are always fraught with difficulty since it is *never* possible to attribute a change to a particular cause. But they are potentially much sounder when based on answers from the same people than when divined from successive cross-sectional measures, which – as we have seen – may contain a variable (and unquantifiable) number of compensating 'changes'.

Probably the most important national event in Britain between the 1983 and 1984 surveys was the General Election of June 1983. In 1983 we collected respondents' party identification. In 1984, early in the interview we asked the identification question again, then towards the end of the interview we asked how respondents voted in the General Election. This analysis is only possible with the panel survey since it has two measures of party identification for the same people. As the tables show, reported voting was more strongly associated with 1984 than with 1983 party identification. Of those who said they voted, 87% claimed to have voted for the party they identified with in 1984, compared with only 78% for the party they identified with in 1983.

Numbers identifying with party in 1983:

Numbers reporting voting for party in General Election:	Conservative	Labour	Liberal/ SDP/ Alliance	Other	None	Refused/ not answered	Total
Conservative	**169**	7	10	1	6	3	196
Labour	3	**124**	8	2	5	1	143
Liberal/SDP/Alliance	16	18	**50**	2	4	6	96
Other	0	2	0	**1**	1	0	4
Didn't vote	32	23	16	1	**22**	4	98
Refused/ not answered	7	5	1	0	0	2	15
Total	227	179	85	7	38	16	552

Numbers identifying with party in 1984:

Numbers reporting voting for party in General Election:	Conservative	Labour	Liberal/ SDP/ Alliance	Other	None	Refused/ not answered	Total
Conservative	**177**	7	7	1	1	4	197
Labour	0	**140**	3	0	0	0	143
Liberal/SDP/Alliance	4	21	**67**	1	2	1	96
Other	0	2	1	**0**	1	0	4
Didn't vote	30	26	11	1	**23**	7	98
Refused/ not answered	7	6	1	0	0	1	15
Total	218	202	90	3	27	13	553

Given that many of the 1983 interviews were conducted in the six weeks prior to the General Election, we might have expected the stronger relationship to be between 1983 identification and vote. The fact that it was not, raises a number of questions: respondents may have altered reports of their voting behaviour to make them consistent with their party identification; alternatively, when interviewed in 1984, respondents may have recalled the General Election and used their choice then to determine their current party identification. A third possibility is that the General Election did indeed serve to crystallise party preferences. The panel survey is in a position to raise these questions but, unfortunately, cannot provide the answers. Further research is required to explore the stability of party identification and its relationship to voting behaviour.

Amplifying the cross-sectional findings

A major benefit of a panel is that it can identify precisely whose reported attitudes have changed. Thus, irrespective of whether or not there has been any net change, panel data can locate, identify and classify the characteristics of those whose views have changed. This enables more complex research hypotheses to be examined.

For example, a substantial change that took place between 1983 and 1984 was that the proportion of people who thought that health should be the first priority for additional government spending increased considerably (from 37% to 51% on the cross-section and from 36% to 50% on the panel).

The shortage of resources in the NHS was an issue of considerable importance during 1983/84. Substantial media coverage was given to discussions about, for example, the possible privatisation of certain NHS functions, the closure of a few specialist hospital units, the over-burdening of doctors and nurses, and the debate about which areas for research and development should take priority. Given a topic of such universal concern, we hypothesised that any increase in the proportion choosing health as the top priority for extra spending would cut across all age, class and party groupings.

The 14% net increase in the panel concealed some changes in the opposite direction. While 139 respondents chose health as a first priority in 1984 but not in 1983, 55 respondents chose health in 1983 but not in 1984. We examined the age and party identification of these two groups in some detail and compared them with the profiles of all those choosing health in both years, and with the

	Panel	Those choosing health in both years	Those choosing health in 1983 only	Those choosing health in 1984 only
Age in 1983:	%	%	%	%
18-24	12	9	14	14
25-34	18	18	11	15
35-44	20	22	20	17
45-54	17	21	9	17
55-64	15	12	24	19
65 or over	17	17	22	18
Party identification in 1983:	%	%	%	%
Conservative	41	37	33	40
Labour	32	39	38	35
SDP/Lib/All	15	15	24	13
Other/Don't Know	11	9	5	12
Base	552	140	55	139

panel as a whole. As is apparent from the table above, although those who move in either direction are more likely to be in the young (18-24) or older (55+) age group, and those choosing health for the first time in 1984 are more likely to be Conservative identifiers, the differences do not approach statistical significance. Thus, they tend to support our hypothesis that the change in priority cuts across all subgroups. To have produced such a conclusion using the cross-section would have been more difficult because of the fact that people's movements tend to be in both directions.

Conclusions

Over time, with continued measurement, further benefits can be expected to accrue from the panel. Modelling may enhance our understanding of attitude formation and change, and enable us to separate simple response variance from 'real' changes in attitudes. Cases may be cumulated in order to look at how rare life events (such as the birth of a child or the death of a spouse) affect attitudes. In addition the effect of ageing on attitudes or behaviour may be explored by comparing the panel, adjusted for attrition and conditioning, with the appropriate subset of the cross-section. Pressure on interview length inevitably means that topics have to be rotated in and out of the cross-section over the years. And although the same is true of the panel survey, the fact that we possess data on the same people enables us to cross-analyse topics asked in different years.

In addition to enhancing the explanatory power of the survey the panel will continue to assist in monitoring the quality of the cross-sectional survey and in providing guidance on such issues as the frequency with which particular questions or groups of questions should reappear.

Thus the panel and the cross-section complement one another: the cross-sectional data provide the means by which the effects of attrition and conditioning on the panel may be identified and disentangled, while the panel provides many analytic benefits including the ability to explore the cross-sectional findings in greater depth. Moreover, for certain purposes the two datasets (appropriately weighted) may be combined in order to boost sample size.

References

BOCHEL, J. and DENVER, D., 'Canvassing, turnout and party support', *British Journal of Political Science 5* (1971) pp. 257-269.
DUNCAN, G., *Years of Poverty, Years of Plenty*, Institute for Social Research, Michigan (1984).
KEMSLEY, W. F. F., 'Family Expenditure Survey: a study of differential response based on a comparison of the 1971 sample with the Census', *Statistical News* (1975).
LAZARSFELD, P., 'Repeated interviews as a tool for studying changes in opinion and their causes', *American Statistical Association Bulletin* (1941).

SOBOL, M. G., 'Panel Mortality and Panel Bias', *Journal of the American Statistical Association* (1959) pp. 52-68.
SMITH, T. W., 'Retrospective questions on the 1982 GSS', *Public Opinion Quarterly 48* (1984) pp. 639-649.
TRAUGOTT, M. and KATOSH, J., 'Response Validity in Surveys of Voting Behaviour', *Public Opinion Quarterly 43* (1979) pp. 359-378.

Acknowledgements

We are grateful to Martin Collins, Harvey Goldstein, Roger Jowell and Sharon Witherspoon for their assistance in the design and reporting of this study. Our thanks are also extended to the ESRC for funding it.

Technical note

Response summary

The following figures trace the progress of the panel from its selection through various stages of non-response to successful recruitment and interview. As can be seen, we successfully recruited and interviewed 80% of those who were available for recruitment in 1984.

A	Selected for interview	769
B	Out of scope (dead, senile, emigrated, in hospital)	38
C	In scope in 1984	731
D	Refused interview in advance, i.e. in 1983 interview	43
E	Non-response (non-traceables, refusals, non-contacts in 1984)	135
F	Successful interviews	553
G	Response rate $\left(\frac{F}{C}\right)$	76%
H	Response rate excluding advance refusals $\left(\frac{F}{C-D}\right)$	80%

Precision of measures of change

The panel design provides more precise measures of aggregate change than repeated cross-sectional surveys of the same size. Consider two contrasting designs: at one extreme, when two samples are completely independent, the variance of the difference is the sum of the two variances; at the other extreme, when the two samples overlap completely, the variance of the difference will be reduced by a factor $(1-r)$ where r is the year-on-year correlation coefficient.

Neither the cross-section nor the panel are at these extremes. The 1983 and 1984 cross-sectional samples are not completely independent as they were deliberately selected in the same areas. Nevertheless, as we would expect the effect of this to be very small, it seems reasonable to treat them as independent samples.

Similarly the panel does not achieve complete overlap from year to year because of non-response among panel members. The precision of the panel will lie somewhere between the original panel sample and the achieved sample in any year. For the moment it seems sensible to calculate measures of precision for our maintained sample of about 550.

Table 7.1 shows for two independent cross-sectional samples of about 1,650 each the minimum difference between two percentages to produce significance at the five per cent level. This is done for several values of p, where p is the smaller of the percentages endorsing the given category in the two years. For example, if we wish to compare the percentage giving a specified reply in 1984 with that found in 1983 – supposing the percentages are around 30% – then we will be looking for a difference of at least 3.7% between the two figures.

Table 7.1

Estimates of change from two cross-sectional samples
(Two independent samples of approximately 1,650 each)

p – percentage in category of interest

	50%	60% (40%)	70% (30%)	80% (20%)	90% (10%)
Difference required for 5% significance:	4.0%	3.9%	3.7%	3.2%	2.4%

Note: The Design Factor is assumed to be about 1.2. This estimate is based on our experience of the clustering effects found for attitudinal variables, but is probably an underestimate for demographic variables.

Table 7.2 illustrates the precision of the panel approach, depending upon the level of year-on-year correlation. Using the same example and assuming a correlation of 0.7, we would be looking for a difference of about 3.6% despite the fact that the sample size is only one third of that of the cross-sectional samples. In general, a correlation of about 0.7 is required for our smaller panel to achieve similar precision to that obtained in the two cross-sectional studies.

Table 7.2

Estimates of change from a panel sample
(A panel with approximately 550 members)

p – percentage in category of interest

	50%	60% (40%)	70% (30%)	80% (20%)	90% (10%)
Difference required for 5% significance when r =	%	%	%	%	%
0	7.1	6.9	6.5	5.7	4.3
0.1	6.7	6.6	6.2	5.4	4.0
0.3	5.9	5.8	5.4	4.7	3.6
0.5	5.0	4.9	4.6	4.0	3.0
0.7	2.9	3.8	3.6	3.1	2.3
0.9	2.2	2.2	2.1	1.8	1.3

Note: The Design Factor is assumed to be about 1.2.

We have calculated year-on-year correlation coefficients for a number of variables. Since many of our variables are unordered categorical measures, however, the correlation coefficients cannot be calculated. So in these cases we have calculated an alternative measure of correlation, the 'index of agreement'. Some examples of correlation coefficents and indices of agreement are shown below:

Variable	Correlation measure
Main daily newspaper	0.77
Economic status of respondent	0.76
Self-rated income level	0.64
Withdrawal of British troops from Northern Ireland	0.53
Obeying the law	0.47
Overall satisfaction with the NHS	0.42
Expectations about unemployment in a year from now	0.42
Nuclear disarmament	0.41
Self-rated social class	0.39

Appendix I
Technical details of the survey

Sample design

The survey was designed to yield a representative sample of people aged 18 or over living in Britain.

For practical reasons, the sample was confined to those living in private households whose addresses were included in the electoral registers. Thus we excluded people living in institutions and those living in private households whose addresses were not on the electoral registers. Owing to the timing of fieldwork (March/April 1984), it was necessary to sample from registers that had just reached the end of their period of currency.

The sampling method involved a multi-stage design, with four separate stages of selection.

Selection of parliamentary constituencies

103 of the 552 constituencies in England and Wales were selected with probability proportionate to their electorates.

Prior to selection, constituencies were stratified according to the classification of the Centre for Environmental Studies Planning and Applications Group (PRAG). This system groups constituencies into 'clusters' (30), and ultimately into 'families' (6), that are broadly homogeneous in terms of demographic, socio-economic and other characteristics derivable from census data.

For Scotland a different procedure was followed. The local authority districts there were grouped into 12 strata, on the basis of region and degree of urbanisation. Districts within the Highlands and Islands Region (one stratum) were excluded. From the remainder, 11 districts were selected with probability proportionate to the electorate within them.

Selection of polling districts

Within each of the selected constituencies/districts a single polling district was selected, again with probability proportionate to electorate.

Selection of addresses

Twenty-two addresses were selected in each of the 114 polling districts. The sample issued to interviewers was therefore $114 \times 22 = 2,508$ addresses. The selection was made from a random starting point and, treating the list of electors as circular, a fixed interval was applied to generate the required number of addresses for each polling district. By this means, addresses were chosen with probability proportionate to their number of listed electors. At each sampled address the names of all electors given on the register were listed, and the name of the individual on which the sampling interval landed was marked with an asterisk (this person is known as the 'starred elector').

Selection of individuals

In order to convert this sample of addresses into a sample of individuals, the interviewers called at the address of each 'starred elector'. They listed all those eligible for inclusion in the sample, that is all persons currently aged 18 or over and resident at the selected household. Where the listing revealed a difference between the register entry and the current members of the household (because there had been movement in or out of the address since the register was compiled, or if some people were not registered), the interviewer selected one respondent by means of a random selection grid. In households where there had been no change, the interviewer attempted to interview the 'starred elector'. Where there were two or more households at the selected address, interviewers were required to identify the household of the elector whose name had led to the selection of that address, or the household occupying that part of the address where he or she used to live, before following a similar procedure.

Prior to analysis, the data were weighted to take account of any differences between the number of eligible persons listed on the register and those found at the address. Such differences occurred in approximately 25% of cases, in each of which the data were weighted by the number of persons aged 18 or over living at the household divided by the number of electors listed on the register for that address. The vast majority of such weights fell within a range between 0.25 and 2.0; in only seven cases were weights greater than 2.0 applied, ranging from 3.0 to 10.0.

In the remaining 75% of cases the number of persons listed on the register and those found at the address matched, so the effective weight was one.

Fieldwork

Interviewing was carried out largely during the months of March and April 1984, with approximately six per cent of interviews (some of them re-issued addresses) carried out mainly in May and June.

The interviews were carried out by 114 interviewers drawn from SCPR's regular interviewing panel, all of whom attended a one-day briefing about the questionnaires and sampling procedures. Interview length averaged 61 minutes.

The response achieved is shown below:

	No.	%
Addresses issued	2,508	
Vacant, derelict, out of scope	101	
In scope	2,407	100
Interview achieved	1,675	70
Interview not achieved	732	30
Refused	567	24
Non-contact	89	4
Other non-response	76	3

There were some regional variations in achieved response. The highest levels of response were achieved in the West Midlands (79%) and East Anglia (76%) with the lowest levels in the North (67%), the North West (66%) and Greater London (55%).

In 113 instances (seven per cent of the achieved sample), the self-completion questionnaire was not returned by the respondent, and is therefore absent from the dataset. Those not returning a self-completion questionnaire included a higher proportion of respondents aged 65 or over (39% of those who did not complete a self-completion questionnaire were over 65, compared with 19% of the sample as a whole). These elderly non-respondents were also slightly more likely to be those who formerly worked in semi-skilled or unskilled manual occupations.

Since the overall proportion returning a self-completion questionnaire was very high, however (93%), these slight non-response biases did not warrant corrective weighting of the self-completion questionnaire.

Analysis variables

A number of standard analyses were used in the tabulation of the data. Many of these appear in the tables included in this report.

Where appropriate, the definitions used in creating these analysis groups are set out below. It should be noted that, in a few cases, definitions have changed slightly from last year in order to enhance long-term analysis capabilities; where this is the case it is noted below.

Region

The Registrar General's 11 Standard Regions have been used. Sometimes these have been grouped. In addition, we divide metropolitan counties (including Glasgow) from other areas.

Social Class

The definition used here is slightly different from last year, although as last year respondents are classified according to their own social class, not that of a putative head of household.

We have classified social class according to each respondent's current or last occupation. Thus, for all respondents classified as being in paid work at the time of the interview, *or* as waiting to take up a paid job already offered *or* as retired *or* as seeking work *or* as looking after the home, the occupation (present, future or last as appropriate) was classified according to the OPCS *Classification of Occupations 1980*. (This differs from last year's practice in that those looking after the home are also classified according to their last occupation.) The combination of occupational classification with employment status generates six Social Classes:

I	– Professional	⎫
II	– Intermediate	⎬ 'Non-manual'
III (non-manual)	– Skilled occupations	⎭
III (manual)	– Skilled occupations	⎫
IV	– Partly skilled occupations	⎬ 'Manual'
V	– Unskilled occupations	⎭

The remaining respondents were grouped as 'never worked/not classifiable'.

In some cases responses are more sensibly analysed by current Social Class, which classifies according to current employment status only. Where this is the case, in addition to the six Social Classes listed above, the remaining respondents not currently in paid work are grouped into one of the following categories: 'not classified', 'retired', 'looking after the home', 'unemployed' or 'others not in paid occupations'.

The tape includes a Social Class variable directly comparable to the system used last year, labelled 'traditional Social Class'.

Industry

All respondents for whom an occupation was coded were allocated a Standard Industrial Classification Code (CSO as revised 1980). Two digit class codes were applied. Respondents with an occupation were also divided into public sector services, public sector manufacturing and transport, private sector manufacturing, and private sector non-manufacturing. This was done by cross-analysing SIC categories with responses to a question about the type of employer worked for. As with Social Class, SIC may be generated on the basis of current occupation only, or the most recently classifiable occupation.

Party identification

Respondents were classified as identified with a particular political party on one of three counts: if they considered themselves supporters of the party (Q.3a,b), *or* as closer to it than to others (Q.3c,d), *or* as more likely to support it in the event of a general election (Q.3e). The three groups are described respectively in both text and tables as *partisans, sympathisers* and *residual identifiers*. The three groups combined are referred to as *identifiers*. Alliance identifiers included those nominating the Social Democratic Party or the Liberal Party or the Alliance. Those who indicated no party preference were classified as *non-aligned*.

Other analysis groupings

These groupings are taken directly from the questionnaire, and to that extent are self-explanatory.

Sex (Q.94a)	Household type (Q.94a, b, c)
Age (Q.94b)	Ethnic group (Q.78a)
Household income (Q.103a)	Age of completing continuous
Employment status (Q.25, 26, 27)	full-time education (Q.96)
Religion (Q.75a)	Types of school attended (Q.95)
Housing tenure (Q.97)	Self-assigned social class (Q.74a)
Marital status (Q.82)	Self-rated racial prejudice (Q.76e)
	Trade union membership (Q.100a, b)

Sampling errors

No sample reflects precisely the characteristics of the population it represents because of both sampling and non-sampling errors. As far as sampling error is concerned, if a sample were designed as a simple random sample – i.e. if every adult had an equal and independent chance of inclusion in the sample – then we could calculate the sampling error of any percentage, p, using the formula

$$\text{s.e. (p)} = \sqrt{\frac{p\,(1-p)}{n}} \qquad \qquad \ldots.1$$

where n is the number of respondents on which the percentage is based. Once the sampling error had been obtained, it would be a straightforward exercise to calculate a confidence interval for the true population percentage. For example, a 95% confidence interval would be given by the formula

$$p \pm 1.96 \times \text{s.e. (p)} \qquad \qquad \ldots.2$$

Clearly, for a simple random sample (srs), the sampling error depends only on the values of p and n. However, simple random sampling is almost never used in practice because of its inefficiency in terms of time and cost.

As noted above, the Social Attitudes sample, like most large-scale surveys, was clustered according to a stratified multi-stage design into 114 polling districts. With a complex design like this, the sampling error of a percentage is not simply a function of the number of respondents in the sample and the size of the percentage, but also depends on how the characteristic is spread within and between polling districts. The complex design may be assessed relative to simple random sampling by calculating a range of *design factors*, DEFTs, associated with it, where

$$DEFT = \sqrt{\frac{\text{Variance of estimator with complex design, sample size n}}{\text{Variance of estimator with srs design, sample size n}}}$$

. . . .3

and represents the multiplying factor to be applied to the simple random sampling error to produce its complex equivalent. A design factor of one means that the complex sample has achieved the same precision as a simple random sample of the same size. A design factor greater than one means the complex sample is less precise than its simple random sample equivalent.

If the DEFT for a particular characteristic is known, a 95% confidence interval for a percentage may be calculated using the formula

$$p \pm 1.96 \times \text{complex sampling error (p)}$$

$$= \quad p \pm 1.96 \times DEFT \times \sqrt{\frac{p(1-p)}{n}}$$

. . . .4

In order to assess the impact of clustering the Social Attitudes sample in 114 polling districts, sampling error computations were carried out for a range of variables which were expected to exhibit different degrees of clustering; these included some classification variables, some behavioural variables and some attitudinal variables. These have been calculated by SCPR's Survey Methods Centre using the World Fertility Survey 'Clusters' program.

The table overleaf contains examples of the DEFTs calculated. The vast majority lie in the interval 1.0-1.5.

In general, classification variables have DEFTs in the range 1.0-1.5 with the important exception of housing tenure, which has a high DEFT because tenure is strongly related to area. The design factors for behavioural variables lie in the range 1.3-1.6. The attitudinal variables exhibit low design factors in the range 1.0-1.3. In the case of attitudinal variables, then, the fact that DEFTs are close to 1.0 means that the use of standard statistical tests of significance (based on the assumption of simple random sampling) is unlikely to be seriously misleading. For classification and behavioural variables, however, more care needs to be taken in the interpretation of test statistics and the estimation of parameter values.

It should be noted that these calculations are based on the total sample (n = 1,675) and that errors for proportions based on subgroups would be larger.

	%(p)	Complex standard error of p (%)	DEFT	95% confidence interval
Q.3 Party identification				
Conservative	38.6	1.8	1.54	34.9 - 42.3
Alliance	13.3	1.0	1.22	11.3 - 15.3
Labour	34.9	2.0	1.68	31.0 - 38.9
Q.97 Housing tenure				
Rented from local authority	25.6	2.4	2.29	20.7 - 30.5
Rented from housing association	0.9	0.3	1.41	0.3 - 1.6
Other rented	7.4	1.0	1.58	5.4 - 9.4
Q.96 Age of completing full-time education				
16 or under	70.4	2.0	1.54	66.4 - 74.3
17 or 18	13.6	1.1	1.25	11.5 - 15.7
19 or over	7.3	0.9	1.40	5.5 - 9.1
Q.8a Would obey law without exception	56.9	1.4	1.13	54.1 - 59.6
Q.8b Might break law in some circumstances	29.4	1.6	1.46	26.1 - 32.7
Q.12 Britain should rid itself of nuclear weapons	22.8	1.2	1.16	20.4 - 25.2
Q.16a Expect inflation to go up	83.0	1.2	1.28	80.6 - 85.3
Q.17 Expect unemployment to go up	55.3	1.8	1.51	51.6 - 59.0
Q.61 Government should increases taxes and spend more on social benefits	39.2	1.4	1.21	36.3 - 42.1
Q.81 Support law against sex discrimination	79.8	1.7	1.17	76.5 - 83.2

Appendix II
Notes on the tabulations

1. Tables at the end of chapters are percentaged vertically; tables within the text are percentaged as indicated.

2. In *end-of-chapter* tables percentages of less than 0.5 are indicated as zero, and percentages have been omitted when the base size is smaller than 50.

3. When bases of fewer than 50 respondents occur in tables *within the text,* reference is made to the small base size. Zero frequencies and percentages are denoted within these tables by –, and percentages of less than 0.5 by *.

4. Percentages equal to or greater than 0.5 have been rounded up in all tables.

5. Owing to the effects of rounding weighted data, the weighted bases shown in the tables may not always add to 1,645.

6. The self-completion questionnaire was not completed by seven per cent of respondents (see Appendix III, p.205). These non-respondents have been excluded from the appropriate bases.

7. Notes on breakdowns:

    (i)   Certain respondents have been omitted from some *end-of-chapter* tables because of missing data or unclassifiable responses. These omissions (indicated by the symbol †) occur in the following breakdowns:

Economic position within sex: 1 man and 1 woman
(Tables 3.1, 3.2, 3.3, 3.4, 3.7, 3.8.)

Age within sex: 3 men and 11 women
(Tables 3.5, 3.6, 3.9, 3.10, 3.11,
3.12, 3.13, 3.14.)

School-leaving age within sex: 17 men and 17 women
(Tables 3.9, 3.10, 3.11, 3.12, 3.13,   respondents to the self-completion
3.14.)   questionnaire

Marital status within sex: 2 men and 3 women
(Tables 3.3, 3.4, 3.7, 3.8.)

Non-manual/manual employment   5 men and 2 women employees
within sex:
(Table 3.6.)

Full-time or part-time working   1 man and 1 woman
within sex:
(Table 3.5.)

(ii) Certain respondents have been included in *residual* categories in
      some *end-of-chapter* tables. When this occurs, as in the following
      breakdowns, it is denoted by the symbol φ:

Economic position within sex: 1 man whose position was 'looking
(Tables 3.1, 3.2, 3.3, 3.4, 3.7, 3.8.) after the home'. This residual
                                       category (Other/N.C.) also
                                       includes those waiting to take up
                                       paid work, the unemployed, those
                                       in full-time education or on
                                       government training or
                                       employment schemes, those
                                       permanently sick and disabled,
                                       and those not classifiable.

(iii) Employment status: The category 'Total in paid work'
      (Tables 2.2, 2.4, 2.6, 2.8, 2.10, includes only people whose
      2.11.)   employment status was known;
                                       4 people in paid work for whom
                                       this information was not available
                                       have been included in the category
                                       'Other/no information'.

Appendix III
The questionnaires

The two questionnaires (interview and self-completion) are reproduced on the following pages. We have removed the punching codes and inserted instead the percentage distribution of answers to each question.

Figures do not necessarily add up to 100% because of weighting and rounding, or for one or more of the following reasons.

(i)   We have not included 'not answered' figures here, which are usually very small. They are, of course, included in the tables and on the tape.

(ii) Some sub-questions are filtered, that is they are asked of only a proportion of respondents. In these cases the percentages add up (approximately) to the proportions who were asked them. Where, however, a series of questions is filtered (for instance in Section Two of the interview questionnaire), we have inserted the unweighted total at the beginning of the series, and derived percentages throughout from that base. In the case of medians where the unweighted base was less than 50, figures have not been given.

(iii) At a few questions respondents were invited to give more than one answer. In these cases, the percentages usually add to well over 100%. Where this is the case, it is clearly marked by interviewer instructions on the questionnaire.

(iv) The self-completion questionnaire was not completed by seven per cent of respondents. In order to allow for comparisons over time, the answers have been re-percentaged on the base of those respondents who returned a self-completion questionnaire (unweighted 1,562; weighted 1,522). This means that the figures cannot be directly compared to those given in last year's Social Attitudes Report, without re-percentaging.

scpr

SOCIAL AND COMMUNITY PLANNING RESEARCH

Head Office: 35 Northampton Square London EC1V 0AX. Tel: 01-250 1866
Northern Field Office: Charazel House Gainford Darlington Co. Durham DL2 3EG. Tel: 0325 730 888

P.770   March 1984

BRITISH SOCIAL ATTITUDES:
1984 SURVEY

Serial number ☐☐☐☐   Area number ☐☐☐

Time interview started (24 hour clock) ☐☐☐☐

		N=1675	
		Col./ Code	Skip to
		%	

SECTION ONE

1a) Do you normally read any daily morning newspaper at least 3 times a week?

	Col./Code	Skip to
Yes	72	b)
No	28	Q2

IF YES

b) Which one do you normally read?
   IF MORE THAN ONE ASK: Which one do you read <u>most</u> frequently?

ONE CODE ONLY

	Code
(Scottish) Daily Express	9
Daily Mail	8
Daily Mirror/Record	18
Daily Star	4
The Sun	16
Daily Telegraph	5
Financial Times	*
The Guardian	2
The Times	2
Morning Star	*
Other Scottish/Welsh/regional or local <u>daily</u> morning paper (SPECIFY) _____	5
Other (SPECIFY) _____	*
Two or more with equal frequency	2
None	28

IF ANY PAPER NAMED

c) Suppose you saw or heard conflicting or different reports of the same news story on radio, television and in the .... (PAPER NAMED AT Q1b). Which of the three versions do you think you would be <u>most</u> likely to believe ... READ OUT ...

	Code
... the one on radio,	15
the one on television,	57
or the one in the newspaper?	16
(Don't know)	10

2. Can you tell me where you usually get <u>most</u> of your news about what's going on in Britain today: is it from the newspapers, or radio, or television, or where?

ONE CODE ONLY

	Code
Newspapers	20
Radio	15
Television	61
Other (SPECIFY) _____	1
Don't know	*
All three equally	2
Television and newspaper equally	1
Radio and television equally	1

		Col./ Code	Skip to
		%	

3.a) Generally speaking, do you think of yourself as a supporter of any one political party?

	Col./Code	Skip to
Yes	48	b)
No	50	c)

IF YES, ASK b).   IF NO ASK c)

b) Which one? RECORD ANSWER BELOW AND GO TO Q.4

c) Do you think of yourself as a little closer to one political party than to the others?

	Col./Code	Skip to
Yes	26	d)
No	24	e)

IF YES, ASK d).   IF NO, ASK e)

d) Which one? RECORD ANSWER AND GO TO Q.4

IF NO AT a) AND c)

e) If there were a general election tomorrow which political party do you think you would be <u>most</u> <u>likely</u> to support?

ONE CODE ONLY

Other party (SPECIFY) _____

    Other answer (SPECIFY) _____

	(b) %	(d) %	(e) %
Conservative	23	10	5
Labour	19	10	6
Liberal			
SDP/Social Democrat (Alliance)	4	5	4
Scottish Nationalist			1
Plaid Cymru			
Other party			*
Other answer			2
None			6
Don't know			2

ASK ALL

4.a) On the whole, would you describe the <u>Conservative Party</u> nowadays as extreme or moderate?

b) And the <u>Labour Party</u> nowadays, is it extreme or moderate?

c) And the <u>SDP/Liberal Alliance</u> nowadays, is it extreme or moderate?

RECORD IN APPROPRIATE COL.

	(a) Conservative %	(b) Labour %	(c) Alliance %
Extreme	48	41	6
Moderate	37	41	55
(Neither or both)	6	7	9
(Don't know)	10	11	30

5.a) Do you think that <u>local councils</u> ought to be controlled by <u>central government</u> more, less or about the same amount as now?

	Col./Code
More	14
Less	36
About the same	42
Don't know	7

b) And do you think the <u>level of rates</u> should be up to the local council to decide, or should central government have the final say? RECORD BELOW

c) How about the level of <u>council rents</u>? Should that be up to the local council to decide or should central government have the final say?

	Local council	Central gov't	Don't know
b)%Rates	74	19	7
c)%Rents	76	17	7

	Col./ Code	Skip to

CARD A

6.a) Suppose a law was now being considered by <u>Parliament</u>, which you thought was really unjust and harmful. Which, if any, of the things on this card do you think you would do? Any others? <u>RECORD IN COL a)</u> <u>BELOW, THEN ASK b). MORE THAN ONE CODE MAY BE RINGED</u>

b) Which <u>one</u> of the things on the card do you think would be the most effective in influencing a government to change its mind? <u>ONE CODE ONLY IN COL b)</u>

	(a) Would do	(b) Most effec- tive
	%	%
Contact my MP	55	43
Speak to influential person	15	4
Contact a government department	9	4
Contact radio, TV or newspaper	18	16
Sign a petition	57	12
Raise the issue in an organisation I already belong to	8	2
Go on a protest or demonstration	9	6
Form a group of like-minded people	8	3
NONE OF THESE	8	7
Don't know	*	1

CARD B

7.a) Now suppose your <u>local council</u> was proposing a scheme which you thought was really unjust and harmful. Which, if any, of the things on this card do you think you would do? Any others? <u>RECORD IN COL a) BELOW, THEN ASK b).</u> <u>MORE THAN ONE CODE MAY BE RINGED</u>

b) And which <u>one</u> of the things on the card do you think would be the most effective in influencing your local council to change its mind? <u>ONE CODE ONLY IN COL b)</u>

	(a) Would do	(b) Most effec- tive
	%	%
Contact my councillor	61	38
Speak to influential person	14	5
Contact a council official	26	8
Contact local newspaper or radio	18	16
Sign a petition	50	15
Raise the issue in an organisation I already belong to	6	2
Go on a protest or demonstration	8	4
Form a group of like-minded people	10	5
NONE OF THESE	5	5
Don't know	*	1

		Col./ Code	Skip to
		%	

8.a) In general would you say that people should obey the law without exception, or are there exceptional occasions on which people should follow their consciences even if it means breaking the law?

	Col./Code
Obey law without exception	57
Follow conscience on occasions	42
Don't know	1

b) Are there any circumstances in which <u>you</u> might break a law to which you were very strongly opposed?

	Col./Code	Skip to
Yes	29	c)
No	63	Q.9
Don't know	7	Q.9

<u>IF YES</u>

c) Can you say what those circumstances might be?   <u>PROBE FULLY.</u>   <u>RECORD VERBATIM.</u>

Now a few questions about Britain's relationships with other countries.

9.a) Do you think Britain should continue to be a member of the EEC - the Common Market - or should it withdraw?

b) And do you think Britain should continue to be a member of NATO - the North Atlantic Treaty Organisation - or should it withdraw?

	(a) EEC %	(b) NATO %
Continue	48	79
Withdraw	45	11
Don't know	6	9

---

10. On the whole, do you think that Britain's interests are better served by ... <u>READ OUT</u> ...

	Col./Code
... closer links with Western Europe,	53
or - closer links with America?	21
(Both equally)	16
(Neither)	3
(Don't know)	7

		Col./ Code	Skip to

11.a) Do you think that the siting of <u>American</u> nuclear missiles in Britain makes Britain a safer or a less safe place to live? <u>RECORD IN COL (a)</u>

b) And do you think that having our <u>own</u> independent nuclear missiles makes Britain a safer or a less safe place to live? <u>RECORD IN COL (b)</u>

	(a) American nuclear missiles	(b) Own nuclear missiles
	%	%
Safer	36	56
Less safe	51	33
No difference	3	2
Don't know	10	9

CARD C

12. Which, if either, of these two statements comes closest to your own opinion on British nuclear policy?

Britain should rid itself of nuclear weapons while persuading others to do the same	23
Britain should keep its nuclear weapons until we persuade others to reduce theirs	73
Neither of these	3
Don't know	1

---

13. Which political party's views on defence would you say comes <u>closest</u> to your own views?

Conservative	41
Labour	24
Liberal	4
SDP/Social Democrat	4
(Alliance)	2
Other (SPECIFY) _____	1
Don't know	21
None	3

CARD D

14. Which of the phrases on this card is closest to your opinion about threats to world peace?

America is a greater threat to world peace than Russia	11
Russia is a greater threat to world peace than America	26
Russia and America are equally great threats to world peace	54
Neither is a threat to world peace	5
Don't know	3

15.a) Do you think the long term policy for Northern Ireland should be for it ... <u>READ OUT</u> ...

... to remain part of the United Kingdom,	27
or - to reunify with the rest of Ireland?	58
Other answer (SPECIFY) _____	7
Don't know	4

b) Some people think that government policy towards Northern Ireland should include a complete withdrawal of British troops. Would you personally <u>support</u> or <u>oppose</u> such a policy? Strongly or a little?

Support strongly	37
Support a little	22
Oppose strongly	17
Oppose a little	16
Withdrawal in long term/not immediately	1
Other answer (SPECIFY) _____	3
Don't know	4

		Col./ Code	Skip to

<u>SECTION TWO</u>

Now I would like to ask you about two of Britain's
economic problems - <u>inflation</u> and <u>unemployment</u>.   %

16.a)   First, inflation: In a year from now, do you
expect prices generally to have gone up, to
have stayed the same, or to have gone down?

	Col./Code	Skip to
To have gone up by a lot	31	b)
To have gone up by a little	52	
To have stayed the same	13	
To have gone down by a little	3	Q.17
To have gone down by a lot	*	
(Don't know)	2	

<u>IF GONE UP OR GONE DOWN</u>

By a lot or a little?

<u>IF EXPECT PRICES TO GO UP (CODES 1 OR 2)</u>   [N=1386]

b)   You say that you expect prices generally to go up in
the next 12 months.   If we look back over the <u>last</u>
12 months prices went up by about 5p in the £, that
is by 5%.   By about what figure would you expect
prices to go up in the <u>next</u> 12 months?   MEDIAN

ENTER IN APPROPRIATE BOX TO | 0 | 5 | p in the £
<u>NEAREST WHOLE NUMBER.</u>

IF 100 OR OVER, ENTER 99   OR | 0 | 5 | %

OR   <u>CODE</u>   Don't know   6

17.   Second, unemployment: in a year from now, do
you expect unemployment to have gone up, to have
stayed the same, or to have gone down?

	Col./Code
To have gone up by a lot	25
To have gone up by a little	31
To have stayed the same	31
To have gone down by a little	11
To have gone down by a lot	1
(Don't know)	2

<u>IF GONE UP OR GONE DOWN</u>

By a lot or a little?

18.a)   If the government <u>had</u> to choose between keeping
down inflation or keeping down unemployment, to
which do you think it should give highest priority?

	Col./Code
Keeping down inflation	26
Keeping down unemployment	69
Both equally/can't separate	2
Other answer	1
Don't know	2

b)   Which do you think is of most concern
to <u>you and your family</u> ... <u>READ OUT</u> ...

	Col./Code
... inflation,	52
or— unemployment?	44
Both equally/can't separate	2
Neither	1
Other answer	*
Don't know	1

			Col./ Code	Skip to

19.	Looking ahead over the next year, do you think Britain's general industrial performance will improve, stay much the same, or decline?		%	
		Improve a lot	4	
	IF IMPROVE OR DECLINE	Improve a little	34	
	By a lot or a little?	Stay much the same	41	
		Decline a little	11	
		Decline a lot	4	
		(Don't know)	6	

20. Here are a number of policies which might help Britain's economic problems. As I read them out will you tell me whether you would support such a policy or oppose it?
READ OUT ITEMS i)-ix) AND CODE IN GRID

			SUPPORT	OPPOSE	DON'T KNOW
i)	Control of <u>wages</u> by legislation	%	42	53	4
ii)	Control of <u>prices</u> by legislation	%	66	30	4
iii)	Reducing the level of Government spending on health and education	%	11	87	1
iv)	Introducing import controls	%	67	27	6
v)	Increasing Government subsidies for private industry	%	60	33	7·
vi)	Devaluation of the pound	%	13	74	13
vii)	Reducing Government spending on defence	%	51	45	3
viii)	Government incentives to encourage job sharing or splitting	%	60	35	5
ix)	Government to set up construction projects to create more jobs	%	89	8	2

21.	On the whole, would you like to see more or less state ownership of industry, or about the same amount as now?			
		More	10	
		Less	36	
		About the same amount	50	
		Don't know	4	

			Col./ Code	Skip to
22.	Thinking of income levels generally in Britain today, would you say that the <u>gap</u> between those with high incomes and those with low incomes is ... <u>READ OUT</u> ...		%	
		... too large,	75	
		about right,	19	
		or too small?	4	
		Don't know	2	
23.a)	Among which group would you place yourself ... <u>READ OUT</u> ...	... high income,	2	
		middle income,	48	
		or low income?	50	
	<u>CARD E</u>	Don't know	*	
b)	Which of the phrases on this card would you say comes closest to your feelings about your household's income these days?			
		Living comfortably on present income	24	
		Coping on present income	50	
		Finding it difficult on present income	18	
		Finding it very difficult on present income	8	
		Other (SPECIFY) _____	*	
		Don't know	*	
24.a)	Looking back over the <u>last year</u> or so, would you say your household's income has ... <u>READ OUT</u> ...			
		... fallen behind prices,	46	
		kept up with prices,	44	
		or - gone up by more than prices?	8	
		(Don't know)	2	
b)	And looking forward to the <u>year ahead</u>, do you expect your household's income will ... <u>READ OUT</u> ...			
		... fall behind prices,	43	
		keep up with prices,	45	
		or - go up by more than prices?	8	
		(Don't know)	4	

	Col./Code	Skip to

CARD F

25. Which of these descriptions applies to what you were doing last week, that is in the seven days ending last Sunday? (Multiple)
PROBE: Any others?   CODE ALL THAT APPLY IN COLUMN I
IF ONLY ONE CODE AT I, TRANSFER IT TO COLUMN II
IF MORE THAN ONE AT I, TRANSFER HIGHEST ON LIST TO II

Description	COL I %	COL II ECONOMIC POSITION %	Skip to
In full-time education (not paid for by employer, including on vacation)	2	2	Q.47
On government training/employment scheme (e.g. Community Programme, Youth Training Scheme, etc.)	*	*	Q.45
In paid work (or away temporarily) for at least 10 hours in the week	52	52	Q.26
Waiting to take up paid work already accepted	*	*	Q.45
Unemployed and registered at a benefit office			Q.49
Unemployed, not registered, but actively looking for a job	7	6	
Unemployed, wanting a job (of at least 10 hrs per week), but not actively looking for a job			Q.51
Permanently sick or disabled	4	4	Q.57
Wholly retired from work	19	17	Q.52
Looking after the home	38	19	Q.53
Doing something else (SPECIFY) ___	2	*	Q.57
FOLLOW SKIP INSTRUCTIONS TO GO TO APPROPRIATE QUESTIONS Don't know	-	*	

IF IN PAID WORK OR AWAY TEMPORARILY (CODE 03 ABOVE)   N=867

26. In your (main) job are you ... READ OUT ...

	Col./Code	Skip to
... an employee,	90	Q.27
or self-employed?	10	Q.40

ALL EMPLOYEES (CODE 1): ASK Qs 27-39   N=778

27. In this (main) job do you normally work ... READ OUT ...
(IF RESPONDENT CANNOT ANSWER, ASK ABOUT LAST WEEK)

	Col./Code
... 10-15 hours a week,	7
16-23 hours a week,	6
24-29 hours a week,	3
or - 30 hours a week or more?	84
Don't know	*

28.a) How would you describe the wages or salary you are paid for the job you do - on the low side, reasonable, or on the high side?   IF 'On the low side': Very low or a bit low?

	Col./Code
Very low	10
A bit low	31
Reasonable	55
On the high side	4
Other answer (SPECIFY) ___	*
Don't know	-

CARD G

b) Thinking of the highest and the lowest paid people at your place of work, how would you describe the gap between their pay, as far as you know?   Please choose a phrase from this card?

	Col./Code
Much too big a gap	15
Too big	23
About right	49
Too small	3
Much too small a gap	1
Don't know	9

		Col./ Code	Skip to

29.a) If you stay in this job would you expect your wages or salary over the coming year to ... READ OUT ...

	Col./Code	Skip to
	%	
... rise by <u>more</u> than the cost of living,	13	
rise by the <u>same</u> as the cost of living,	47	
rise by <u>less</u> than the cost of living,	26	
or - <u>not</u> to rise at all?	10	
(Will not stay in job)	1	
(Don't know)	3	

b) Over the coming year do you expect your workplace will be ... READ OUT ...

	Col./Code
... increasing its number of employees,	18
reducing its number of employees,	29
or - will the number of employees stay about the same?	51
Other answer (SPECIFY) _____	1
(Don't know)	1

c) Thinking now about your own job. How likely or unlikely is it that you will leave this employer over the next year for any reason? Is it ... READ OUT ...

	Col./Code	Skip to
... very likely,	13	d)
quite likely,	13	d)
not very likely,	26	Q.30
or - not at all likely?	48	Q.30
(Don't know)	*	

IF VERY OR QUITE LIKELY

CARD H

d) Why do you think you will leave? Please choose a phrase from this card or tell me what other reason there is.

MORE THAN ONE
CODE MAY BE RINGED

	Col./Code
Firm will close down	2
I will be declared redundant	5
I will reach normal retirement age	2
My contract of employment will expire	1
I will take early retirement	2
I will decide to leave and work for another employer	12
I will decide to leave and work for myself, as self-employed	2
I will leave to look after home/children/relative	2
Other answer (SPECIFY) _____	3
(Don't know)	-

IF RESPONDENT IS MALE, ASK ABOUT "WOMEN"
IF RESPONDENT IS FEMALE, ASK ABOUT "MEN"

30. Where you work are there any (women/men) doing the same sort of work as you?

	Col./Code
Yes	36
No	63
Works alone	1
No-one else doing same job	*

31. Do you think of your work as ... READ OUT ...

	Col./Code
... mainly men's work,	29
mainly women's work,	16
or - work that either men or women do?	56
Other (SPECIFY) _____	*
(Don't know)	-

		Col./ Code	Skip to

CARD J

32.a) Now I'd like you to look at the statements on the card and tell me which ones best describe your own reasons for working at present. CODE ALL THAT APPLY.   RECORD IN COL (a).

IF MORE THAN ONE REASON ASK b).   OTHERS GO TO Q.33

b) And which one of these would you say is your main reason for working?   RECORD IN COL (b)

	(a) Reasons for working %	(b) Main Reason %
Working is the normal thing to do	35	6
Need money for basic essentials such as food, rent or mortgage	71	62
To earn money to buy extras	37	8
To earn money of my own	28	6
For the company of other people	25	1
Enjoy working	51	9
To follow my career	28	6
For a change from my children or housework	6	1
Otl.er reason (SPECIFY) _____	1	1
Don't know	-	-

33.a) Suppose you lost your job for one reason or another, would you start looking for another job, would you wait for several months or longer before you started looking, or would you decide not to look for another job?

	Col./Code	Skip to
Start looking	88	b)
Wait several months or longer	4	Q.34
Decide not to look	8	Q.34
Don't know	*	Q.34

IF START LOOKING

b) How long do you think it would take you to find an acceptable replacement job?

MONTHS   YEARS

MEDIAN: | 0 | 2 | | | |

Don't know   19

IF 3 MONTHS OR MORE ASK c) TO e):   OTHERS GO TO Q.34

c) How willing do you think you would be in these circumstances to retrain for a different job ... READ OUT ...

... very willing,	16
quite willing,	10
or - not very willing?	5
Would find job in less than 3 months or don't know how long	57
would not start looking immediately	13

d) And how willing do you think you would be to move to a different area to find an acceptable job ... READ OUT ...

... very willing,	6
quite willing,	7
or - not very willing?	17
(Don't know)	*
Would find job in less than 3 months or don't know how long	57
would not start looking immediately	13

e) And how willing do you think you would be in these circumstances to take what you now consider to be an unacceptable job ... READ OUT ...

... very willing,	5
quite willing,	11
or - not very willing?	15
(Don't know)	*
Would find job in less than 3 months or don't know how long	57
would not start looking immediately	13

		Col./ Code	Skip to
34.	If without having to work, you had what you would regard as a reasonable living income, do you think you would still prefer to have a paid job, or wouldn't you bother?	%	
	Still prefer paid job	69	
	Wouldn't bother	29	
	Do voluntary/service work	1	
	Other answer (SPECIFY) _____	1	
	Don't know	*	
35.	Have you in the past year done any regular paid work outside your main job?		
	Yes	7	
	No	93	
36.a)	During the last five years (that is since March 1979) have you been unemployed and seeking work for any period?		
	Yes	23	b)
	No	77	Q.37
	IF YES		
	b) For how many months in total during the last five years? MONTHS YEARS MEDIAN: 0 6 OR		
37.a)	For any period during the last five years have you worked as a self-employed person as your main job?		
	Yes	5	b)
	No	95	c)
	IF YES, ASK b). IF NO, ASK c)		
	b) In total, for how many months during the last five years have you been self-employed? MONTHS YEARS OR NOW SKIP TO Q.38		Q.38
	IF NO AT a)		
	c) How seriously in the last five years have you considered working as a self-employed person ... READ OUT ...		
	... very seriously,	6	d)&e)
	quite seriously,	10	d)&e)
	not very seriously,	12	Q.38
	or not at all seriously?	67	Q.38
	IF VERY OR QUITE SERIOUSLY, ASK d) & e)		
	d) What were the main reasons you did not become self-employed? PROBE FULLY. RECORD VERBATIM.		
	Cost/Lack of capital/money	9	
	Risk	4	
	Recession/Economic climate	1	
	Other answer	7	
	Don't know	-	
	e) How likely or unlikely is it that you will work as a self-employed person as your main job in the next five years ... READ OUT ...		
	... very likely,	3	
	quite likely,	5	
	not very likely,	4	
	or not at all likely?	4	
	(Don't know)	*	

		Col./ Code	Skip to
38.a)	At your place of work are there unions, staff associations, or groups of unions recognised by the management for negotiating pay and conditions of employment?	%	
	Yes	63	
	No	37	b)
	Don't know	*	Q.39
	IF YES		
b)	On the whole, do you think these unions or staff associations do their job well or not? Yes	39	
	No	21	
	Don't know	2	
39.a)	In general how would you describe relations between management and other employees at your workplace ... READ OUT ...		
	... very good,	36	
	quite good,	47	
	not very good,	13	
	or - not at all good?	3	
b)	And in general, would you say your workplace was ... READ OUT ...		
	... very well managed,	28	
	quite well managed,	51	Q.57
	or - not well managed?	19	
	NOW GO TO SECTION 3 (GREY) Don't know	*	

ALL SELF-EMPLOYED (CODE 2 AT Q.26): ASK Qs 40-44   N=89

40.a)	In your (main) job do you normally work ... READ OUT ... ... 10-15 hours a week,	5	
	(IF RESPONDENT CANNOT ANSWER, ASK ABOUT LAST WEEK) 16-23 hours a week,	-	
	24-29 hours a week,	4	
	or - 30 hours a week or more?	89	
	Don't know	-	
b)	During the last 5 years (that is since March 1979) have you been unemployed and seeking work for any period? Yes	14	c)
	No	86	Q.41
	IF YES		
c)	For how many months in total during the last 5 years?	MONTHS [ ][ ] OR YEARS [ ][ ]	
41.	If without having to work, you had what you would regard as a reasonable living income, do you think you would still prefer to do paid work, or wouldn't you bother? Still prefer paid work	77	
	Wouldn't bother	18	
	Other answer (SPECIFY) _____	3	
	Don't know	2	

		Col./ Code	Skip to
	CARD J		

42. Now I'd like you to look at the statements on the card and tell me which ones best describe your own reasons for working at present.   CODE ALL THAT APPLY.   RECORD IN COL (a)

IF MORE THAN ONE REASON ASK b).   OTHERS GO TO Q.43

b) And which one of these would you say is your main reason for working?   RECORD IN COL (b)

	(a) Reasons for working %	(b) Main Reason %
Working is the normal thing to do	49	11
Need money for basic essentials such as food, rent or mortgage	73	62
To earn money to buy extras	34	5
To earn money of my own	35	5
For the company of other people	16	1
Enjoy working	60	12
To follow my career	23	1
For a change from my children or housework	8	1
Other reasons (SPECIFY) _____	1	2
Don't know	–	–

43.a) Have you, for any period in the last five years, worked as an employee as your main job rather than as self-employed?

	Col./Code	Skip to
Yes	37	b)
No	63	c)

IF YES, ASK b).   IF NO, ASK c)

b) In total for how many months during the last five years have you been an employee?

MONTHS   YEARS
☐☐   OR   ☐☐   Q.44

NOW SKIP TO Q.44

IF NO AT a)

c) How seriously in the last five years have you considered getting a job as an employee ... READ OUT ...

	Col./Code	Skip to
... very seriously,	1	d)&e)
quite seriously,	4	d)&e)
not very seriously,	5	Q.44
or – not at all seriously?	54	Q.44

IF VERY OR QUITE SERIOUSLY ASK d) AND e)

d) What were the main reasons you did not become an employee?
PROBE FULLY.   RECORD VERBATIM.

e) How likely or unlikely is it that you will work as an employee, in your main job, in the next five years ... READ OUT ...

	Col./Code
... very likely,	–
quite likely,	–
not very likely,	1
or – not at all likely?	4
(Don't know)	–

	Col./Code	Skip to

44.a) Compared with <u>a year ago</u>, would you say your business is doing ... <u>READ OUT</u> ...

	Col./Code	Skip to
... very well,	% 17	
quite well,	19	
about the same,	47	
not very well,	8	
or - not at all well?	1	
(Business not in existence then)	9	

b) And over <u>the coming year</u>, do you think your business will do ... <u>READ OUT</u> ...

	Col./Code	Skip to
... better,	40	
about the same,	46	
or - worse than this year?	3	Q.57
Other (SPECIFY) _____	2	
(Don't know)	9	

NOW GO TO SECTION 3 (GREY)

ALL ON GOVERNMENT SCHEMES OR WAITING TO TAKE UP PAID WORK (CODES 02 OR 04 AT Q.25): ASK Qs 45-46   N=9

45.a) During the last five years (that is since March 1979) have you been unemployed <u>and</u> seeking work for any period?

	Col./Code	Skip to
Yes		b)
No		Q.46

IF YES ASK b). IF NO, GO TO Q.46

b) For how many months in total during the last five years?

MONTHS   YEARS
[   ][   ] OR [   ][   ]

---

46. If without having to work, you had what you would regard as a reasonable living income, do you think you would still prefer to have a paid job or wouldn't you bother?

	Col./Code	Skip to
Still prefer paid job		
Wouldn't bother		Q.57
Other answer (SPECIFY) _____		
Don't know		

NOW GO TO SECTION 3 (GREY)

		Col./ Code	Skip to
	ALL IN FULL TIME EDUCATION (CODE 01 AT Q.25): ASK Q.47-48		

47.a) When you leave full-time education, do you
think you will start looking for a job, will
you wait several months or longer before you
start looking, or will you decide not to look
for a job?

[N=27]

Start looking .... b)

Wait several months or longer

Decide not to look

Other answer (SPECIFY) _____   Q.48

Don't know

IF START LOOKING ASK b): OTHERS GO TO Q.48

b) How long do you think it will take
you to find an acceptable job?

MONTHS   YEARS

☐☐ OR ☐☐

Don't know

IF 3 MONTHS OR MORE AT b) ASK c): OTHERS GO TO Q.48

c) How willing do you think you would be in
these circumstances to take what you now
consider to be an unacceptable job?
... READ OUT ...   ... very willing,

quite willing,

or - not very willing?

(Don't know)

48. If without having to work, you had
what you would regard as a reasonable living
income, do you think you would prefer to
have a paid job, or wouldn't you bother?   Prefer paid job

Wouldn't bother   Q.57

Other answer (SPECIFY) _____

Don't know

NOW GO TO SECTION 3 (GREY)

		Col./ Code	Skip to

ALL UNEMPLOYED AND LOOKING FOR JOB - (CODES 05 AND 06 AT Q.25): ASK Qs49-50

49.a) In total how many months <u>in the last five years</u> (that is, since March 1979) have you been unemployed and seeking work?

N=98

%

MEDIAN: MONTHS |1|8| OR YEARS | |

b) How long has this <u>present</u> period of unemployment and seeking work lasted so far?

MONTHS |0|9| OR YEARS | |

c) How confident are you that you will find a job to match your qualifications ... <u>READ OUT</u> ...

... very confident,	10
quite confident,	9
not very confident,	44
or - not at all confident?	37

d) Although it may be difficult to judge, how long <u>from now</u> do you think it will be before you find an acceptable job?

MEDIAN: MONTHS |0|6| OR YEARS | |

Don't know

IF LESS THAN 3 MONTHS, SKIP TO Q.50.   ALL OTHERS(INC. DK) ASK e) - g)

e) How willing do you think you would be in these circumstances to retrain for a different job ... <u>READ OUT</u> ...

... very willing,	41
quite willing,	11
or -not very willing?	26
would find a job in less than 3 months or don't know how long	19

f) How willing would you be to move to a different area to find an acceptable job ... <u>READ OUT</u> ...

... very willing,	16
quite willing,	9
or -not very willing?	53
would find a job in less than 3 months or don't know how long	17

g) And how willing do you think you would be in these circumstances to take what you now consider to be an <u>unacceptable</u> job ... <u>READ OUT</u> ...

... very willing,	24
quite willing,	18
or -not very willing?	36
would find a job in less than 3 months or don't know how long	16

50. If without having to work, you had what you would regard as a reasonable living income, do you think you would still prefer to have a paid job or wouldn't you bother?

Still prefer paid job	70	
Wouldn't bother	21	Q.57
Other answer (SPECIFY) _____	-	
Don't know	-	

NOW GO TO SECTION 3 (GREY)

		Col./ Code	Skip to

ALL WHO ARE UNEMPLOYED BUT NOT ACTIVELY LOOKING FOR A JOB (CODE 07 AT Q.25): ASK Q.51   N=8

51.a) In total how many months in the <u>last five years</u> (that is, since March 1979) have you been unemployed and seeking work?   %

MONTHS   YEARS

b) How long has this <u>present</u> period of unemployment lasted so far?

MONTHS   YEARS

c) You said you were unemployed but not actively looking for a job. Could you explain why not? <u>PROBE FULLY</u>. RECORD VERBATIM.

NOW GO TO SECTION 3 (GREY)

ALL WHOLLY RETIRED FROM WORK (CODE 09 AT Q.25): ASK Q.52

52.a) Do you (or does your husband/wife) receive a pension from any past employer?   N=294   Yes 51
No 49

b) (Can I just check) are you over 65 (men)/ 60 (women)?   Yes 92   c)
No   8   e)

IF YES ASK c) AND d). IF NO GO TO e) AND f)

c) On the whole would you say the present <u>state</u> pension is on the low side, reasonable, or on the high side? IF 'On the low side': Very low or a bit low?

Very low	32
A bit low	36
Reasonable	23
On the high side	–

d) Do you expect your state pension in a year's time to purchase more than it does now, less, or about the same?

More	4	
Less	52	Q.57
About the same	31	
Don't know	5	

IF NO AT b)   f)
e) At what age did you retire from work?   YEARS
IF EVER WORKED   Never worked   Q.57
f) Why did you decide to retire at that age? PROBE FULLY. RECORD VERBATIM.

Q.57

Q.57

NOW GO TO SECTION 3 (GREY)

		Col./ Code	Skip to
	ALL LOOKING AFTER HOME (CODE 10 AT Q.25). ASK Qs53-56 N=312	%	
53.	What are the main reasons you do not have a paid job outside the home?		
	Looking after children at home	40	
	Above retirement age/OAP/too old to work	27	
	Prefer to look after home/family	14	
	No jobs available	9	
	Not suitable for available jobs	8	
	Other reasons	27	
54.a)	Have you, during the last five years, ever had a full or part time job of 10 hours per week or more? Yes	32	b)
	No	68	Q.55
	IF YES		
	b) How long ago was it that you left that job? NO. OF MONTHS AGO NO. OF YEARS AGO		Q.56
	MEDIAN: 2 4 OR		
	NOW SKIP TO Q.56		
55.a)	IF NO AT Q.54a)		
	How seriously in the past five years have you considered getting a full-time job? ... READ OUT ... ... very seriously,	3	Q.56
	PROMPT, IF NECESSARY: FULL TIME quite seriously,	3	Q.56
	IS 30 HRS+ PER WEEK not very seriously,	3	b)
	or - not at all seriously?	59	b)
	IF NOT VERY OR NOT AT ALL SERIOUSLY ASK b)		
	b) How seriously, in the past five years, have you considered getting a part time job? ... READ OUT ... ... very seriously,	2	
	quite seriously,	5	
	not very seriously,	6	
	or - not at all seriously?	48	
56.	Do you think you are likely to look for a paid job in the next 5 years?		
	IF YES: Full-time or part-time? Yes - Full-time	6	
	Yes - Part-time	32	
	No	59	
	Other (SPECIFY) _____	-	
	Don't know	2	

	Col./ Code	Skip to

SECTION THREE

ASK ALL

CARD K

57. Here are some items of government spending. Which of them, if any, would be your highest priority for <u>extra</u> spending? And which next? Please read through the whole list before deciding.

ONE CODE ONLY IN EACH COL.

	1st Priority	2nd Priority
	%	%
Education	20	29
Defence	3	3
Health	51	25
Housing	6	12
Public transport	*	1
Roads	1	3
Police and prisons	1	5
Social security benefits	7	8
Help for industry	10	10
Overseas aid	*	1
NONE OF THESE	*	1
Don't know	1	2

CARD L

58. Thinking now only of the government's spending on <u>social benefits</u> like those on the card. Which, if any, of these would be your highest priority for <u>extra</u> spending? And which next?

ONE CODE ONLY IN EACH COL.

	1st Priority	2nd Priority
	%	%
Retirement pensions	43	23
Child benefits	9	13
Benefits for the unemployed	18	17
Benefits for disabled people	21	34
Benefits for single parents	7	10
NONE OF THESE	1	2
Don't know	1	1

59. I will read two statements. For each one please say whether you agree or disagree? Strongly or slightly?

		(a) Falsely claim	(b) Fail to claim
a) Large numbers of people these days <u>falsely</u> claim benefits.		%	%
	Agree strongly	37	46
	Agree slightly	27	33
b) Large numbers of people who are eligible for benefits these days <u>fail</u> to claim them.	Disagree slightly	14	9
	Disagree strongly	12	4
	Don't know	10	8

		Col./ Code	Skip to

60. Opinions differ about the level of benefits for
the unemployed. Which of these two statements
comes closest to your own ... READ OUT ...

%

... Benefits for the unemployed are too low and cause hardship,   49

OR

Benefits for the unemployed are too high and discourage people
from finding jobs?   28

(Neither)   8

Other (SPECIFY)_____   9

(Don't know)   6

CARD M

61. Suppose the government had to choose between the
three options on this card. Which do you think
it should choose?

Reduce taxes and spend less on health, education and social benefits   6

Keep taxes and spending on these services at the same level as now   50

Increase taxes and spend more on health, education and social
benefits   39

None   2

Don't know   4

---

62. Turning now to the National Health Service.
On the whole, which of these three types of family
would you say gets best value from their taxes out
of the National Health Service ... READ OUT ...

... those with high incomes,   28

those with middle incomes,   15

or - those with low incomes?   41

(Don't know)   13

CARD N

63. All in all, how satisfied or dissatisfied would you say
you are with the way in which the National Health Service
runs nowadays? Choose a phrase from this card.

Very satisfied   11

Quite satisfied   40

Neither satisfied nor dissatisfied   19

Quite dissatisfied   19

Very dissatisfied   11

			Col./ Code	Skip to
64.a)	Are you covered by a private health insurance scheme, that is an insurance scheme that allows you to get private medical treatment?		%	
		Yes	11	b)
		No	89	Q.65
	IF YES			
	b) Does your employer (or your husband's/wife's employer) pay the majority of the cost of membership of this scheme?	Yes	6	
		No	5	
		Don't know	*	
65.a)	Now thinking of <u>private medical treatment</u> in hospitals. Do you think that the existence of private medical treatment in National Health Service hospitals is a good or bad thing for the National Health Service, or doesn't it make any difference to the NHS?			
		Good thing	23	
		Bad thing	42	
		No difference	30	
		Don't know	5	
b.)	And do you think the existence of private medical treatment in <u>private</u> hospitals is a good thing or bad thing for the <u>National Health Service</u>, or doesn't it make any difference to the NHS?			
		Good thing	35	
		Bad thing	19	
		No difference	42	
		Don't know	4	
	CARD P			
c.)	Which of the views on this card comes <u>closest</u> to your own about private medical treatment in hospitals?			
	Private medical treatment in all hospitals should be abolished		9	
	Private medical treatment should be allowed in private hospitals, but not in National Health Service hospitals		48	
	Private medical treatment should be allowed in both private and National Health Service hospitals		39	
		Don't know	3	

		Should	Should not	Don't know
66.a)	Now thinking of GPs and dentists. Do you think that National Health Service GPs should or should not be free to take on <u>private patients</u>?	%	%	%
		59	36	5
b.)	And do you think that National Health Service dentists should or should not be free to give <u>private treatment</u>?	64	31	5

		Col./ Code	Skip to

67. It has been suggested that the National Health Service should be available <u>only to those with lower incomes.</u> This would mean that contributions and taxes could be lower and most people would then take out medical insurance or pay for health care. Do you support or oppose this idea?

%

Support — 23
Oppose — 70
Don't know — 7

Now a few questions on education.

68. Do you think that what is taught in schools should be up to ... <u>READ OUT</u> ...

... the <u>local</u> education authority to decide — 53
or— should <u>central</u> government have the final say? — 39
(Don't know) — 7

69. In general, how would you compare the overall standards of education in schools today with the standards when you were at school. Would you say that standards today are higher, lower, or about the same? <u>IF HIGHER OR LOWER</u>: A lot or a little?

A lot higher now — 20
A little higher — 17
About the same — 18
A little lower now — 17
A lot lower — 21
Not educated here — 2
Don't know — 4

70. Some people think it is best for secondary schoolchildren to be separated into grammar and secondary modern schools according to how well they have done when they leave primary school. Others think it is best for secondary schoolchildren <u>not</u> to be sep- arated in this way, and to attend comprehensive schools.

On balance, which system do you think provides the best all-round education for secondary schoolchildren ... <u>READ OUT</u> ...

... a system of grammar and secondary modern schools, — 50
or - a system of comprehensive schools? — 40

Other (SPECIFY) _____ — 3

(Don't know) — 8

		Col./ Code	Skip to
71.a)	Generally speaking, what is your opinion about private schools in Britain? Should there be ... READ OUT ...	%	
	... more private schools,	9	
	about the same number as now,	68	
	fewer private schools,	10	
	or – no private schools at all?	9	
	Other answer (SPECIFY) _____	2	
	(Don't know)	2	
b)	If there were <u>fewer</u> private schools in Britain today do you think, on the whole, that state schools would ... READ OUT ... ... benefit,	17	
	suffer,	14	
	or – would it make no difference?	64	
	(Don't know)	4	
72.	On the whole, which of these three types of family would you say gets best value from their taxes out of government spending on education ... READ OUT ...		
	... those with high incomes,	31	
	those with middle incomes,	21	
	or – those with low incomes?	31	
	no difference	2	
	(Don't know)	14	

		Col./ Code	Skip to

SECTION FOUR

Now moving on to the subject of social class in Britain.

73.a) To what extent do you think a person's social class affects his or her opportunities in Britain today ... READ OUT ...

	Col./Code %
... a great deal,	25
quite a lot,	38
not very much,	28
or – not at all?	6

Other answer (SPECIFY) _____ 1

Don't know	2

b) Do you think social class is more or less important now in affecting a person's opportunities than it was 10 years ago, or has there been no real change?

More important now	22
Less important now	30
No change	45
Don't know	2

c) Do you think that in 10 years time social class will be more or less important than it is now in affecting a person's opportunities, or will there be no real change?

More important in 10 years time	19
Less important in 10 years time	27
No change	50
Don't know	3

CARD Q

74.a) Most people see themselves as belonging to a particular social class. Please look at this card and tell me which social class you would say you belong to? RECORD ANSWER IN COL (a)

b) And which social class would you say your parents belonged to when you started at primary school? RECORD ANSWER IN COL (b)

	(a) Self %	(b) Parents %
Upper middle	2	2
Middle	25	19
Upper working	19	11
Working	48	59
Poor	3	8
Don't know	2	1

	Col./ Code	Skip to

75.a) Do you regard yourself as belonging to any particular religion? <u>IF YES:</u> Which? <u>IF 'Christian'</u> PROBE FOR DENOMINATION

%

     <u>ONE CODE ONLY</u>

No religion	32	Q.76
Christian – no denomination	2	
Roman Catholic	12	
Church of England/Anglican	39	
<u>CHRISTIAN : DENOMINATIONS</u> United Reform Church (URC) /Congregational	1	
Baptist	2	
Methodist	3	
Presbyterian/Church of Scotland	5	
Other Christian (SPECIFY)_____		b)
Hindu	1	
Jew	*	
<u>OTHER RELIGIONS</u> Islam/Muslim	*	
Sikh	*	
Buddhist	–	
Other non-Christian (SPECIFY)_____	*	

<u>IF RELIGION ENTERED AT a) ASK b). OTHERS SKIP TO Q.76</u>

b) Apart from such special occasions as weddings, funerals and baptisms, how often nowadays do you attend services or meetings connected with your religion?

Once a week or more	12	
Less often but at least once in two weeks	3	
Less often but at least once a month	5	
Less often but at least twice a year	12	
Less often but at least once a year	7	
Less often	5	
Never or practically never	23	
Varies	1	

		Col./ Code	Skip to

ASK ALL

Now I would like to ask you some questions about racial prejudice in Britain.

76.
a) First, thinking of <u>Asians</u> - that is people originally from India and Pakistan - who now live in Britain. Do you think there is a lot of prejudice against them in Britain nowadays, a little or hardly any? <u>RECORD IN COL (a)</u>

b) And black people - that is West Indians and Africans - who now live in Britain. Do you think there is a lot of prejudice against them in Britain nowadays, a little, or hardly any? <u>RECORD IN COL (b)</u>

	(a) Asians %	(b) Blacks %
A lot	56	51
A little	35	39
Hardly any	6	7
Don't know	1	2

c) Do you think there is generally <u>more</u> racial prejudice in Britain now than there was 5 years ago, <u>less</u>, or about the <u>same</u> amount?

More now	40
Less now	20
About the same	37
Other answer (SPECIFY) _____	*

d) Do you think there will be <u>more</u>, <u>less</u> or about the <u>same</u> amount of racial prejudice in Britain in 5 years time compared with now?

Don't know	2
More in 5 years	40
Less	18
About the same	38
Other answer (SPECIFY) _____	2
Don't know	2

e) How would you describe yourself: ... <u>READ OUT</u> ...

... as very prejudiced against people of other races,	3	f)
a little prejudiced,	34	f)
or not prejudiced at all?	62	Q.77
Other answer (SPECIFY) _____	1	Q.77
	*	

<u>IF 'VERY' OR 'A LITTLE' PREJUDICED</u>

f) Against any race in particular? <u>PROBE AND RECORD. IF 'BLACK' OR 'COLOURED' MENTIONED, PROBE FOR WHETHER WEST INDIAN, ASIAN, GENERAL, ETC. RECORD VERBATIM EVERYTHING MENTIONED</u>

_____

_____

77.   There is a law in Britain against racial discrimination, that is against giving unfair preference to a particular race in housing, jobs and so on. Do you generally support or oppose the idea of a law for this purpose?

Support	70
Oppose	26
Don't know	3

		Col./ Code	Skip to
78.a)	INTERVIEWER: CODE FROM OBSERVATION FOR ALL RESPONDENTS	%	
	White/European	98	b)
	Indian/East African Asian/Pakistani/Bangladeshi/Sri Lankan	1 ⎫	
	Black/African/West Indian	1 ⎬	Q.79
	Other (inc. Chinese)	* ⎭	
b)	INTERVIEWER: REFER TO RESPONDENT SELECTION DIGIT. IF ODD, ASK VERSION A. IF EVEN OR 0, ASK VERSION B. RING CODE FOR WHICH VERSION USED. VERSION A VERSION B		

VERSION A

c) Do you think most white people in Britain would mind or not mind if a suitably qualified person of Asian origin were appointed as their boss? IF 'WOULD MIND': A lot or a little? RECORD IN COL. c)

d) And you personally? Would you mind or not mind? IF 'WOULD MIND': A lot or a little?   RECORD IN COL. (d)

e) Do you think that most white people in Britain would mind or not mind if one of their close relatives were to marry a person of Asian origin? IF 'WOULD MIND': A lot or a little?
          RECORD IN COL. (e)

f) And you personally? Would you mind or not mind? IF 'WOULD MIND': A lot or a little?   RECORD IN COL. (f)
          THEN GO TO Q.79

VERSION B

c) Do you think most white people in Britain would mind or not mind if a suitably qualified person of black or West Indian origin were appointed as their boss? IF 'WOULD MIND': A lot or a little?
          RECORD IN COL. (c)

d) And you personally? Would you mind or not mind? IF 'WOULD MIND': A lot or a little?   RECORD IN COL. (d)

e) Do you think that most white people in Britain would mind or not mind if one of their close relatives were to marry a person of black or West Indian origin? IF 'WOULD MIND': A lot or a little?
          RECORD IN COL. (e)

f) And you personally? Would you mind or not mind? IF 'WOULD MIND': A lot or a little?   RECORD IN COL. (f)

		BOSS				MARRIAGE			
		(c) Most people		(d) Self		(e) Most people		(f) Self	
		Asian	Black	Asian	Black	Asian	Black	Asian	Black
		%	%	%	%	%	%	%	%
	Mind a lot	26	26	11	9	41	47	30	29
	Mind a little	28	32	11	12	35	35	22	22
	Not mind	43	38	76	79	20	15	46	47
	Other answer	1	1	1	*	1	1	1	1
	Don't know	2	3	1	*	3	3	1	1

(SPECIFY) c) _____

d) _____

e) _____

f) _____

		Col./ Code %	Skip to

79. Now I would like to ask you about the obligations that people who have been married have if they divorce.

a) Consider a married couple, both aged about 45, with no children at home. They are both working at the time of the divorce.

In your opinion should the man make maintenance payments to support the wife?

		Col./Code %
	Yes	14
	No	79
Other answer (SPECIFY) _____		6
	Don't know	1

b) Consider a similar couple, also aged about 45 with no children at home. They are both working at the time of the divorce, but the woman's earnings are much lower than the man's.

In your opinion, should the man make maintenance payments to support the wife?

	Yes	44
	No	44
Other answer (SPECIFY) _____		10
	Don't know	1

c) Finally, consider another couple, also aged about 45 with no children at home. The man is working at the time of the divorce, but the woman has never worked in a paid job outside the home.

In your opinion, should the man make maintenance payments to support the wife?

	Yes	72
	No	18
Other answer (SPECIFY) _____		9
	Don't know	1

IF INTERVIEWING IN ENGLAND OR WALES, ASK ABOUT "BRITAIN".
IF INTERVIEWING IN SCOTLAND, ASK ABOUT "SCOTLAND".

80. Do you think that divorce in (Britain/Scotland) should be ... READ OUT ...

... easier to obtain than it is now,		13
more difficult,		30
or - should things remain as they are?		54
(Don't know)		3

81. There is a law in Britain against sex discrimination, that is against giving unfair preference to men - or to women - in employment, pay and so on. Do you generally support or oppose the idea of a law for this purpose?

	Support	80
	Oppose	17
	Don't know	2

		Col./ Code	Skip to
82.	Can I just check your own marital status.	%	
	At present are you ... READ OUT ... Married or living as married,	68	Q.83
	PRIORITY CODE separated or divorced,	6	
	widowed,	10	Q.85
	or - not married?	16	

83.	IF MARRIED OR LIVING AS MARRIED N = 1120		
	Are there any children under 16 years old in this household? Yes	43	
	No	57	

84. IF MARRIED OR LIVING AS MARRIED AT Q.82   OTHERS GO TO Q.85

I would like to ask about how you and your (husband/wife/partner) generally share some family jobs. Who does the household shopping: mainly the man, mainly the woman or is the task shared equally?
RECORD ANSWER IN GRID BELOW AND CONTINUE WITH ii) - ix)
ONE CODE FOR EACH ITEM

		MAINLY MAN	MAINLY WOMAN	SHARED EQUALLY	DON'T KNOW
i)	Household shopping %	6	54	39	-
ii)	Makes the evening meal %	5	77	16	-
iii)	Does the evening dishes %	18	37	41	-
iv)	Does the household cleaning %	3	72	23	-
v)	Does the washing and ironing %	1	88	9	-
vi)	Repairs the household equipment %	83	6	8	-
vii)	Organises the household money and payment of bills %	32	38	28	-

IF CHILD(REN) AT Q.83, ASK viii)-ix).   OTHERS GO TO Q.85

		MAINLY MAN	MAINLY WOMAN	SHARED EQUALLY	DON'T KNOW
viii)	N = 479 Looks after child(ren) when they are sick %	1	63	35	-
ix)	Teaches the child(ren) discipline %	10	12	77	-

85. ASK ALL

(Now) I would like to ask about how you think family jobs should generally be shared between men and women. For example, who do you think should do the household shopping: mainly the man, mainly the woman, or should the task be shared equally?
RECORD ANSWER IN GRID BELOW AND CONTINUE WITH ii)-ix)
ONE CODE FOR EACH ITEM

		MAINLY MAN	MAINLY WOMAN	SHARED EQUALLY	DON'T KNOW
i)	Household shopping %	*	34	63	*
ii)	Make the evening meal %	1	57	39	*
iii)	Do the evening dishes %	12	20	66	*
iv)	Do the household cleaning %	*	49	48	*
v)	Do the washing and ironing %	*	75	22	*
vi)	Repair the household equipment %	78	2	19	*
vii)	Organise the household money and payment of bills %	21	16	59	*
viii)	Look after children when they are sick %	*	50	47	*
ix)	Teach children discipline %	12	6	79	*

	ASK ALL			Col./ Code	Skip to
86.	There are a number of laws which aim at giving women greater equality with men, particularly at work. I am going to read out some of them, and I would like you to tell me for each one, whether you support or oppose it.				
	ONE CODE FOR EACH ITEM	Support	Oppose	Don't know	
i)	Laws giving men and women equal pay for equal work	%	94	5	1
ii)	The right to six weeks maternity pay if a woman has been in her job for two years	%	88	8	4
iii)	The opportunity for boys and girls to study the same subjects at school.	%	96	2	1
iv)	The right for a woman to return to her job within six months of having a baby	%	77	18	5
v)	Laws making it illegal to treat men and women differently at work	%	81	14	5

		Col./ Code	
87.	Some people think that women are generally less likely than men to be promoted at work, even when their qualifications and experience are the same. Do you think this happens ... READ OUT ...	%	
	... a lot,	40	
	a little,	42	
	or – hardly at all?	10	
	Don't know	7	

88.a) CARD R

I'd like you to look at the statements on this card.
In general, which ones do you think best describe the
reasons why many married women work? Any others?
CODE ALL THAT APPLY. RECORD IN COL. (a)

IF MORE THAN ONE REASON MENTIONED AT a) ASK b)   OTHERS GO TO Q.89

b) And which one of these would you say is generally the
main reason why married women work? RECORD IN COL (b)

	(a) Reasons for working	(b) Main Reason
	%	%
Working is the normal thing to do	6	1
Need money for basic essentials such as food, rent or mortgage	64	45
To earn money to buy extras	71	35
To earn money of their own	46	8
For the company of other people	38	2
Because they enjoy working	28	2
To follow a career	30	2
For a change from children or housework	41	3
Other (SPECIFY) _____	1	*
Don't know	1	1

		Col./ Code	Skip to

CARD S
Now I would like to ask you some questions about sexual relations.

89.a) If a man and a woman have sexual relations before marriage, what would your general opinion be? Please choose a phrase from this card.
RECORD IN COL (a)

b) What about a <u>married person</u> having sexual relations with someone other than his or her partner? Please choose a phrase from this card. RECORD IN COL (b)

c) What about sexual relations between two adults of the same sex? Please choose a phrase from this card. RECORD IN COL (c)

	(a) BEFORE MARRIAGE	(b) EXTRA MARITAL	(c) SAME SEX
	%	%	%
Always wrong	15	59	54
Mostly wrong	12	26	13
Sometimes wrong	19	10	7
Rarely wrong	6	1	2
Not wrong at all	42	1	16
Depends/varies	4	2	6
Don't know	*	*	1

		NOTHING WRONG	BIT WRONG	WRONG	SERIOUSLY WRONG	DON'T KNOW	Col./ Code	Skip to

90. CARD T
I am now going to read out some situations that might come up. As I read out each one, please say which of the phrases on this card comes closest to what you think of the situation.

READ OUT ...

	Situation	NOTHING WRONG	BIT WRONG	WRONG	SERIOUSLY WRONG	DON'T KNOW
i)	A company employee exaggerates his claims for travel expenses over a period and makes £50. %	4	17	54	23	1
ii)	A company manager accepts a Christmas present worth £50 from a firm from which he buys products. %	39	23	29	7	1
iii)	A manager asks a firm from which he % buys products for a £50 gift for himself	2	6	46	44	1
iv)	A firm selling products to another company regularly takes a manager in that company to expensive lunches. %	39	27	26	6	1
v)	A council official accepts a Christmas present worth £50 from a private firm that supplies services to the council.%	13	14	43	28	2
vi)	A council official asks a firm that supplies services to the council for a £50 gift for himself. %	1	4	38	56	1
vii)	A firm supplying services to the Council regularly takes a council official to expensive lunches. %	22	22	41	13	1
viii)	A council official uses his influence to get a relative a job with the council. %	11	19	45	23	1
ix)	A council official exaggerates his claims for travel expenses over a period and makes £50. %	2	12	52	33	1
x)	A council tenant applies for a transfer to a better house. An official in the housing department notices that the application is from an old friend. He decides to put the application near the front of the queue. %	2	11	52	33	1
xi)	A council tenant applies for a transfer to a better house. An official in the housing department asks for £50 to put the application near the front of the queue. %	*	1	26	72	*
xii)	A council tenant applies for a transfer to a better house. He offers an official in the housing department £50 to put the application near the front of the queue. %	1	4	41	53	*
xiii)	A policeman stops a driver for speeding. The policeman asks for £50 to forget the incident. %	*	1	17	81	*
xiv)	A policeman stops a driver for speeding. The driver offers £50 to forget the incident. %	1	4	36	59	*
xv)	A policeman stops a driver for speeding. The driver is an old friend. The policeman decides simply to forget the incident.	3	14	51	31	*

				Col./Code	Skip to

STILL CARD T

Still using the card to say what comes closest to what you think about the situation ...

		Nothing wrong	Bit wrong	Wrong	Seriously wrong	Don't know
91.a)	A man offers the dustmen £5 to take away rubbish they are not supposed to pick up	% 32	35	29	3	2

b)	Might you do this if the situation came up?		%
		Yes	58
		No	38
		Don't know	3

STILL CARD T

		Nothing wrong	Bit wrong	Wrong	Seriously wrong	Don't know
92.a)	A householder is having a repair job done by a local plumber. He is told that if he pays cash he will not be charged VAT. So he pays cash.	% 31	31	32	4	2

b)	Might you do this if the situation came up?		%
		Yes	66
		No	27
		Don't know	5

STILL CARD T

		Nothing wrong	Bit wrong	Wrong	Seriously wrong	Don't know
93.a)	A man gives a £5 note for goods he is buying in a big store. By mistake, he is given change for a £10 note. He notices but keeps the change.	% 6	15	61	16	1

b)	Might you do this if the situation came up?		%
		Yes	18
		No	77
		Don't know	4

SECTION FIVE

Finally, a few details about you and your household.

	PERSON NO.	Resp-ondent	1	2	3	4	5	6	7	8	9
		%									
94.a)	Sex: Male	47									
	Female	53									
b)	Age last birthday:										
c)	Relationship to respondent:										
	Spouse/partner										
	Son/daughter										
	Parent/parent-in-law										
	Other relative										
	Not related										
d)	HOUSEHOLD MEMBER(S) WITH LEGAL RESPON-SIBILITY FOR ACCOMMODATION (INC. JOINT AND SHARED)	SOLE 30% SHARED: 46% NONE 23%									
	ASK ONLY FOR RESPONDENT AND SPOUSE/PARTNER, AND EACH OF RESPONDENT'S SONS/DAUGHTERS OVER 5 IN HOUSEHOLD. CARD V	%									
95.	Which of these types of school have you (has he/she) ever attended?										
	PRIMARY State or LA	88									
	Private	6									
	Voluntary/maintained	7									
	SECON-DARY State or LA	79									
	Private	7									
	Voluntary/maintained	5									
	No secondary school attended	9									

96. RESPONDENT ONLY

AGE OF COMPLETING FULL TIME EDUCATION:

	%
15 or under}	77
16}	
17}	14
18}	
19 or over	7
Still at school}	2
Still at college, polytechnic, or university}	

Other answer (SPECIFY) _____ -

		Col./ Code	Skip to
97.	Does your household own or rent this accommodation? PROBE AS NECESSARY TO CLASSIFY	%	
	ONE CODE ONLY Owned/being bought leasehold or freehold	66	
	RENTED FROM: Local authority (include GLC)	25	
	New Town Development Corporation	1	
	Housing Association	1	
	Property Company	1	
	Employer	2	
	Other organisation	1	
	Relative	*	
	Other individual	4	
	Don't know	*	

IS THIS A SINGLE PERSON HOUSEHOLD?   Yes → SKIP TO c)
                                       No → ASK a)

		Col./ Code	Skip to
98.a)	Who is the person <u>mainly</u> responsible for general domestic duties in this household? Respondent mainly	37	
	Someone else mainly (SPECIFY RELATIONSHIP TO RESPONDENT) _____	36	
	Duties shared equally (SPECIFY BY WHOM) _____	12	
	Single person household	12	

IS THERE A CHILD UNDER 16 IN THE HOUSEHOLD?   Yes → ASK b)
                                               No → SKIP TO c)

		Col./ Code	Skip to
	b) Who is the person <u>mainly</u> responsible for the general care of the child(ren) here? Respondent mainly	14	
	Someone else mainly (SPECIFY RELATIONSHIP TO RESPONDENT) _____	13	
	Duties shared equally (SPECIFY BY WHOM) _____	7	
	No children under 16 in household	64	

ASK ALL

		Col./ Code	Skip to
c)	Some people have responsibilities for looking after a disabled, sick, or elderly friend or relative. Is there anyone like this who depends on you to provide some regular care for them?		
	Yes	13	
	No	85	

	Col./ Code	Skip to

REFER TO ECONOMIC POSITION OF RESPONDENT (Q.25) PAGE 9

IF IN PAID WORK (CODE 03) → ASK a) TO h) ABOUT <u>PRESENT</u> MAIN JOB
IF WAITING TO TAKE UP JOB OFFERED (<u>CODE 04</u>) → ASK a) TO h) ABOUT
<u>FUTURE</u> JOB.

O.U.O.

IF UNEMPLOYED (<u>CODES 05, 06 OR 07</u>) OR RETIRED (<u>CODE 09</u>) OR LOOKING
AFTER HOME (<u>CODE 10</u>) → ASK a) TO h) ABOUT <u>LAST</u> JOB.   IF NEVER HAD A
JOB, WRITE IN AT a)

O.C.

OTHERS GO TO Q.100

99.   Now I want to ask you about your (present/future/last) job.   E.S.
       CHANGE TENSES FOR (BRACKETED) WORDS AS APPROPRIATE.

   a) What (is) your job?   PROBE AS NECESSARY: S.E.G.
       What is the name or title of the job? _____
       _____ SC/M.NM
       _____

   b) What kind of work (do) you do most of the time?   IF RELEVANT: What   SIC
       materials/machinery (do) you use? _____
       _____
       _____

   c) What training or qualifications (do) you have that (are) needed for
       that job? _____
       _____

   d) (Do) you supervise or (are) you responsible for the   %
       work of any other people?   IF YES: How many?
                            Yes: WRITE IN NO. [   ][   ][   ][   ]
                            No: (RING)   0000

   e) Can I just check: are you ... READ OUT ...   ... an employee   83
                                             or, self-employed?   7
                                               never worked   3
       IF EMPLOYEE (CODE 1)   [N=1391]
       CARD W
       f) Which of the types of organisation on this card
           (do) you work for?

                                    Private firm or company   63
                          Nationalised industry/public corporation   9
                    Local Authority/Local Education Authority   14
                              Health Authority/hospital   7
                          Central Government/Civil Service   6
                                        Charity or trust   1
       Other (SPECIFY) _____   1

       ASK ALL

   g) What (does) your employer (IF SELF-EMPLOYED: you) make or do at the
       place where you usually (work)?   IF FARM, GIVE NO. OF ACRES.
       _____
       _____

   h) Including yourself, how many people (are)
       employed at the place you usually (work) (from)?   Under 10   21
                                                               10-24   13
                                                               25-99   20
                                                               100-499   20
                                                               500 or more 14
                                                               never worked 3

		Col./ Code	Skip to
ASK ALL		%	
100.a) Are you <u>now</u> a member of a trade union or staff association?	Yes	26	c)
IF NO AT a)	No	73	b)
b) Have you <u>ever</u> been a member of a trade union or staff association?	Yes	30	c)
	No	43	Q.101

IF NOW OR EVER TRADE UNION· MEMBER (CODE 1 AT a) or b)	%	%	% DON'T KNOW
c) Have you ever ... READ OUT ... RING ONE CODE FOR EACH	YES	NO	
... attended a union or staff association meeting?	37	19	–
voted in a union or staff association election or meeting?	34	22	*
put forward a proposal or motion at a union or staff association meeting?	11	44	–
gone on strike?	20	36	–
stood in a picket line?	6	50	–
served as a lay representative such as a shop steward or branch committee member?	9	47	–

IF RESPONDENT IS MARRIED OR LIVING AS MARRIED, ASK Q.101 AND Q.102
ABOUT HUSBAND/WIFE/PARTNER.   OTHERS GO TO Q.103.

CARD X

101. Which of these descriptions applies to what your (husband/wife/ partner) was doing last week, that is the seven days ending last Sunday? PROBE: Any others? CODE ALL THAT APPLY IN COL. I.

IF ONLY ONE CODE AT I, TRANSFER IT TO COL. II   N=1120
IF MORE THAN ONE AT I, TRANSFER HIGHEST ON LIST TO II.

(Multiple)

	COL. I	COL. II ECONOMIC POSITION	
In full-time education (not paid for by employer, including on vacation)	% *	% *	Q.103
On government training/employment scheme (e.g. Community Programme, Youth Training Scheme etc.)	*	*	Q.103
In paid work (or away temporarily) for at least 10 hours in the week	57	57 ⎫	
Waiting to take up paid work already accepted	*	*	
Unemployed and registered at a benefit office	4	4 ⎬	Q.102
Unemployed, <u>not</u> registered, but actively looking for a job	1	1	
Unemployed, wanting a job (of at least 10 hrs per week), but not actively looking for a job	1	1 ⎭	
Permanently sick or disabled	3	3	Q.103
Wholly retired from work	13	13 ⎫	Q.102
Looking after the home	36	21 ⎭	
Doing something else (SPECIFY) _____	1	*	Q.103

	Col./Code	Skip to
REFER TO ECONOMIC POSITION OF RESPONDENT'S SPOUSE/PARTNER (Q.101) P.39		

IF SPOUSE IS IN PAID WORK (CODE 03) - ASK a) to i) ABOUT PRESENT MAIN JOB.
IF SPOUSE IS WAITING TO TAKE UP JOB OFFERED (CODE 04) - ASK a) to i) ABOUT FUTURE JOB.
IF SPOUSE IS UNEMPLOYED (CODES 05, 06, OR 07), OR RETIRED (CODE 09), OR LOOKING AFTER HOME (CODE 10) ASK a) to i) ABOUT LAST JOB.
IF NEVER HAD A JOB WRITE IN AT a). OTHERS GO TO Q.103

O.U.O.

OC.

E.S.

S.E.G.

SC/M.NM

SIC

102.

Now I want to ask you about your (husband's/wife's/partner's) job.

a) What (is) the name or title of that job? _____

b) What kind of work (does) he/she do most of the time? IF RELEVANT: What materials/machinery (does) he/she use? _____

c) What training or qualifications (does) he/she have that (are) needed for that job? _____

%

d) (Does) he/she supervise or (is) he/she responsible for the work of any other people? IF YES: How many?   YES: WRITE IN NO. [   ]
NO: (RING)   0000

e) (Is) he/she ... READ OUT ...   N=1120   ... an employee, 83
or self-employed? 9
IF EMPLOYEE (CODE 1)   N=930   never worked 4
CARD Y

f) Which of the types of organisation on this card does he/she work for?

Private firm or company	63
Nationalised industry/public corporation	11
Local Authority/Local Education Authority	13
Health Authority/hospital	7
Central Government/Civil Service	4
Charity or trust	2
Other (SPECIFY) _____	1

ASK ALL

g) What (does) the employer (IF SELF-EMPLOYED: he/she) make or do at the place where he/she usually (works)? IF FARM GIVE NO. OF ACRES

_____

h) Including him/her self, roughly how many people (are) employed at the place where he/she usually (works) (from)?

Under 10	24
10-24	12
25-99	19
100-499	20
500 or more	14
never worked	4

i) (Is) the job ... READ OUT ...

... full-time (30 hours+)	71
or part-time (10-29 hours)?	18
never worked	4

			Col./ Code	Skip to
ASK ALL **CARD Z**				

103.a) Which of the letters on this card represents the <u>total income</u> from <u>all</u> sources of your household?   **ONE CODE IN COLUMN a)**

IF IN PAID WORK (ECONOMIC POSITION CODE 03 AT Q 25. OTHERS GO TO Q.104

b) Which of the letters on this card represents your <u>own</u> gross or total <u>earnings, before</u> deduction of income tax and national insurance? **ONE CODE IN COLUMN b)**

GROSS ANNUAL INCOME:	% a) House- hold	% b) Earn- ings	N=867
Less than £2,000	6	9	
£2,000 - £2,999	8	6	
£3,000 - £3,999	9	8	
£4,000 - £4,999	7	11	
£5,000 - £5,999	8	13	
£6,000 - £6,999	8	9	
£7,000 - £7,999	8	8	
£8,000 - £9,999	9	10	
£10,000 - £11,999	9	8	
£12,000 - £14,999	8	5	
£15,000 +	9	3	
Refused	12	8	

104.a) **ASK ALL**

Is there a telephone in (your part of) this accommodation?

IF NO ASK b)

b) Do you have easy access to a 'phone where you can receive incoming calls?   **IF YES, ASK:** Is this a home or a work number?

                    IF BOTH, CODE HOME ONLY

IF YES AT a) OR b)

c) A few interviews on any survey are checked by a supervisor to make sure that people are satisfied with the way the interview was carried out.   In case my supervisor needs to contact you, it would be helpful if we could have your telephone number.

RECORD HOME OR WORK NUMBER ON
ADDRESS SLIP ONLY - NOT HERE.

	Col./Code	Skip to
Yes	80	c)
No	19	b)
Yes - home	1	c)
Yes - work	1	c)
No		Q.105
Number given		
Number refused		

105.a) In a year's time we will be doing a similar interview and we may wish to include you again.   Would this be alright?

IF NO AT a)

b) Can you tell me why that is?   **RECORD VERBATIM**

c) This interview has lasted about .... If next year's interview were going to last only <u>half</u> an hour, might you then have agreed to be included?
Other (SPECIFY) _____

	Col./Code	Skip to
Yes	91	Q.106
No	9	b)
Yes		Q.107
No		

	Col./Code	Skip to
IF WILLING TO BE INTERVIEWED AGAIN (CODE 1 AT Q.105a)		

106.a) Suppose we try to call at this address in a year's time and for some reason have difficulty in contacting you. Is there any other address or telephone number you could give us of someone else who might be likely to know your whereabouts?

IF NECESSARY, PROMPT: Perhaps the address or 'phone number of a relative who is unlikely to move, or your workplace?

— Another address/'phone number given

No other information given

RECORD OTHER ADDRESS/PHONE NO., NAME OF CONTACT OR ANY OTHER INFORMATION OFFERED.

IF TELEPHONE NUMBER GIVEN AT Q.104c)

b) If we were trying to reach you again, would you prefer us ...
READ OUT ...
... simply to come round again,
to phone first,
to write first,
or - doesn't it matter?

SELF-COMPLETION QUESTIONNAIRE

107.a) Was it ... ... filled in before main interview,
filled in immediately after interview in interviewer's presence,
or left behind to be filled in after interview?
Other (SPECIFY) _____

b) Was it ... ... (to be) collected by interviewer,
or to be posted back?

24 hour clock

Time interview completed ☐☐|☐☐

minutes

TOTAL DURATION OF INTERVIEW ☐☐☐

Name of interviewer _____ No: ☐☐☐☐ P/N

DATE OF INTERVIEW: DAY ☐☐ MONTH ☐ O ☐ YEAR ☐ 8 4

scpr

SOCIAL AND COMMUNITY PLANNING RESEARCH

Head Office: 35 Northampton Square London EC1V 0AX. Tel: 01-250 1866
Northern Field Office: Charazel House Gainford Darlington Co. Durham DL2 3EG. Tel: 0325 730 888

SELF COMPLETION QUESTIONNAIRE

BRITISH SOCIAL ATTITUDES: 1984 SURVEY

March 1984   P.770

Interviewer
to enter

Serial No.

To the selected respondent

We hope very much that you will agree to participate in this important study -
the second in an annual series of surveys to be published each summer.   The
study consists of this self-completion questionnaire and an interview.

Completing the questionnaire

The questions inside cover a wide range of subjects, but each one can be answered
simply by placing a tick (√) or a number in one or more of the boxes provided.
No special knowledge is required: we are confident that everyone will be able
to offer an opinion on all questions.   And we want *all* people to take part, not
just those with strong views or particular viewpoints.   The questionnaire should
not take up much of your time and should be completed by the person selected by
the interviewer at your address.   We hope you will find it interesting and
enjoyable and you may be assured that participation is confidential and anonymous.

Returning the questionnaire

Your interviewer will arrange with you the most convenient way of returning
the questionnaire.   If he or she has arranged to call back for it, please
complete it and keep it safely until then.   If not, please complete it and
post it back in the stamped, addressed envelope *as soon as you possibly can*.

*Social and Community Planning Research is an independent social research
institute registered as a charitable trust.   Its projects are funded by
government departments, local authorities, universities and foundations to
provide information on social issues in Britain.   SCPR interviewers carry
out around 50,000 interviews per year.   This study has been funded mainly
by the Monument Trust (one of the Sainsbury foundations), with contributions
also from industry and government.   Please contact us if you require further
information.*

N=1562

1. Please tick one box for *each* country below to show
    whether you think its <u>standard of living</u> is higher,
    about the same, or lower than Britain's.

PLEASE TICK ONE BOX ON EACH LINE   STANDARD OF LIVING

	Higher than Britain's	About the same as Britain's	Lower than Britain's	Don't know
France %	26 ₁	53 ₂	14 ₃	3
East Germany %	12 ₁	18 ₂	61 ₃	5
West Germany %	66 ₁	23 ₂	3 ₃	3
Japan %	38 ₁	21 ₂	32 ₃	4
Canada %	65 ₁	26 ₂	2 ₃	3
Australia %	52 ₁	37 ₂	3 ₃	3

2. Now thinking of <u>influence on world events</u>. Please
    tick one box for <u>*each*</u> country below to show whether
    it generally has more influence, about the same
    amount of influence, or less influence than Britain
    has nowadays.

PLEASE TICK ONE BOX ON EACH LINE   INFLUENCE

	More than Britain	About the same amount as Britain	Less than Britain	Don't know
France %	16 ₁	58 ₂	19 ₃	3
China %	27 ₁	22 ₂	42 ₃	4
East Germany %	14 ₁	25 ₂	50 ₃	4
West Germany %	27 ₁	56 ₂	10 ₃	4
Canada %	10 ₁	50 ₂	31 ₃	4
Australia	7 ₁	47 ₂	37 ₃	4
Israel	20 ₁	21 ₂	50 ₃	4
India	4 ₁	14 ₂	73 ₃	4

/Continued over ...

3.a) | Suppose you were advising a 16 year old girl school leaver on the two most important things she should look for in a job. Please put a '1' in the box next to the *most* important thing in the list below, and a '2' next to the *second most* important in column (a).

b) | And if you were advising a 16 year old boy school leaver, which would be the *first* and which the *second* most important? Please place a '1' and '2' in the boxes in column (b).

	% GIRL 1st	% BOY 1st	% GIRL 2nd	% BOY 2nd
High starting wage or salary	4	3	5	5
Secure job for the future	42	53	13	17
Opportunities for career development	24	25	27	40
Satisfying work	19	10	23	17
Good working conditions	3	1	16	9
Pleasant people to work with	1	*	7	1
Short working hours	*	–	1	*
A lot of responsibility	*	*	1	2
Not answered/Don't know	7	8	7	8

4. | Here are a number of circumstances in which a woman might consider an abortion. Please say whether or not you think the law should allow an abortion in each case.

Should abortion be allowed by law?

PLEASE TICK ONE BOX ON EACH LINE

	Yes	No	Don't know
The woman's health is seriously endangered by the pregnancy %	92 1	5 2	1
The woman became pregnant as a result of rape %	89 1	8 2	*
There is a strong chance of a defect in the baby %	82 1	13 2	1
The couple cannot afford any more children %	37 1	58 2	1
The woman is not married and does not wish to marry the man %	32 1	64 2	1
The couple agree they do not wish to have the child %	32 1	63 2	1
The woman decides on her own she does not wish to have the child %	29 1	66 2	1

5.a)   Suppose a person has a painful incurable disease.
       Do you think that doctors should be allowed by law
       to end the patient's life if the patient requests
       it?

       PLEASE TICK ONE BOX   Yes | 75 |

                                                          No | 24 |

  b)   And if a person is not incurably sick but simply Don't know   1
       tired of living, should doctors be allowed by law
       to end that person's life if he or she requests it?

       PLEASE TICK ONE BOX   Yes | 11 |

                                                          No | 87 |
                                                   Don't know   1

---

6.   Are you in favour of or against the death penalty for ...

     PLEASE TICK ONE BOX ON EACH LINE

	IN FAVOUR	AGAINST	DON'T KNOW
... murder in the course of a terrorist act	78	20	*
... murder of a policeman	73	24	1
... other murders	66	31	1

---

7.   Listed below are a number of organisations or services.
     From what you know or have heard about each one, can
     you say whether you are generally satisfied or not
     satisfied with the service that each one provides.

     PLEASE TICK ONE BOX ON EACH LINE

	SATISFIED	NOT SATISFIED	DON'T KNOW
The press	62	34	1
Local government	49	47	1
The civil service	53	42	2
Banks	82	13	1
The BBC	66	30	1
Independent TV and radio	76	21	*
The police	79	17	*
Local doctor	84	13	*
The postal service	75	22	*
British Rail	52	42	2
The telephone service	80	16	1

/Continued over ...

8.	How serious an effect on our environment do you think each of these things has?	VERY SERIOUS	QUITE SERIOUS	NOT VERY SERIOUS	NOT AT ALL SERIOUS	DON'T KNOW
	PLEASE TICK ONE BOX ON EACH LINE					
	Noise from aircraft %	7 ₄	24 ₃	50 ₂	17 ₁	*
	Lead from petrol %	45 ₄	39 ₃	11 ₂	2 ₁	*
	Industrial waste in the rivers and sea	67 ₄	25 ₃	6 ₂	1 ₁	*
	Waste from nuclear electricity stations	69 ₄	18 ₃	9 ₂	2 ₁	1
	Industrial fumes in the air	46 ₄	40 ₃	11 ₂	2 ₁	*
	Noise and dirt from traffic	20 ₄	45 ₃	29 ₂	4 ₁	*

9.a) Which one of these three possible solutions to
Britain's electricity needs would you favour most?

PLEASE TICK ONE BOX

%
(✓)

We should make do with the power stations
we have already 38 ₁

We should build more coal-fuelled power stations 44 ₂

We should build more nuclear power stations 15 ₃

Don't know 1

b) As far as nuclear power stations are concerned,
which of these statements comes closest to your
own feelings?

*PLEASE TICK
ONE BOX*

%
(✓)

They create very serious risks for the future 37 ₁

They create quite serious risks for the future 30 ₂

They create only slight risks for the future 23 ₃

They create hardly any risks for the future 8 ₄

Don't know 1

10. Which one of these two statements comes closest
to your own views?

PLEASE TICK ONE BOX

%
(✓)

Industry should be prevented from causing damage to the
countryside, even if this sometimes leads to higher prices 77 ₁

OR

Industry should keep prices down, even if this sometimes
causes damage to the countryside 22 ₂

Don't know 1

11. Here is a list of predictions.   For each one, please say
how likely or unlikely you think it is to come true *within
the next ten years?*

PLEASE TICK ONE BOX FOR EACH PREDICTION	VERY LIKELY	QUITE LIKELY	NOT VERY LIKELY	NOT AT ALL LIKELY	DON'T KNOW
Acts of political terrorism in Britain will be common events %	20 4	42 3	30 2	5 1	1
Riots and civil disturbance in our cities will be common events %	16 4	40 3	34 2	6 1	1
There will be a world war involving Britain and Europe %	3 4	18 3	50 2	25 1	2
There will be a serious accident at a British nuclear power station %	13 4	40 3	36 2	8 1	2
The police in our cities will find it impossible to protect our personal safety on the streets %	18 4	34 3	35 2	11 1	1
The government in Britain will be overthrown by revolution	2 4	8 3	33 2	54 1	1
A nuclear bomb will be dropped somewhere in the world %	9 4	26 3	38 2	24 1	1

12.a) How much influence would you say the trade unions
have on the lives of people in Britain these days?   %
                                                                                       (✓)
PLEASE TICK ONE BOX   A great deal of influence | 28 1 |
                                            Quite a bit of influence | 39 2 |
                                                     Some influence | 27 3 |
                                                                                       %
                                                 Not much influence | 6 4 | Don't know *

b) Do you think they have too much influence,   %
about the right amount, or too little   (✓)
influence?   Too much influence | 57 1 |

PLEASE TICK ONE BOX   About the right amount | 34 2 |
                                                                                       %
                                                Too little influence | 8 3 | Don't know *

13.a) And how much influence would you say big business
has on the lives of people in Britain these days?   (✓)
PLEASE TICK ONE BOX   A great deal of influence | 42 1 |
                                            Quite a bit of influence | 38 2 |
                                                     Some influence | 16 3 |
                                                                                       %
                                                 Not much influence | 3 4 | Don't know 1

b) Do you think big business has too much
influence, about the right amount, or   (✓)
too little influence?   Too much influence | 46 1 |

PLEASE TICK ONE BOX   About the right amount | 50 2 |
                                                                                       %
                                                Too little influence | 2 3 | Don't know 1

/Continued over ...

14.	New kinds of technology are being introduced more and more in Britain: computers and word processors, robots in factories and so on.			
a)	Please tick a box in the first column to show what effect you think this technology will have over the next *three years or so*?			Don't know % 1
b)	Now tick one box in the second column to say what effect you think this technology will have over the next *ten years or so*?			Don't know % 1

PLEASE TICK ONE BOX IN EACH COLUMN

	THREE YEARS % (✓)	TEN YEARS % (✓)
It will increase the number of jobs available	13 (1)	18 (1)
It will reduce the number of jobs available	63 (2)	66 (2)
It will make no difference to the number of jobs available	19 (3)	12 (3)

---

15. Some people say that British governments nowadays - of whichever party - can actually do very little to change things.   Others say they can do quite a bit.   Please say whether you think that British governments nowadays can do very little or quite a bit ...

PLEASE TICK ONE BOX ON EACH LINE

	VERY LITTLE	QUITE A BIT	DON'T KNOW
to <u>keep prices down</u>?	% 38 (1)	59 (2)	*
to <u>reduce unemployment</u>?	% 46 (1)	51 (2)	1
to <u>improve the general standard of living</u>?	% 30 (1)	66 (2)	*
to <u>improve the health and social services</u>?	% 19 (1)	77 (2)	*

---

16. Although the cost of living has been going up for several years now, the prices of some things have been rising faster than others.   For each of the items below, please say whether you think it has gone up more, the same, or less than the average rise in prices over the past few years.

PLEASE TICK ONE BOX ON EACH LINE

HAS GONE UP IN PRICE:

	More than average	Same	Less than average	Don't know
Fresh fruit and vegetables	% 40 (1)	50 (2)	7 (3)	1
British Rail fares	% 67 (1)	23 (2)	2 (3)	3
Electrical products for the home	% 38 (1)	43 (2)	14 (3)	1
Electricity	% 78 (1)	18 (2)	2 (3)	1
House prices	% 65 (1)	27 (2)	4 (3)	1
Rents	% 60 (1)	32 (2)	3 (3)	2
The television licence	% 58 (1)	34 (2)	4 (3)	1
Clothes	% 44 (1)	47 (2)	6 (3)	1
Bus fares	% 58 (1)	31 (2)	6 (3)	2
Petrol	% 80 (1)	14 (2)	2 (3)	1
Postal charges	% 56 (1)	37 (2)	4 (3)	1
Your local rates	% 63 (1)	30 (2)	2 (3)	1

17. Central government provides financial support to housing
in two main ways.   First, by means of allowances
to low income tenants;   second by means of tax relief
to people with mortgages.   On the whole, which of
these three types of family would you say benefits
most from central government support for housing?

PLEASE TICK ONE BOX

%
(✓)

Families with high incomes   37₁

Families with middle incomes   20₂

Families with low incomes   38₃

Don't know   2

18. Britain controls the numbers of people from abroad that are
allowed to settle in this country.   Please say for *each* of
the groups below, whether you think Britain should allow more
settlement, less settlement, or about the same amount as now.

PLEASE TICK ONE BOX ON EACH LINE	MORE SETTLEMENT	LESS SETTLEMENT	ABOUT THE SAME AS NOW	DON'T KNOW
Australians and New Zealanders %	12₁	35₂	51₃	1
Indians and Pakistanis %	2₁	73₂	22₃	1
People from common market countries %	5₁	49₂	43₃	1
West Indians %	2₁	69₂	26₃	1

19. For each of the jobs below, please tick a box to show whether
you think the job is particularly suitable for men only,
particularly suitable for women only, or suitable for both
men and women equally?

PLEASE TICK ONE BOX ON EACH LINE	Particularly suitable for men	Particularly suitable for women	Suitable for both equally	Don't know
Social worker %	1₁	11₂	87₃	*
Police officer %	49₁	*₂	49₃	*
Secretary %	1₁	60₂	38₃	*
Car mechanic %	72₁	1₂	25₃	*
Nurse %	*₁	41₂	57₃	*
Computer programmer %	6₁	3₂	89₃	*
Bus driver %	49₁	1₂	49₃	*
Bank manager %	39₁	1₂	58₃	*
Family doctor/GP %	10₁	1₂	87₃	*
Local councillor %	12₁	1₂	85₃	*
Member of Parliament %	16₁	*₂	82₃	*

/Continued over ...

20.   Finally, please tick one box for *each* statement below
      to show how much you agree or disagree with it.

	AGREE STRONGLY	JUST AGREE	NEITHER AGREE NOR DISAGREE	JUST DISAGREE	DISAGREE STRONGLY	DON'T KNOW
Having a job is the best way for a woman to be an independent person	% 30 5	36 4	22 3	7 2	4 1	*
Most married women work only to earn money for extras rather than because they need the money	% 16 5	30 4	13 3	22 2	18 1	*
New technology will benefit the rich more than the poor in Britain	% 28 5	24 4	27 3	13 2	7 1	*
British people should try to buy British goods even when they have to pay a bit more for them	% 36 5	30 4	14 3	13 2	6 1	*
A husband's job is to earn the money; a wife's job is to look after the home and family	% 23 5	20 4	19 3	16 2	22 1	*
Women should be paid the same as men for doing the same work	% 68 5	23 4	4 3	2 2	2 1	*
The days when Britain was an important world power are over	% 22 5	34 4	17 3	17 2	9 1	*
The welfare state makes people nowadays less willing to look after themselves	% 23 5	28 4	16 3	19 2	12 1	*
People receiving social security are made to feel like second class citizens	% 26 5	27 4	19 3	17 2	10 1	*
The welfare state encourages people to stop helping each other	% 14 5	24 4	22 3	25 2	13 1	*
In times of high unemployment married women should stay at home	% 18 5	17 4	17 3	21 2	26 1	*

Subject index

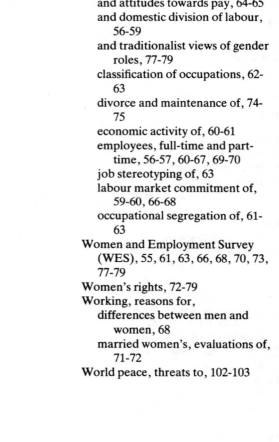